comfort + able = comfortable
drink + able = drinkable
laugh + able = laughable
read + able = readable
unthink + able = unthinkable

BARRON'S
E-Z
SPELLING

Linda Eve Diamond
Author and Educator
http://LindaEveDiamond.com
http://ListenersUnite.com
http://NationalPictureBookWeek.com

Joseph Mersand
Former Associate Professor of Education
York College of the City University of New York

Francis Griffith
Former Emeritus Professor of Education
Hofstra University,
Hempstead, New York

Kathryn O'D. Griffith
Former Chair, Speech Department
George Washington High School,
New York City

BARRON'S

Better Grades or Your Money Back!

As a leader in educational publishing, Barron's has helped millions of students reach their academic goals. Our E-Z series of books is designed to help students master a variety of subjects. We are so confident that completing all the review material and exercises in this book will help you, that if your grades don't improve within 30 days, we will give you a full refund.

To qualify for a refund, simply return the book within 90 days of purchase and include your store receipt. Refunds will not include sales tax or postage. Offer available only to U.S. residents. Void where prohibited. Send books to **Barron's Educational Series, Inc., Attn: Customer Service** at the address on this page.

ACKNOWLEDGMENTS

I acknowledge, with deep appreciation, the original authors of *Spelling the Easy Way*—Joseph Mersand, Francis Griffith, and Kathryn Griffith—who created the foundations for *E-Z Spelling*. I am especially grateful to Kevin Ryan for inviting me to join the *E-Z* team.

All inquiries should be addressed to:
Barron's Educational Series, Inc.
250 Wireless Boulevard
Hauppauge, New York 11788
www.barronseduc.com

Library of Congress Catalog Card No. 2010033243
ISBN: 978-0-7641-4459-2

Library of Congress Cataloging-in-Publication Data
Diamond, Linda Eve
    E-Z spelling / Linda Eve Diamond...[et al.].—5th ed.
        p. cm.
    Easy spelling
    "Prior editions under the title Spelling the Easy Way."
    Includes bibliographical references.
    ISBN: 978-0-7641-4459-2
    1. English language—Orthography and spelling.   I. Title. II. Title: Easy spelling.
PE1145.2.M39 2011
428.1'3—dc22

                                                2010033243

PRINTED IN THE UNITED STATES OF AMERICA
9 8 7 6 5 4 3 2 1

Contents

Introduction v

Pretest vi

THE IMPORTANCE OF SPELLING / 1

1 Why Learn to Spell? 3
Five Reasons to Take Spelling Seriously 4
Spelling Issues in the "Communication Age" 4
Spell-Check Isn't Always ~~Write~~ *Right!* 5
Quick, E-Z, and Clever vs. Proper Spelling 6

2 Why Is Spelling So Difficult? 7
Confusing English 8
How Did This Happen? 8
Sounds Complicated! 9
Homonyms and Homophones 11

3 Learning Techniques 17
Study Spelling Rules and Exceptions 18
Use and Develop Memory Techniques 18
Consult the Dictionary 18
Learn "New" Words 20
Use Spelling Lists 20
Read, Speak, and Listen with Care 21
Try This Six-Step Method 21

4 Mnemonics 23
Memory Techniques for Difficult Words 24
Acronyms 24
Acronyms as Memory Devices 25

RULES FOR SPELLING / 29

5 Better Spelling by Ear 31
Syllables: Breaking It Down 32
One Syllable at a Time 34
Common Mix-ups 35
More Common Mix-ups 38

6 Some Special Problems 39
IE and *EI* 40
-SEDE, *-CEED*, and *-CEDE* 43

7 Prefixes 45
The Prefix Rule 46
A List of Common Prefixes 46
Pay Attention to *PER-*, *PRE-*, *PRO-* 49

8 Confusing Suffixes 53
Words Ending in *-ABLE*, *-IBLE* 54
Adding *-LY* to Words Ending in *-AL* 57
Words Ending in *-OUS* 58
Troublesome Affixes *-AL*, *-EL*, *-LE* 60
Words Ending in *-ER* or *-OR* 64
Words Ending in *-AR* 64
Words Ending in *-ANCE*, *-ENCE* 65
Words Ending in *-ENSE* 66
Words Ending in *-ARY*, *-ERY* 68
Words Ending in *-ISE*, *-IZE* 69

9 Plural Nouns 71
Regular Plurals 72
Nouns Ending in a Sibilant Sound 72
Nouns Ending in Long $\bar{O}$ 73
Nouns Ending in *-F* or *-FE* 73
Nouns Ending in *-Y* 76
Special Situations 77

10 The Final *-Y* 83
The *-Y* Preceded by a Vowel 84
The *-Y* Preceded by a Consonant 85

11 The Final *-E* 89
Dropping the Final *-E* 90
Retaining the Final *-E* 94
Unusual Situations 97

12 Doubling Final Consonants 101
One-Syllable Words 102
Words of More Than One Syllable 104
Special Situations 105
How Consonants Determine Meaning 106

13 English as a Second Language 111
A Guide to Pronunciation and Spelling 112

SPECIAL DEVICES / 127

14 The Hyphen 129
Compound Adjectives 130
Compound Nouns 132
Compound Numbers and Fractions 133
Compounds with Certain Particles 134
Used for Clarity 136
Used to Divide Words 136

15 The Apostrophe 139
Show Contraction 140
Show Possession 140
Indicate Double Ownership 142

16 Capital Letters 145
Basic Principles 146
Proper Nouns 146
Books, Plays, Music 147

17 Spelling Abbreviations 149
Date and Time 150
Business Terms 151
Personal Titles 152
Measurement Terms 153

TROUBLESOME WORDS / 157

18 More Homonyms and Homophones and Other Confusing Word Pairs 159
Homonyms and Homophones 160
Other Confusing Word Pairs 169

19 Word Building 175
Word Families 176

20 Most Frequently Misspelled Words 179
One Hundred Pests 180
Business Terms 180
Commonly Misspelled Professions 185

21 Computer Terms 187
Computer Acronyms 188
One Word or Two? 188
Computer-age Generated Words 189
Common Computer Words 189

22 More Commonly Misspelled Words 193
Foods and Food-related Words 194
Household, Community, and School Words 195

23 Medical and Health Terms 197
Medical and Health Terms 198

MEASURING YOUR PROGRESS / 203

24 Achievement Tests 205
Achievement Test 1 205
Achievement Test 2 207
Achievement Test 3 208
Achievement Test 4 211
Achievement Test 5 214
Achievement Test 6 217
Achievement Test 7 219

25 Answer Key 223
For Chapters 3–23 223
For Achievement Tests 1–7 237

26 10,000 Word Ready Reference Spelling List 243
Spelling Reminders 243
Using the 10,000 Words as Practice 244
About the List 244
10,000 Words 245

INTRODUCTION

In this age of spell-checkers, the need for a spelling book may seem out of date. However, spelling is still a necessary skill. As you will see in Chapter 1, spell-check programs have their limitations. Beyond these issues, situations still arise (rare as they may be) that require writing by hand. An over-reliance on spell-checkers may even hurt our spelling abilities. Anyone who expects the computer to pick up any and all errors will easily put less focus on the importance of actually knowing proper spelling and even grammar. Spell-checkers are helpful, but knowledge is still essential.

Although spelling is filled with complexities, oddities, and exceptions, you may be surprised by how quickly you can strengthen your spelling skills and confidence. *E-Z Spelling* simplifies spelling rules and exceptions with clear explanations, simple learning and memory techniques, and ample opportunities for practice.

E-Z Spelling includes:

• A pretest in the beginning to highlight areas of learning that need extra attention.

• Achievement Tests to assess improvement and reinforce successful learning.

• Helpful instruction and comprehensive exercises throughout.

• A reference list of 10,000 Commonly Misspelled Words.

• Professor boxes with spelling tips, quotes, fun facts, and stories.

PRETEST

When you complete the Pretest, check your answers and make note of those that were incorrect. Take some time to review the correct answers. As you continue to work through the book, you will find rules, tips, and tricks that will help you spell these words correctly in the future.

The Spelling Pretest is designed to help you:

1. Assess where you are now, which will help you better evaluate your progress as you work to strengthen your skills.

2. Recognize some of the kinds of words that are especially difficult for you.

3. Follow the instructions in the Pretest Answer Key to begin a list of those words to help you learn them.

4. Be ready to pay close attention to those troublesome words as you reach chapters that offer explanations, warnings, and memory devices related to them.

SPELLING PRETEST

Directions: Circle the letter of the incorrectly spelled word in each group.

1. A. efficient
    B. patience
    C. recieve
    D. audience

2. A. equally
    B. authorities
    C. definitely
    D. actualy

3. A. acustomed
    B. illegible
    C. grammar
    D. appearance

4. A. children
    B. analyses
    C. sheeps
    D. pianos

5. A. carried
    B. beautyful
    C. iciness
    D. angrily

6. A. dont
    B. could
    C. you're
    D. she's

7. A. A.M.
    B. Jr
    C. assn.
    D. Capt.

8. A. thirty-one
    B. when-ever
    C. far-fetched
    D. ex-wife

9. A. exceed
   B. recede
   C. proced
   D. succeed

10. A. irrelevant
    B. disolve
    C. misjudge
    D. illiteracy

11. A. prescribe
    B. persist
    C. propose
    D. perpare

12. A. eligible
    B. legible
    C. permissable
    D. intelligible

13. A. drizzel
    B. swivel
    C. brutal
    D. quarrel

14. A. governor
    B. inventer
    C. editor
    D. passenger

15. A. guidance
    B. violence
    C. pleasant
    D. importence

16. A. loveing
    B. owing
    C. becoming
    D. using

17. A. intensity
    B. poreous
    C. sincerity
    D. extremity

18. A. completeness
    B. likeness
    C. vagueness
    D. coarsness

19. A. duly
    B. wholly
    C. truley
    D. awfully

20. A. spinner
    B. omitting
    C. begining
    D. conferring

21. A. inferring
    B. refering
    C. permitting
    D. occurring

22. A. precede
    B. preceede
    C. accede
    D. concede

23. A. superseede
    B. exceed
    C. succeed
    D. proceed

24. A. its
    B. were
    C. theyre
    D. we'll

25. A. produce
    B. perceive
    C. personnel
    D. perpose

26. A. attorney
    B. prinsiple
    C. moral
    D. morale

27. A. certain
    B. extravagant
    C. probuble
    D. dictionary

28. A. liquify
    B. plague
    C. cellar
    D. counselor

29. A. picnicing
    B. trafficking
    C. engaging
    D. colicky

30. A. completeness
    B. amusement
    C. rudness
    D. arrangement

31. A. reversible
    B. collectible
    C. navigable
    D. admissable

32. A. reducable
    B. eligible
    C. readable
    D. permissible

33. A. comprehensible
    B. digestable
    C. combustible
    D. convertible

34. A. divisible
    B. legible
    C. deductable
    D. eatable

35. A. comfortable
    B. accountible
    C. favorable
    D. preventable

36. A. usually
    B. equally
    C. logically
    D. practicaly

37. A. couragous
    B. adventurous
    C. outrageous
    D. analagous

38. A. quarrel
    B. personal
    C. funnal
    D. annual

39. A. regel
    B. legal
    C. arrival
    D. denial

40. A. model
    B. trowal
    C. kernel
    D. cancel

41. A. kisses
    B. buses
    C. losses
    D. clases

42. A. children
    B. women
    C. thiefs
    D. lives

43. A. chiefes
    B. beliefs
    C. shoes
    D. roofs

44. A. vetoes
    B. volcanoes
    C. solos
    D. heros

45. A. lives
    B. knives
    C. leaves
    D. loafs

46. A. solos
    B. pianos
    C. altoes
    D. sopranos

47. A. sisters-in-law
    B. handfuls
    C. cupfuls
    D. mother-in-laws

48. A. oxes
    B. feet
    C. deer
    D. sheep

49. A. sheeps
    B. women
    C. men
    D. geese

50. A. wield
    B. veil
    C. sieze
    D. grieve

PRETEST ANSWER KEY

Check your answers. Total the number of your correct responses at the bottom of the chart. Then read the recommendations that follow.

Item	Answer	Correct Spelling	Item	Answer	Correct Spelling
1.	C.	receive	26.	B.	principle
2.	D.	actually	27.	C.	probable
3.	A.	accustomed	28.	A.	liquefy
4.	C.	sheep	29.	A.	picnicking
5.	B.	beautiful	30.	C.	rudeness
6.	A.	don't	31.	D.	admissible
7.	B.	Jr.	32.	A.	reducible
8.	B.	whenever	33.	B.	digestible
9.	C.	proceed	34.	D.	deductible
10.	B.	dissolve	35.	B.	accountable
11.	D.	prepare	36.	D.	practically
12.	C.	permissible	37.	A.	courageous
13.	A.	drizzle	38.	C.	funnel
14.	B.	inventor	39.	A.	regal
15.	D.	importance	40.	B.	trowel
16.	A.	loving	41.	D.	classes
17.	B.	porous	42.	C.	thieves
18.	D.	coarseness	43.	A.	chiefs
19.	C.	truly	44.	D.	heroes
20.	C.	beginning	45.	D.	loaves
21.	B.	referring	46.	C.	altos
22.	B.	precede	47.	D.	mothers-in-law
23.	A.	supersede	48.	A.	oxen
24.	C.	they're	49.	A.	sheep
25.	D.	propose	50.	C.	seize

How many did you answer correctly? Give yourself two points for each correct answer. (Take the total number correct and multiply by two. For instance: 35 correct = 70% out of a possible 100%.)

To gain the most benefit from your Pretest, consider writing down the most difficult words—correctly spelled—and keep this list by your side as you go through the book. Watch for rules, explanations, and memory tricks that might make these words easier to remember. If your list of difficult words is long, don't worry—you're not alone. As you read on, you will see why spelling is so challenging, and you'll find lots of exercises to help you build your spelling muscles.

Why Learn to Spell?

With Awl My Hart

I hope you no
Eye love ewe sew
With awl my hart
And all my sole
Write from the start
You maid mi hole

WHAT YOU WILL LEARN

Can you find the eleven misspellings in the above poem (not counting the title, which has two errors you'll see again in the poem)? Spell-check couldn't find one! You had a brief introduction to the problems with spell-checkers in the Introduction. In this chapter, you will learn more about why a spell-check feature doesn't replace the need for learning how to spell correctly. You'll also be asked to consider why learning to spell is just as important—if not *more* important—than ever.

SECTIONS IN THIS CHAPTER

- Five Reasons to Take Spelling Seriously
- Spelling Issues in the "Communication Age"
- Spell-Check Isn't Always ~~Write~~ *Right!*
- Quick, E-Z, and Clever vs. Proper Spelling

Five Reasons to Take Spelling Seriously

1. **Your image depends on it.** Many readers are quick to judge when they see misspelled words. They will either draw the conclusion that you don't know how to spell correctly or that you don't care enough to take the time to pay attention to important details. Right or wrong, your writing is seen as a reflection of you.

2. **Non-standard spellings (and even misspellings) can potentially cause confusion.** Written communication can only be clear to people who use the same language, and improper spelling changes the appearance of language—sometimes enough to cause misunderstandings.

3. **Good writing has no distractions.** Misteaks can be terribly distracting and cause readers to lose interest and confidence in the writer. For instance, once you saw *misteaks* instead of *mistakes* in the previous sentence, didn't you find it difficult to pay attention to the rest of the message?

4. **We cannot rely on spell-checkers.** Consider the poem, *With Awl My Hart.*

5. **Knowledge builds confidence.**

Spelling Issues in the "Communication Age"

The so-called "communication age" may be causing as many communication problems as it solves. Our interpersonal communications are changing, and so are our rules and habits for writing. The changes in writing style that have come along with instantaneous, rushed written communication have created an environment that makes learning to spell more difficult than ever before.

Instant messaging has created a style of shorthand that uses misspelled versions of words, or completely avoids spelling out words by turning entire sentences into acronyms (words formed from the initial letters or groups of letters from a set of words). While this shorthand is convenient, clever, and time saving, it should be kept in perspective and not used to completely replace the spelling out of words. Overuse makes learning (and even recognizing) correct spellings more difficult. Some say the answer is to question whether conventional spelling matters so much anymore. However, correct spelling is *not* a quaint, old-fashioned notion; from educational institutions to businesses to Internet pages and e-mails, spelling still counts.

DOES SPELL-CHECK HELP OR HARM EFFORTS TO LEARN? *YOU DECIDE!*

Spell-check may interfere with learning to spell. It's easier to guess words and let spell-check correct them than it is to learn them for next time. As a result, many people type the same words on a regular basis but never learn to spell them. However, you wouldn't want to skip the spell-check step (which *is* essential), and you *can* use it to assist in learning. Instead of sitting back and passively clicking the "Change" button, become more active in the process. When a word is flagged, quiz yourself before checking suggested replacements. How do you think it should be spelled? When you see the correct spelling, take a moment to look at it, jot it down, and even spell it out loud. If you're creating a list of words to study, add it to that list. You don't have to do this each time to begin noticing a difference—you'll find that you're guessing less often and spelling with greater confidence.

Spell-Check Isn't Always ~~Write~~ *Right!*

Our language is filled with confusing word pairs, such as *write* and *right*. You cannot count on computers to correct words that are in the dictionary (even when they're spelled wrong in the context of your sentence). For instance, look at the following paragraph. Every word in bold is a misspelling that would not be corrected.

Spelling rules may be confusing, but they are **their** for a reason. One of **witch**, and the most important reason, is clear communication. **Weather** we know it or not, spellings—or misspellings—present an image, and we are judged (in classes, business, and even our personal lives) based on that image. Spell-checkers cannot tell aisle (a walkway) from isle (an island); alter (to change) from altar (a platform on which religious rites are performed); or rites (ceremonial acts) from rights (directional turns or something to which one has a fair claim) from writes (communicates through the written word).

Spell-check programs don't know about context, and they know odd words we might not think to double-check. Think about the poem in the beginning of this chapter. Were you surprised that spell-check didn't pick up the misspelled word, hart? Most people wouldn't know that hart is a male deer (especially a red male deer that is more than five years old), but the spell-check program knows the word, so it isn't flagged as a misspelling. On one hand, it knows too much to catch that simple error; on the other hand, it simply doesn't know enough to distinguish the correct usage of a word.

Another concern is whether you're using the latest software and whether, even if you are, the program is up-to-date with the most recent dictionaries. As of this book's production in 2010, the spell-check program being used is still highlighting the words *blog* and *podcast* as errors. While this computer's software may not have the latest update, you can see how quickly things are changing—and even the latest updates aren't always up-to-date with the newest words.

Computer spell-checkers are wonderfully helpful assistants, catching errors that could easily be missed—even if you know the correct spellings—and they suggest possible spellings when you're close but don't know exactly how to spell a word. A spell-checker, though, cannot go unchecked or be the final word. While nothing should be typed without running a spell-check, the final spell-checker has to be *you*.

Quick, E-Z, and Clever vs. Proper Spelling

Remember that while abbreviations are accepted in certain kinds of communications, they are not professional or accepted overall. Also, while many people use the same shorthand, others do not. Abbreviated communication is often less clear, even if you don't realize it. Think of Internet shorthand as another language. If you use it, realize that not everyone "speaks" or understands it, and not everyone wants to; if you try to use it in all of your communications, your messages will not be as clear as you intend.

Still, you may ask, isn't it just as E-Z to abbreviate as it is to spell out a word? Sometimes misspellings and abbreviations seem more appealing and more fun than proper spelling. Many of us enjoy playing with words for a spell. In fact, the title of this book, *E-Z Spelling,* plays with the spelling of *easy*. Once you know the rules, it can be fun, attention-getting, or style-enhancing to break the rules when appropriate. When in doubt, though, your reputation is usually safest when you choose to spell correctly.

Why Is Spelling So Difficult?

2

From the song, "Why Can't the English Learn to Speak?"*

One common language I'm afraid we'll never get.
Oh, why can't the English learn to
Set a good example to people whose English
Is painful to your ears?
There even are places where English completely disappears.
In America, they haven't used it for years!

> Henry Higgins, *My Fair Lady,*
> Lyrics by Alan Jay Lerner
> *With slight adaptation

WHAT YOU WILL LEARN

Henry Higgins was already singing this song lamenting the downfall of the English language when *My Fair Lady* first came to the stage in 1956! Higgins was appalled by Eliza Doolittle's grammar and pronunciation, and I'm sure that her spelling wouldn't have been any better. Even accomplished writers struggle with many English-language spellings. In this chapter, you will learn why spelling correctly is such a challenge.

SECTIONS IN THIS CHAPTER

- Confusing English
- How Did This Happen?
- Sounds Complicated!
- Homonyms and Homophones

Confusing English

How do we know which spelling is *write* when we *right*? Pardon my misspellings. What I meant to write was that it can be difficult to know which spelling is *right* when we *write*! And how do we know when to use one *s* or two, when to use an *f* or a *ph*, and when to slip in a silent letter or two? *Their they're* you might say—no, sorry, *there there*. You might tell me to calm down, which would only confuse me more because I'll want to know why *calm* has an *l* if it isn't pronounced. I have my *doubts* about this language; I would rather write *douts*! So much ink and angst are wasted on letters that aren't even meant to be heard!

English presents numerous spelling challenges, and nearly everyone—those whose first language is not English and native speakers alike—has some level of difficulty with spelling. In many languages, words are more often spelled as they are pronounced. In English, certain vowels and consonant sets have one sound in some words and a completely different sound in others. Strong letters, such as *b* and *k* are sometimes silent. Simply put: English spelling is confusing.

READ WHAT ONE LOVER OF WORDS—A GREAT AMERICAN AUTHOR—HAD TO SAY ABOUT SPELLING

"The only stupid thing about words is the spelling of them."

–Laura Ingalls Wilder

How Did This Happen?

The development and complexities of the English language could fill a book, but here are a few key factors that contribute to the difficult spellings we see today:

- The English language has its origins in Anglo-Saxon, which was spoken in Britain between the fifth and twelfth centuries. In 1066, the Normans conquered England and brought with them a form of French that combined with Anglo-Saxon to create a language now called Middle English. Many of these words also came from Latin and Greek and were used very close to their original forms. Many words that were foreign to the language and had unusual spellings were incorporated. *Foreign*, in fact, was one of these words.

- Beyond the mixed origins and pronunciations of words, some pronunciation has changed over time. One distinctive period of change began in the fifteenth century and was known as the "Great Vowel Shift." The pronunciation of many vowels changed. For instance, *leaf* used to be pronounced as we now pronounce *life*. Another change at that time was that the *e* at the end of a word was pronounced. While we changed pronunciation of some vowels and dropped the sound of others, spellings remained largely the same, expanding the gap even further between how a word sounds and how it appears.

- English has continued to incorporate words from other languages to the *chagrin* (originally a French word) of those who study spelling. We have not only added to an already confusing language words with spellings as confounding as *buffet*, *hors d'oeuvres*, and *chauffeur*, we still add foreign words as our language continues its ongoing development.

If you look at the history of the English language, you'll see how we developed such confusing, inconsistent spellings that seem to have more exceptions than rules. Of course, you don't need to know the history of the language to improve spelling or to learn the tips and tricks that can help you along the way.

"WOBBLY" SPELLING

"My spelling is Wobbly. It's good spelling but it Wobbles, and the letters get into the wrong places."

—A.A. Milne, author of the famous *Winnie the Pooh* books

Sounds Complicated!

A good first step in spelling a word correctly is to listen to how it sounds. On the other hand, the sound of a word may be of little help and can even be misleading. The English language has over forty sounds, but only twenty-six letters.

Some letters or letter combinations represent multiple sounds. For example, the letter *a* represents six different sounds and the letter *s* four:

SINGLE LETTERS WITH SEVERAL SOUNDS

A	S
p<u>a</u>t (ă)	<u>s</u>ea (s)
b<u>a</u>ke (ā)	no<u>s</u>e (z)
c<u>a</u>re (â)	<u>s</u>ure (sh)
f<u>a</u>ther (ä)	plea<u>s</u>ure (zh)
<u>a</u>ll (a)	
<u>a</u>bout (ə)	

The *-ough* words show how many different pronunciations may result from identical spelling.

-OUGH HAS MANY SOUNDS

Word	Sound
thr*ough*	(oo)
r*ough*	(uff)
c*ough*	(awf)
pl*ough*	(ow)
thor*ough*	(oh)
hicc*ough*	(up)

Many letters or letter combinations also represent multiple sounds. For example, the sound of *a* may be spelled as follows:

SINGLE SOUNDS REPRESENTED BY DIFFERENT LETTERS

"ā" Sound

ay—as in say	*e*—as in beta
a—as in page	*ey*—as in obey
ai—as in maid	*ei*—as in weight
au—as in gauge	

Think about how many ways there are to represent the *sh* sound.

"sh" Sound

sh—as in shine	*s*—as in sure
ch—as in panache	*ss*—as in assure
tion—as in motion	*c*—as in ocean
cion—as in suspicion	

To see the strangeness of English spelling, consider the word *potato*. Using some of the unusual combinations in English it would be possible to spell the word: *ghoughpteighbteau*.

Here is the key:

P	*gh*	as pronounced in hiccou*gh*		
O	*ough*	as pronounced in th*ough*		
T	*pt*	as pronounced in *pt*omaine	}	*gh/ough/pt/eigh/bt/eau*
A	*eigh*	as pronounced in w*eigh*		(potato)
T	*bt*	as pronounced in de*bt*		
O	*eau*	as pronounced in b*eau*		

Try to discover why someone might want to spell the word *fish* as *ghoti*!

HIDDEN COMPLICATIONS

Letters may have multiple sounds—or no sound at all. If the number of different sounds or combination of letters can complicate spelling, think about silent letters. How many different letters can be silent? Take a moment of silence to consider just a few: ras*p*berry, recei*p*t, de*b*t, crum*b*, *p*sychiatrist, *k*nife, desi*g*n, cas*t*le, balle*t*, ya*c*ht, autum*n*, debr*i*s, as*t*hma, and ans*w*er.

Homonyms and Homophones

Homonyms and homophones confuse the language even more—and to make matters worse, not all dictionaries agree on their definitions. Most will agree that homonyms have the same spelling but a different meaning; others say they may or may not be spelled the same and they may or may not sound the same. Homophones are typically thought of as words that sound the same but have different meanings and spellings, but some will classify those with the same spelling as homophones also. The meaning of the words homonyms and homophones is not as important as learning to distinguish words that can be easily confused with one another because they are spelled and/or pronounced the same.

MULTIPLE MEANINGS

Our language is filled with multiple meanings for words with the exact same spellings. Just open any dictionary to see how many different definitions you will find for one word. Try looking up the word *run*. How many definitions do you see?

JUST FOR FUN!

To appreciate the variety of multiple meanings words have, try this little exercise just for fun. Fill in the blanks below. Each number uses the same word (same spelling) on every blank. You'll find the answers below.

1. You can feel it, and it's also a color of the rainbow: _____

2. It's a compliment when someone says you *have it*, but it may or may not be a compliment if someone says you *are one*: _____

3. You can wear one, spin one, or reach for it: _____

4. You can swim in one, bet in one, or play it as a game: _____

5. Your houseplant might have one in it, and your house might have one planted in it: _____

1. blue 2. character 3. top 4. pool 5. bug

SAME PRONUNCIATION, SAME SPELLING, DIFFERENT MEANING

pool (a body of water)	pool (a game)
fair (light-colored)	fair (a market)
bug (insect)	bug (virus) bug (secretly record)
bank (embankment)	bank (place where money is kept)
mouse (rodent)	mouse (computer component)
long (lengthy)	long (yearn for)
surf (ride a wave)	surf (scan the Internet)
fire (flames)	fire (discharge from work)
run (campaign)	run (jog)
dog (a kind of animal)	dog (follow persistently)
spam (canned meat)	spam (junk e-mail)

SAME PRONUNCIATION, DIFFERENT SPELLING, DIFFERENT MEANING

air	heir	
aisle	I'll	isle
allowed	aloud	
ate	eight	
be	bee	
beat	beet	
blue	blew	
bow	bough	
bye	buy	by
compliment	complement	
flower	flour	
for	four	fore
knew	new	
know	no	
pale	pail	
right	write	
sink	synch	
site	sight	
sum	some	
Sunday	sundae	
their	there	their
to	two	too
wait	weight	
weather	whether	
week	weak	
won	one	

DIFFERENT PRONUNCIATION, SAME SPELLING, DIFFERENT MEANING

wind (breeze)	wind (turn, as with a clock)
invalid (not valid)	invalid (disabled person)
present (give)	present (gift)
produce (make)	produce (fruits and vegetables)
object (a thing)	object (voice disagreement)
lead (take charge)	lead (a metal element)
dove (a bird)	dove (jumped off)
close (shut)	close (near)
tear (rip)	tear (from crying)

The abundance of homonyms and homophones in English is a source of difficulty, especially to students for whom English is a second language.

MISPRONUNCIATION

We have a tendency to spell words as we hear them. Even with all of the exceptions, many words are spelled as they sound. However, words are quite often mispronounced, which results in some of our common spelling errors. Some words drop a syllable in common pronunciation. The pronunciation may not be incorrect, but it makes these words hard to spell by ear.

NOTE:

A syllable is the smallest unit of speech and generally contains only one vowel sound. Syllables are referred to often as ways to sound out words and even apply certain spelling rules. You will find syllables explained in Chapter 5.

The table below shows some words in which syllables or letters are commonly omitted. The number of syllables of both the actual word and the common pronunciation are shown in parentheses.

WORDS WITH SYLLABLES COMMONLY OMITTED

Correct Word	Common Pronunciation
in•ter•est•ing (4)	in•tres•ting (3)
priv•i•lege (3)	priv•lege (2)
hy•gi•en•ic (4)	hy•genic (2)
lic•o•rice (3)	lick•rice (2)
di•a•mond (3)	di•mond (2)
mack•er•el (3)	mack•rel (2)
lab•o•ra•to•ry (5)	la•bra•to•ry (4)

When practicing spelling aloud, break the word into syllables. Spell by syllables. You will find this method helpful.

Sometimes when we pronounce a word incorrectly we add a syllable where it does not belong, omit a sound, or substitute one sound for another. The following is a list of words that are commonly mispronounced. The correct pronunciation and spelling is in the left column. The common mispronunciation and subsequent misspelling is in the right column.

WORDS COMMONLY MISPRONOUNCED

Correct Word	Mispronounced Word
athletic	athaletic
February	Febuary
government	goverment
kindergarten	kindergarden
library	libery
strictly	strickly

If you have a habit of slurring consonants, omitting syllables, or running syllables together like a verbal accordion player, you make it difficult for your listeners to understand what you are saying. You will also improve your spelling by making the effort to pronounce words correctly.

NOTE: REGIONAL PRONUNCIATION

In some regions of our country some words are pronounced differently from common usage. For example, creek is pronounced *crik*; sauce, *sass*; film, *filum*; and draw, *drawr*.

Since we tend to spell words as we hear them pronounced, these and similar regional pronunciations cause spelling difficulties. We must be able to discern dialectal pronunciations to avoid spelling errors.

SHORTCUTS TO SPELLING

As mentioned earlier, instant messaging, text messaging, and online chats often include slang expressions, acronyms, and misspellings intended to shorten words and phrases and keep them recognizable. As long as they're short and look similar to how they sound, they enter common use; many do even if they use numbers along with letters. Shortened words and phrases are convenient because of the time they save. Unfortunately, they reinforce the notion that we don't need to learn the actual spellings.

Here are a few examples:

EXAMPLES

nite	=	night
CU	=	see you
bcoz	=	because
2nite	=	tonight
dem	=	them
h8	=	hate
CUL8R	=	see you later
GR8	=	great
ENUF	=	enough

Can this be helping our abilities to learn and retain the proper spellings of words? Many kids today don't write, "I'm going to school." They write, "Im gong 2 skool." When I asked an online instant messaging translator: "Do you know how to spell?" it answered: "Do u know how 2 spel?" If you are inundated with this "language" and are trying to study spelling at the same time, you might want to try slowing down and spelling out more words. Shortcuts to spelling may save a little time, and there's no need to stop using them altogether if they help you communicate in a common "language" with friends. However, these shortcuts are likely to slow you down in achieving the goal of improving your spelling.

Learning Techniques

Aristotle, the great Greek philosopher, was tutor to the future king, Alexander the Great. One day they were doing a lesson in mathematics that required many calculations. Alexander, always impatient, suddenly threw aside his work and exclaimed:

> "Why must I go through all these little steps? Why can't I get the answer immediately? I'm the future king!"
>
> "There is no royal road to knowledge," answered his tutor.

WHAT YOU WILL LEARN

There is no royal road to knowledge. There is no shortcut to any branch of learning, and that is especially true for spelling. We had trouble with spelling in America long before Noah Webster published his famous speller. Nobody was ever born a perfect speller. Spellers are *made*, not born. Everyone can become a good speller by following certain steps.

SECTIONS IN THIS CHAPTER

- Study Spelling Rules and Exceptions
- Use and Develop Memory Techniques
- Consult the Dictionary
- Learn "New" Words
- Use Spelling Lists
- Read, Speak, and Listen with Care
- Try This Six-Step Method

Study Spelling Rules and Exceptions

As complex as spelling can be, most words either follow rules or are notable, memorable exceptions. Learning the rules will take the guesswork out of spelling many words that seem to defy explanation. Trying to remember spellings without understanding the rules behind them is overwhelming, but you can gain confidence and skill by learning and applying the rules. Once you understand these rules, learning the exceptions is less daunting, and many can be easily learned and recalled with a few memory techniques.

Use and Develop Memory Techniques

Memory devices are helpful for remembering difficult words, the differences between confusing homophones, or which vowel to use when multiple possibilities might be correct. For instance, do you have trouble remembering whether the correct spelling is *seperate* or *separate*? Think of the word *part*. When you *separate*, you take things *apart*. Remembering that device will help you recall that *ar* is correct.

You'll learn more techniques in Chapter 4, and you'll also be encouraged to think of your own memory tricks for difficult words.

Consult the Dictionary

The dictionary is an important tool for learning to spell and reinforcing what you learn. Have a dictionary at hand and/or bookmarked online. Any dictionary that you feel comfortable using is fine. Online dictionaries are wonderful references and learning resources, and many offer free access.

Good dictionaries include:

1. A *phonetic spelling* of each word immediately following each main entry, which is often in **boldface**. For example, **grovel** (´gröv-əl): "to creep with the face to the ground." A phonetic spelling translates the printed sight of a word into its spoken sounds. The phonetic spelling and main entry also divide each word into syllables, and use primary and secondary stress marks to show emphasis in pronunciation (e.g., ham´ bur´ ger).

2. An *abbreviated pronunciation key* is also usually printed at the bottom of each page, for the convenience of the reader, or sometimes across the bottom of each pair of facing pages. This key illustrates the sound of each symbol in the phonetic spelling through a short word.

3. A *full Pronunciation Key,* which includes phonetic symbols, is in the front of the dictionary. Phonetic symbols represent every possible sound of speech that individual

letters in the alphabet can represent visually within the many words of a written language. The symbol for each key sound is also illustrated in a key word. Familiarize yourself with the location of this Pronunciation Key in your own dictionary. Computer and online dictionaries will also include an audio button to allow you to hear the proper pronunciation.

Using a dictionary, you learn to pronounce the word through its phonetic spelling. For example, **epitome** is pronounced ĭ-pĭt´-a-mē. The curved and straight lines above ĭ and ē in the phonetic spelling, called diacritical marks, indicate that the vowel is pronounced briefly (˘) or held for a longer sound (¯). The stress mark indicates that the second syllable is emphasized.

A good dictionary is a treasure house of information on language, often containing introductory essays on the history of the language, on spelling and grammar, on dialects, and on usage. (A good dictionary will also contain usage notes within its definitions of those words that are growing, dying, or changing their meaning or social acceptability.)

EXERCISE 1

In the space provided, copy the phonetic spelling of each of the following words from a dictionary, including separation of syllables and diacritical and stress markings.

_____ 1. supercilious

_____ 2. humor

_____ 3. liquid

_____ 4. intricacy

_____ 5. intimidate

_____ 6. naive

_____ 7. gubernatorial

_____ 8. farcical

_____ 9. decadence

_____ 10. review

Learn "New" Words

The dictionary is a living document that is continually changing. Words are added with our changing times, new technologies, expressions coined by new generations, common use, and more. Think of how different the first dictionary would have been. It didn't include the words *telephone*, *bikini*, or *downshifting*. Think of how many words continue to be added with new technologies.

Even clever expressions and new combinations of old words enter the dictionary when they become popular in common use. You might be familiar with some of the latest dictionary additions. If not, you may have fun guessing the new words by seeing their definitions. In Exercise 2, you will find definitions of words that are so new, you may not have heard all of them.

EXERCISE 2

See if you can write the new words after the definitions below. Just by imagining them and going over the answers, you'll be gaining experience with word formations and spelling, including a little preview of prefixes and suffixes (which will be covered later in Chapters 7 and 8.)

1. Educational entertainment _____

2. A person advised by a mentor _____

3. Resembling the Beatles' style _____

4. An online (Web) seminar _____

5. Wrap a gift that was given to you and give it to someone else

   _____

6. The inflation of taxes _____

Use Spelling Lists

Make a list of the words that you find the most challenging to spell. You may have started this list already after taking the Pretest, as suggested. Continue adding to your list and referring back to it. Read the words over to become accustomed to their proper spellings. Pick a few and try the six-step exercise at the end of this chapter. Keeping and reviewing spelling lists will help you master these and other similar words.

You'll also find several categorized lists of difficult words throughout this book and a list of 10,000 difficult words. Use and refer to these lists, highlighting and practicing difficult words and looking back to the rules that will help you learn to spell them correctly.

Read, Speak, and Listen with Care

Reading is one effortless way to improve your spelling skills. Even if you're not trying or thinking about it, the more your eye sees words spelled correctly, the more you will recognize and recall these spellings. While reading won't automatically make you a great speller, it will make a difference.

As you saw in Chapter 2, many misspellings come from mispronunciations. Words such as *government*, *security*, and *conservation* are often misspoken and, as a result, misspelled. Listen to those who enunciate well and pay attention to how their words sound. If you're only listening to those who don't enunciate, or if you're not listening carefully to someone who does, you might hear *guvment* instead of *government*, *scruity* instead of *security*, and *consivation* instead of *conservation*. One of the foundations of learning to spell is to pay attention to language—to speak with clarity and listen with care.

Try This Six-Step Method

If you're having an especially difficult time with a word, try this six-step method.

1. Look at a word. Pronounce each syllable carefully.

   For example: in•de•pen•dent

2. Close your eyes and picture the word in your mind. If you cannot see the word clearly in your mind, look again until you can close your eyes and picture it.

3. Write the word while pronouncing it out loud.

4. Write a sentence using the word but leave a blank in place of the word.

5. Go back the next day and fill in the blank. If you spelled it correctly, your practice paid off!

6. Review in a few days to reinforce what you've learned.

Mnemonics

If a word like mnemonics (pronounced nu-mon-ics) makes you want to give up on spelling altogether, don't despair. It's just another one of those many exceptions that was imported from another language and stays close to its Greek heritage. In Greek, mnemonikos means mindful; in mythology, the goddess, Mnemosyne, was the personification of memory.

Mnemonics refers to specific techniques designed to help us remember things, such as a song, poem, or word that serves as a device to trigger memory. The *Oxford English Dictionary* defines a mnemonic as: "a pattern of letters or words formulated as an aid to memory." For instance, the rules about whether a word is spelled *ie* or *ei* would be hard to remember without this mnemonic device: "*I* before *e* except after *c*…"

WHAT YOU WILL LEARN

You will learn some common mnemonic devices and some other helpful techniques. You also might be inspired to create your own mnemonic devices for things you will need to recall. After all, Mnemosyne was also said to be the mother of the nine muses (the goddesses said to inspire creative arts). Maybe you can even come up with a device to help you memorize the spelling of the word *mnemonics*!

SECTIONS IN THIS CHAPTER

- Memory Techniques for Difficult Words
- Acronyms
- Acronyms as Memory Devices

Memory Techniques for Difficult Words

Below are some useful techniques for helping to avoid a few common mistakes.

- Do you be*lie*ve or be*lei*ve?

  Memory device: Never be*lie*ve a *lie*!

- Is it c*e*m*e*t*e*ry, c*e*m*a*t*e*ry, c*e*m*a*t*a*ry, or c*e*m*e*t*a*ry? They all sound the same!

  Memory device: Think of a cemetery late at night, a haunted scene where you might scream—*eee!* That might help you recall the three *e*'s in c*e*m*e*t*e*ry.

- When is princi*ple* used, and when should it be princi*pal*? One means the person who governs a school and the other is an ideal or stance on an issue. How can you remember that the princi*pal* is the one who governs a school?

  Memory device: You would hope that your princi*pal* would be your *pal*!

- Is it gramm*er* or gramm*ar*? How can you remember the correct spelling is grammar?

  Memory device: Bad gram*mar* will *mar* your professional image.

- When is comple*ment* used, and when should it be compl*iment*?

  Memory device: A comple*ment* comple*tes*, while a compl*iment* adm*ires*.

- When is station*ary* used, and when should it be station*ery*?

  Memory device: Station*a*ry means st*a*nding still; station*e*ry is used for l*e*tters.

- Is it use*ful* or use*full*, resent*ful* or resent*full*, art*ful* or art*full*?

  Memory device: Remember this simple spelling truth: The *only* word that ends in *full* is *full*!

Acronyms

An acronym is a word (or words) formed from the initial letters or groups of letters in a phrase or series of words. Government, business, science, technology, and education make use of acronyms regularly. Following are just a few:

MOMA = Museum of Modern Art

PIN   = Personal Identification Number

Scuba = Self-contained breathing apparatus

Initials that are pronounced individually and not sounded out as new words are also often referred to as acronyms, such as **FAQ** (frequently asked questions) and **WHO** (World Heath Organization). Instant messaging brought acronyms to new levels of use and popularity. Many are in common use (and countless new ones are created regularly by creative texters), though not all will gain widespread use. The most common have been around for a long time, such as **LOL** (laughing out loud) and **BRB** (be right back). Some have less to do with spelling than sound, such as **CU** (see you). Many people use acronyms even for longer, common phrases such as **AAMOF** (as a matter of fact). Some that are used but few people know are long and obscure, such as **ALOTBSOL** (always look on the bright side of life). Don't use that expecting anyone to know! If you come across the **AAAAA**, that's an acronym for the American Association Against Acronym Abuse. If you have any thoughts of escaping this new world of acronyms, you'll be discouraged to know that there's even an acronym for Acronym-Free Zone (**AFZ**)!

IDK: IS IT IMPORTANT TO SPELL THINGS OUT?

The following is a true story: Gloria saw "IDK" being used a lot on blogs and social networking sites.

She asked a friend, who seemed to be much more savvy about Internet shortcuts to spelling, "What does IDK mean?"

He replied, "I don't know."

So she asked another friend, who said, "I don't know."

She started to feel, at least, like she wasn't the only one who didn't know. She asked a third friend, "What does IDK mean?"

He also replied, "I don't know."

Gloria said, "It seems like no one does!"

"No one does what?" asked her friend.

"Knows what IDK means."

"I know!"

"You know what it means? What is it?"

"I don't know."

"See?"

"What?"

"You don't know!"

"No," said Gloria's friend, finally understanding the confusion. "IDK means 'I don't know!'"

Have you heard of Abbott and Costello's "Who's on First?" skit? If you are familiar with it (or look it up online), you'll see how this played out like a real-life Abbott and Costello skit—a "Who's on First" of spelling. As funny as it is, it's also a good reminder of how easily abbreviations can cause confusion!

Acronyms as Memory Devices

Acronyms are extremely helpful as memory devices. HOMES, for instance, is a commonly used memory device for recalling the names of the Great Lakes. The word HOMES tells you the first letter of each of the lakes, which should help when trying to remember all five: **H**uron, **O**ntario, **M**ichigan, **E**rie, and **S**uperior.

Acronyms can help us not only remember words, but remember the correct order in a series. Following are a few other popular acronyms that people use as memory devices:

ROY G. BIV: This nonsense name helps people recall the colors of the rainbow in the order in which they appear: **R**ed, **O**range, **Y**ellow, **G**reen, **B**lue, **I**ndigo, **V**iolet.

UCAN: There's a place in the United States where four states touch. Can you name those four states? Of course *UCAN:* **U**tah, **C**olorado, **A**rizona, **N**ew Mexico.

Sentences work, too. When you want to remember the correct order of mathematical operations, think of **M**y **D**ear **A**unt **S**ally, and you'll recall that it's **M**ultiplication, **D**ivision, **A**ddition, then **S**ubtraction.

CYO! (CREATE YOUR OWN!)

Create your own memory devices. Nothing is more memorable than a device of your own creation.

EXERCISE 1

Look back at the words that were the most challenging for you on the Pretest. Choose three of them and write them below. Can you think of any memory devices to help you remember? There are no right or wrong answers; this is just a warm-up exercise to help you build your muscle for finding solutions for difficult spelling issues.

EXERCISE 2

Do you recall the memory devices from the beginning of this chapter? If you do, choosing the correct spellings of the words below should be easy! Circle the correctly spelled words.

1. be*lie*ve   be*lei*ve?

2. cem*e*tery   cem*a*tery   cem*a*tary   cem*e*tary

3. princi*ple*   princi*pal* (referring to a school administrator)

4. gramm*er*   gramm*ar*

5. comple*ment*   compl*i*ment (words that praise and admire)

6. station*ary*   station*ery* (standing still)

7. use*ful*   use*full*

8. resent*ful*   resent*full*

9. art*ful*   art*full*

10. Do you remember how to spell the original memory device discussed?

    mn*u*monic   mn*e*monic   mn*eu*monic

EXERCISE 3

Businesses often set up phone numbers that can also be remembered as words, such as a loan company whose number is GET CASH (438-2274) or a paving company whose number is ASPHALT (227-4258). Look at your telephone (most land lines and some cell phones) and see what words you can spell from your phone number. Few people remember telephone numbers anymore (as most of us have the numbers we call most often programmed into our phones). Your number will be easy for anyone to remember, though, if you find that it spells a clever word (or words).

Better Spelling by Ear

In ancient Rome, the battle cry was *divide and conquer*. The same strategy works with learning to spell many words. Breaking them down into syllables is often helpful for both sounding a word out and also learning a few helpful spelling rules along the way. While some words can be sounded out with careful pronunciation, others—as you know—cannot be sounded out. In many cases, their vowel sounds are indistinct and it's hard to hear which vowel is used. No matter how carefully you listen to some words, you may not be able to hear the difference between an *e* or an *o* (edit*e*r or edit*o*r?), an *a* or an *e* or an *i* (comp*e*tent or comp*i*tent or comp*e*tant or comp*i*tant?). With a little practice, though, you can be your own edit*o*r and a comp*e*tent speller of difficult words.

WHAT YOU WILL LEARN

In this chapter, you will learn about syllables, how they're broken down, and how to sound out words for better spelling. The practice words are grouped into vowel categories to offer a clue to their spellings when you hear them. You will practice listening, spelling, and double-checking to help you improve your spelling by sounding out difficult words.

SECTIONS IN THIS CHAPTER
• Syllables: Breaking It Down
• One Syllable at a Time
• Common Mix-ups
• More Common Mix-ups

Syllables: Breaking It Down

A syllable is the smallest unit of speech and generally contains only one vowel sound. If you listen to words, hear how many beats each spoken word has. *Spoken* has two beats—two syllables; *word* has one—it's a one-syllable word. A syllable can be either one letter—*a*—or a component of a word, or complete word, such as *laugh*. Syllables are shown in the dictionary and are helpful for learning to spell. You will see syllable breaks in the list of 10,000 words in the back of this book. The word syllable is three syllables: syl•la•ble.

pro—one syllable

speak—one-syllable word

pro•nounce—two-syllable word

pro•nounc•ing—three-syllable word

pro•nounc•a•ble—four-syllable word

pro•nun•ci•a•tion—five-syllable word

Most one-syllable words are short. However, don't break a word into syllables just because it's getting long. The following one-syllable words each have nine letters: stretched, screeched, scratched, and strengths.

DIVIDE A WORD INTO SYLLABLES

The question of how exactly to divide syllables is less important now that computers automatically insert hyphens. In the days of typewriters, we needed to know where the proper word breaks were. It is still, however, helpful to understand how syllables work—where the syllable breaks are and why. The following four rules explain this.

RULE 1

Begin a syllable with a consonant when the consonant is between two vowels and the first vowel is *long*.

EXAMPLE   ro•man•tic

The consonant *m* begins the second syllable because the vowel *o* is long.

The long vowels are pronounced exactly as they are pronounced when you recite the alphabet.

$\bar{a}$—*as in* hay

$\bar{e}$—*as in* bee

ī—*as in* kite

ō—*as in* note

ū—*as in* mute

Other examples of Rule 1 are:

ro•tate   na•ture   re•view

RULE 2

End a syllable with a consonant when the consonant is between two vowels and the first vowel is *short*.

EXAMPLE   hab•it

The consonant *b* ends the first syllable because it is between two vowels and the first vowel is short.

The short vowels are present in this line:

bag, beg, big, bog, bug

Syllables with short vowels:

a—*as in* fash•ion, tap•es•try

e—*as in* nec•es•sa•ry

i—*as in* crit•i•cism

o—*as in* prom•i•nent

u—*as in* sub•urb

Other examples of Rule 2 are:

proph•et   pun•ish   ex•ec•u•tive

RULE 3

Adjoining consonants most often separate into syllables.

EXAMPLES   mur•mur   can•dy   ex•pense

RULE 4

Double consonants are not divided when a suffix is added.

EXAMPLES   mill•er   hiss•ing

WARNING!

The hyphens inserted automatically by computers are often incorrectly placed. They are acceptable because of common use (or misuse), so you don't need to worry that they're wrong or try to fix them. However, if you're trying to improve your spelling by recognizing syllables, learn the rules and check your dictionary, but pay atttention to where your computer places a hyphen!

One Syllable at a Time

While many words are not spelled as they sound, many actually are. Some longer words sound intimidating until we break them down into simple syllables, and then the difficulty disappears.

EASY AS 1-2-3!

1. Read each of the following six words slowly.

2. Spell them out loud.

3. Pronounce each one slowly two more times, writing them down as you do.

   mag•nif•i•cent

   mag•a•zine

   ar•tic•u•late

   priv•i•lege

   per•pet•u•ate

   mon•u•men•tal

EXERCISE 1

Divide the following words into syllables.

_____   1. bonanza

_____   2. refresh

_____   3. fatigue

_____   4. punishment

_____   5. ordeal

_____   6. rummage

_____   7. missing

_____   8. gasoline

_____   9. excavate

_____   10. tyrannical

Common Mix-ups

Have someone dictate these words to you. Spell them. Then compare your spelling with those in the book. What errors did you make? Practice the words until you can spell them correctly without thinking twice about them.

DIFFICULT "A" WORDS

Each of the following words has *a* trouble. People forget the existence of *a* and substitute another letter:

captain	certain	criminal
finally	grammar	dictionary
maintain	plain	liberal
preparations	probable	justifiable
separate	straight	equally
usually	villain	congressional
balance	equivalent	professional
performance	salary	temperature
actually	extravagant	similar
village	calendar	
partially	illegal	

DIFFICULT "E" WORDS

Each of the words below has an *e* difficulty. Writers frequently forget the *e* and use another letter incorrectly.

apparently	coherent	audience
dependent	current	correspondence
prominent	efficient	existence
machinery	experience	magnificent
independent	opponent	patience
privileges	permanent	superintendent
luncheon	cafeteria	description
competent	conscience	

DIFFICULT "I" WORDS

In the following words, the *i*'s have it:

acquainted	auxiliary	exhibition
compliment	definite	until
criticized	sympathized	principle
participle	peculiar	respectively
quantities	quiet	hosiery
physical	individual	anticipate
articles	business	

DIFFICULT "O" WORDS

Do you omit these *o*'s? In the words below, the letter *o* comes in for much abuse and neglect. Be kind to these words:

attorney	surgeon	proprietor
conspicuous	authorize	competitors
favorable	conqueror	editor
notorious	memorial	senator
society	organization	tailor
odor	strenuously	authority
colonel	aviator	interior
colors	accustomed	motorist
humorist	favorite	successor
precious	memory	

SILENT LETTERS

The following are just a few common words with silent letters. The only way to learn them is to practice!

government	promptly	February
indebted	pamphlet	pledged
psychiatrist	condemn	solemn
campaign	foreign	resign
fasten	gourmet	depot
debut	salmon	autumn
column	climb	

EXERCISE 2

Some of the following words are spelled correctly and some are misspelled.
Put a check on the blank if a word is spelled correctly. Rewrite it correctly if it
is misspelled.

_____	1. grammar
_____	2. seperate
_____	3. usally
_____	4. village
_____	5. calender
_____	6. existence
_____	7. description
_____	8. editer
_____	9. attorney
_____	10. senator
_____	11. odor
_____	12. tailer
_____	13. cafateria
_____	14. goverment
_____	15. promptly
_____	16. existence
_____	17. discription
_____	18. equivelent
_____	19. conquorer
_____	20. successer

More Common Mix-ups

A common type of misspelling occurs when letters are interchanged. For example, *l* and *v* are often reversed in *relevant* so that the word is misspelled *revelant*. This type of error is called *metathesis*. Observe the correct spelling of the following ten words:

Correct	Incorrect
cava*l*ry	calvary
child*ren*	childern
hund*red*	hunderd
jew*elry*	jewlery
lar*ynx*	larnyx
mod*ern*	modren
patt*ern*	pattren
*pers*piration	prespiration
re*lev*ant	revelant
west*ern*	westren

EXERCISE 3

Fill in the missing letters:

1. hund _____ _____ d

2. mod _____ _____ n

3. p _____ _____ spiration

4. west _____ _____ n

5. re _____ e _____ ant

6. ca _____ a _____ ry

7. child _____ _____ n

8. jew _____ _____ _____ y

9. lar _____ _____ x

10. patt _____ _____ n

Some Special Problems

The *Saturday Review of Literature* once published the following story:

> A neophyte copy editor in a large advertising agency was slowly
> going out of his mind because his copy chief was constantly taking
> a small slip of paper from his breast pocket, looking at it, leering,
> then putting it back. After watching this for months he managed
> one day, when the copy chief was taking a nap, to steal the secret
> paper from the jacket in back of the chief's chair. He opened the
> slip of paper with trembling hands.
>
> It read:
>
> "*I* before *E* except after *C*"[1]

WHAT YOU WILL LEARN

In this chapter, you will learn the value of the little mnemonic device used by the
editor in the story above. You'll also learn some additional lines to that helpful
device (which account for more exceptions to the *i* before *e* rule). This chapter will
also help you determine how to pro*ceed* when you're not sure whether a word ends
in *-sede*, *-ceed*, or *-cede*.

SECTIONS IN THIS CHAPTER
• *IE* and *EI*
• *-SEDE*, *-CEED*, and *-CEDE*

[1]*Reprinted by permission of* Saturday Review of Literature.

IE and *EI*

RULE

Put *i* before *e*,
Except after *c*,
Or when sounded like *a*,
As in *neighbor* and *weigh*;
And except *seize* and *seizure*
And also *leisure*,
Weird, *height*, and *either*,
Forfeit and *neither*.

IE

Examine the list below. Notice that in no case below does a *c* precede the *ie*.

achieve	befriend	field	grief	hygiene
aggrieve	belief	fiend	grievance	interview
alien	believe	fierce	grieve	mischievous
chief	besiege	fiery	mischief	piece
niece	brief	friend	pierce	retrieve
quiet	lieu	relieve	reprieve	thievery
review	relief	shield	shriek	yield
siege	series	sieve	thief	
view	wield	frontier	handkerchief	

EXERCISE 1

Study the list above. Notice that never does a c *directly precede the* ie. *Any other letter in the alphabet may do so, but not the* c. *Write five of the above words once, one word to a line; pronounce it; then write it once in a sentence; follow this scheme.*

Word	*Pronounce*	*Sentence*
achieve	a chēē v	I hope to achieve my goal.

EXERCISE 2

When you feel certain that you know the preceding words, copy and fill in the missing letters in the following:

1. aggr __ __ ve

2. br __ __ f

3. fr __ __ nd

4. gr __ __ ve

5. front __ __r

6. misch __ __ f

7. sh __ __ ld

8. shr __ __ k

9. w __ __ ld

10. spec __ __ s

11. rel __ __ ve

12. l __ __ sure

13. handkerch __ __ f

14. rec __ __ pt

15. s __ __ ze

16. perc __ __ ve

17. gr __ __ f

18. n __ __ ce

19. conc __ __ ve

EI

Now we can master the other combinations. Study the following chart:

| | HANDLING *EI* | |
| | EI because the sound | |
EI follows C	is ā as in HAY	Special Cases
dec*ei*t	fr*ei*ght	*ei*ther
perc*ei*ve	v*ei*l	h*ei*ght
rec*ei*ve	sl*ei*gh	l*ei*sure
	w*ei*gh	forf*ei*t
		n*ei*ther
		s*ei*ze
		w*ei*rd
		s*ei*zure

EXAMPLE   *EI* **follows C**

Read this list carefully and notice that in each case the *ei* follows *c*.

c*ei*ling	dec*ei*tful
conc*ei*t	dec*ei*ve
conc*ei*ted	rec*ei*pt
conc*ei*ve	rec*ei*ve

EXAMPLE   *EI* **Sounds as Ā**

The following list has the *ei* because it sounds like ā in *bay*.

reign	vein
sleigh	weigh
surveillance	weight
veil	

EXAMPLES   **Special Cases**

1. The final *feit* is pronounced *fit*.

   forfeit
   counterfeit
   surfeit

2. These are pronounced *ī* as *kite*. Be sure to put the *e* in.

> height
> sleight

3. A few words have *cie*, but in all cases the *c* is pronounced as *sh*.

> ancient   glacier
> conscience   proficient
> deficient   species
> efficient   sufficient

EXERCISE 3

Have the following passage read aloud to you. Ask the reader to stress the italicized words and to pause for you to write those words. Then, study those that were difficult or that you misspelled.

> A *thief* was planning to *deceive* the clerk with a *counterfeit* bill. He saw a *surveillance* camera, but his *conceit* made him *believe* he could never be caught. He knew the clerk would be in trouble if the bill was discovered, leaving *receipts* short at the end of the day. The clerk was so *friendly*, the thief's *conscience* made him *forfeit* his plan.

-SEDE, -CEED, and *-CEDE*

Knowing which of these word endings to use may seem confusing, but it's surprisingly simple to learn and remember. Memorize the endings of four words and you'll know the right answer when determining whether a word ends in *-sede, -ceed,* or *-cede.*

-SEDE

The only word in English that ends in *-sede* is *supersede.*
Try this memory trick to remember: It *supersedes* all others to stand alone in this category.

-CEED

Only three words end in *-ceed.*

> proceed   exceed   succeed

Try this memory trick: Think of a boxer who is first a *pro*fessional, then an *ex*-fighter, replaced by a *suc*cessor. If another similar example will work better for you, modify so that you'll remember. Even if you simply have to learn these words without a memory device, it's easy to memorize a set of three words that comprise the entire *-ceed* group.

-CEDE

All other words in this class end in *-cede*. The following are a few examples:

accede	precede	recede
concede	secede	intercede

NOTE:

Super*cede* is listed in dictionaries as a spelling variant of super*sede*. However, it is not the traditional spelling and may be seen as an error. The most commonly accepted spelling is super*sede*.

WARNING! *-ed* Alert!

The rules in this chapter *only* apply to *present tense* words. Though they are rare, any verb ending in *cee* would have a past tense ending of *-ceed*. For instance, *emceed*, the past tense of *emcee* (a variation of MC, which means *to serve as the master of ceremonies*), ends in *-ceed*.

EXERCISE 4

Have the following passage read aloud to you. Ask the reader to stress the italicized words and to pause for you to write those words. Then, study those that were difficult or that you misspelled.

Without practice, the spelling rules you learn will *recede* in your memory. But if you *proceed*, you will *succeed*. You may even *exceed* your expectations. Your confidence will *supersede* any fears you have about misspellings.

Prefixes

"Pre" is a prefix meaning before. A *prefix* is a letter or set of letters added to the beginning of a word. Prefixes add important shades of meaning. A prefix might change the word's meaning, its placement in time or in relation, or its intensity; it may even turn a word upside-down so that it means the opposite. Just a few little letters change someone from being *active* to *in*active or *pro*active. The difference between being *moral* and *a*moral is as stark as the difference between day and night.

WHAT YOU WILL LEARN

This chapter contains only one simple rule and a few pointers for dealing with confusing prefixes.

SECTIONS IN THIS CHAPTER

- The Prefix Rule
- A List of Common Prefixes
- Pay Attention to *PER-*, *PRE-*, *PRO-*

The Prefix Rule

This rule is simple and easily learned. It will help you avoid many misspellings.

A prefix is one or more syllables attached to the beginning of a word. Prefixes, as those below, change the meaning of words to which they are attached.

dis + agree = disagree

il + logical = illogical

un + kind = unkind

mis + spell = misspell

super + vision = supervision

THE PREFIX RULE

Do *not* change the spelling of either the prefix or the original word.

A List of Common Prefixes

Here is a list of some common prefixes. Become familiar with them to discover the meaning and spelling of words that are new to you.

COMMON PREFIXES

Prefix	Meaning	Examples
a-	in a state	aglow
		afire
	not, without	asexual
		amoral
		asocial
ab-	away, from	abject
		abduct
ante-	before	anteroom (a room before another)
anti-	against	antiaging
		antioxidant
circum-	around	circumscribe (to draw a line around)
		circumnavigate (to sail around)
		circumlocution (act of talking around a topic rather than directly)
com-, con-	with, together	conjoin (to join together)
		commingle (to combine)
de-	down	devalue
		demotivate

Prefix	Meaning	Examples
dis-	apart	disgrace
		disagree
		disorder
hyper-	above, beyond	hyperactive
		hypercritical
hypo-	under, beneath	hypothesis
il-, im-,	not	illogical
in-, ir-		immoral
		indecisive
		irrelevant
inter-	among, between	interview
		intercollegiate
		international
intra-	within	intracoastal
		intravenous (within a vein)
mis-	wrongly, unfavorably	misjudge
		misunderstand
		misappropriate
non-	not	nonsense
		noncombatant
		nonconformist
over-	excessive, on top	overcharge
		overcoat
per-	through	perception
		perspire
		persevere
post-	behind, after	postmortem (after death)
		postpone
		postgraduate
pre-	before	precaution
		prefix
		preamble
pro-	forward, instead of, before	procession
		pronoun
		proclaim
		proactive
re-	again, against	react
		restore
		reevaluate
sub-	under	subway
		subtract
super-	above	superintendent
		superficial
		superstar
trans-	across	transcontinental
		transfer
		transplant
un-	not	unnatural
		unnoticeable
		unoccupied

WARNING!

Most errors occur when a prefix ends with the same letter with which the word begins. For example:

un + natural = unnatural (*not* unatural)
dis + satisfied = dissatisfied (*not* disatisfied)
mis + step = misstep (*not* mistep)

Remember, when you add a prefix, do *not* change the spelling of either the prefix or the original word.

EXERCISE 1

How many s's in:

_____ 1. di ___?___ olve

_____ 2. di ___?___ imilar

_____ 3. mi ___?___ pell

_____ 4. di ___?___ appear

_____ 5. mi ___?___ take

EXERCISE 2

Try your skill in building your own words. Take, for example, scribe, *meaning a writer.*

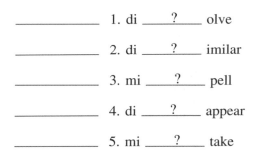

circum
trans
sub   } scribe
de
pre

Give the meaning of each.

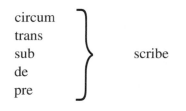

EXERCISE 3

By adding the proper Latin prefixes to the following italicized words, spell the new formations correctly. Some require changing the word form.

EXAMPLES not *satisfied*   *dissatisfied*
            not *legible*   *illegible*

_____ 1. A *step* wrongly taken

_____ 2. not to *understand*

_____ 3. not *similar*

_____ 4. to *start* again

_____ 5. below the *standard*

_____ 6. across the *Atlantic*

_____ 7. before *marriage*

_____ 8. against the *establishment*

_____ 9. *navigates* around the globe

_____ 10. after an *operation*

Pay Attention to *PER-, PRE-, PRO-*

Some difficulties with the spelling of prefixes may be due to carelessness in pronunciation. Thus, if you don't pronounce *prescription* properly, you may not spell the prefix with *pre*. The reverse error may come with a word like *per*spiration, in which the initial *per* may be misspelled.

Knowing the meaning of certain prefixes, as indicated earlier in this chapter, will help you to both know the meaning of the word and its spelling.

PER-, PRE-, PRO-

PER- MEANS "THROUGH"

Word	Meaning
permeate	to penetrate through and through
perforate	to pierce through
perpetual	through the years
persist	to continue through a project
persecute	to follow through
perspective	to see through to a distant point or from one point of view

PRE- MEANS "BEFORE"

Word	Meaning
precocious	to develop earlier
prefer	to place before
prepare	to make ready beforehand
prejudice	a judgment before the evidence is in
prescribe	to write before

PRO- MEANS "FORWARD"

Word	Meaning
propose	to put forward an offer
prophesy	something stated before it happens
proceed	to move forward
proclaim	to shout before
produce	to bring forth
prognosis	forecast of the probable outcome of a disease

EXERCISE 4

Underline the correct spelling of the pairs of words in the following sentences.

1. The protesting students felt they had been (persecuted, presecuted).

2. Let us (preceed, proceed) with the trial.

3. This bright child was obviously (precocious, percocious).

4. We must look at world affairs from the proper (perspective, prospective).

5. The patient asked the doctor to (proscribe, prescribe) something for her cough.

6. The illness was diagnosed as a (perforated, proferated) ulcer.

7. It costs a great deal to (perduce, produce) a musical comedy.

8. We must (persist, presist) in our efforts to find ways to peace.

9. Searching for the truth requires (perpetual, prepetual) effort.

10. Let us (propose, perpose) a toast.

Confusing Suffixes

A suffix is added to the end of a word to change the meaning or form. The most common problems with suffixes are knowing which one to choose and whether the root word changes when the suffix is added. Unlike prefixes—which follow one, simple rule—suffixes follow a number of rules.

EXAMPLES

desire + *able* = desir*able*
move + *ing* = mov*ing*
kind + *ly* = kind*ly*
mean + *ness* = mean*ness*
fame + *ous* = fam*ous*

WHAT YOU WILL LEARN

In this chapter, you will learn how to make the right choice between *-able* and *-ible*, *-ary* and *-ery*, *-ance*, and *-ence*. You'll also learn when a root word should not change, and when letters should be doubled or dropped. While suffixes can be confusing, taking the time to learn these rules will help you build your spelling knowledge and skill immensely.

SECTIONS IN THIS CHAPTER

- Words Ending in *-ABLE, -IBLE*
- Adding *-LY* to Words Ending in *-AL*
- Words Ending in *-OUS*
- Troublesome Affixes *-AL, -EL, -LE*
- Words Ending in *-ER* or *-OR*
- Words Ending in *-AR*
- Words Ending in *-ANCE, -ENCE*
- Words Ending in *-ENSE*
- Words Ending in *-ARY, -ERY*
- Words Ending in *-ISE, -IZE*

Words Ending in -*ABLE*, -*IBLE*

The endings -*able* and -*ible* are often confused. Not only do they look the same—they both add the meaning *able*, having the ability to or quality of.

-*ABLE*

1. Our most familiar words add -*able* to form the adjective.

$$comfort + able = comfortable$$
$$drink + able = drinkable$$
$$laugh + able = laughable$$
$$read + able = readable$$
$$unthink + able = unthinkable$$

-*ABLE* RULES

1. The ending -*able* is more common than -*ible*. If in doubt, use -*able*.

2. Nouns ending in -*ation* will most often use the suffix -*able*. Example: abomina*tion* and naviga*tion* become abomin*able* and navig*able*. However, you'll find six exceptions to this in the next section, including diges*tion* (which becomes digest*ible*) and collec*tion* (which becomes collect*ible*).

3. Rule #1 is the most important to remember. When in doubt, remember that far more words end in -*able* than -*ible*.

-*IBLE*

-*IBLE* RULES

1. -*ible* is not used after vowels. Example: If the root words are *agree* and *replace*, you know that the correct ending is -*able*: *agreeable, replaceable*.

2. Words ending in *ss* will often use the suffix -*ible*. Example: *accessible, permissible*.

3. Words ending in -*ion* will often use the suffix -*ible*. Example: *destruction, destructible; division, divisible*.

4. -*ible* is often used in words to keep the soft sound of *g* or *c*. These are more difficult to notice. Example: *legible* (if we were to use *legable*, the sound of the *g*, which is now pronounced as a *j* sound, would sound more like the *g* in *gum*.)

The last rule may be very difficult to recognize, but not all of the -*able* and -*ible* rules are perfect every time.

MORE EXAMPLES

- Words preceded by a double *ss* before the *-ible*.

acce*ss*ible	permi*ss*ible
admi*ss*ible	transmi*ss*ible
compre*ss*ible	

- Words ending in *-ible* with a noun form ending in *-sion*. Drop the *-ion* and add *-ible*.

admission	expansion	extension
admiss*ible*	expans*ible*	extens*ible*
compression	reversion	division
compress*ible*	revers*ible*	divis*ible*
permission	coercion	reprehension
permiss*ible*	coerc*ible*	reprehens*ible*
transmission	comprehension	conversion
transmiss*ible*	comprehens*ible*	convert*ible*

- Words ending in *-ible* with a noun form ending in *-tion*.

combustion	digestion	corruption
combust*ible*	digest*ible*	corrupt*ible*
destruction	collection	perception
destruct*ible*	collect*ible*	percept*ible*

- Words that end in *-ible* to keep the soft sound of *g* or *c*.

deduc*ible*	produc*ible*	incorrig*ible*
conduc*ible*	corrig*ible*	irasc*ible*
elig*ible*	inelig*ible*	leg*ible*
intellig*ible*	invinc*ible*	

EXERCISE 1

Add -able or -ible to the following words:

account	depend	perish
avoid	detest	reason
comfort	fashion	return
download	favor	review
credit	market	season

Did you add -able to each of these? Then you were 100% correct. Now add -able or -ible to the roots of these words:

HINT: consol-*a*-tion   consol-*a*ble

      commendation
      admiration
      conformation
      appreciation
      consideration

Did you add -able to the roots of each of these words? You were 100% correct. Remember, a noun ending in -ation will have an adjective in -able. As a final task, add the endings -able or -ible to the roots of the following words.

HINT: demonstr-*ation*   demonstr-*a*ble

derivation	exportation	notation
duration	habitation	refutation
estimation	imagination	separation
execration	irritation	taxation
	lamentation	toleration

You should add -able to the roots of each of the words.

EXERCISE 2

   Have someone dictate the following passage that contains many words ending in the suffixes -ible or -able.

    The prosecuting attorney protested that the evidence by the defendant about his *taxable* income was *inadmissible*. In the first place, it was not easily *accessible*. In the second place, although the evidence was originally *acceptable* in a lower court, the decisions in such courts are *reversible*.

    The defendant's attorney objected that such reasoning was *unsupportable* and *intolerable* and that it was *reprehensible* on his opponent's part to bring up such a claim. The tension was increasing *perceptibly*. If this continued, the defending attorney might have to be ejected *forcibly*, or be *eligible* for disbarment. However, it took some time for the atmosphere to be cleared and the case proceeded to its *inevitable* conclusion.

Adding *-LY* to Words Ending in *-AL*

-LY RULE

When adding *-ly* to words ending in *-al* (to change adjectives into adverbs), simply add *-ly* to the original word. Example: *verbal* (adjective), *verbally* (adverb).

EXERCISE 3

Form the adverbs of the following adjectives:

———————————————— 1. accidental

———————————————— 2. critical

———————————————— 3. elemental

———————————————— 4. equal

———————————————— 5. exceptional

———————————————— 6. final

———————————————— 7. general (adj.)

———————————————— 8. incidental

———————————————— 9. intentional

———————————————— 10. radical

———————————————— 11. logical

———————————————— 12. mathematical

———————————————— 13. practical

———————————————— 14. professional

———————————————— 15. real

_____ 16. typical

_____ 17. usual

_____ 18. verbal

_____ 19. global

Words Ending in -*OUS*

-*OUS* AFTER A CONSONANT

-*OUS* RULE FOR WORDS ENDING IN CONSONANTS

When adding -*ous* to a noun ending in a consonant, do not change the spelling of the noun. Simply add -*ous*. Review the examples below.

-*OUS* AFTER A CONSONANT

Noun		Suffix		Adjective
danger	+	ous	=	danger*ous*
hazard	+	ous	=	hazard*ous*
humor	+	ous	=	humor*ous*
libel	+	ous	=	libel*ous*
marvel	+	ous	=	marvel*ous*
moment	+	ous	=	moment*ous*
mountain	+	ous	=	mountain*ous*
murder	+	ous	=	murder*ous*
peril	+	ous	=	peril*ous*
poison	+	ous	=	poison*ous*
riot	+	ous	=	riot*ous*
slander	+	ous	=	slander*ous*

WARNING!

Nouns ending in -*f* change the *f* to *v* when -*ous* is added.

EXAMPLES   grief + *ous* = grievous (*not* grievious)
mischief + *ous* = mischievous (*not* mischievious)

WARNING!

Most nouns ending in *-y* drop the *y* and add *i* or *e* before *-ous*. An exception to this rule is joyous.

EXAMPLES
glory + *ous* = glor*ious*
mystery + *ous* = myster*ious*
victory + *ous* = victor*ious*
joy + *ous* = joy*ous*

-OUS AFTER A VOWEL

-OUS RULE FOR WORDS ENDING IN *-E*

When adding *-ous* to a noun ending in *-e*, drop the *e*.

EXAMPLES
adventure + *ous* = adventur*ous*
analogue + *ous* = analog*ous*
desire + *ous* = desir*ous*

WARNING!

Occasionally the final *e* is left before *ous* to retain the same pronunciation of the last letter.

EXAMPLES
courage + *ous* = courage*ous*
advantage + *ous* = advantage*ous*
outrage + *ous* = outrage*ous*

EXERCISE 4

Write the correct adjectives of the following nouns by adding the suffix -ous.

_____ 1. advantage

_____ 2. courage

_____ 3. peril

———————————— 4. mountain

———————————— 5. fame

———————————— 6. desire

———————————— 7. mischief

———————————— 8. adventure

———————————— 9. bounty

———————————— 10. danger

———————————— 11. grief

———————————— 12. humor

———————————— 13. outrage

———————————— 14. libel

———————————— 15. poison

Troublesome Affixes -*AL*, -*EL*, -*LE*

The endings, -*al*, -*el*, and -*le* are called affixes. They are added to the end of words and are a source of many spelling difficulties because they are pronounced in approximately the same way.

Although there are no hard-and-fast rules governing their use, here are some guidelines that will help you correctly spell most of the words in which they occur.

THE AFFIX -*AL*

-*AL* RULE

The affix -*al* is added to nouns and adjectives only. The affix -*al* means of, belonging to, pertaining to, or appropriate to.

EXAMPLES   person*al* — *of* the person
autumn*al* — *belonging* to autumn
roy*al* — *pertaining* to a king
nautic*al* — *appropriate* to ships

Review the examples below.

COMMON WORDS ENDING IN -AL

Adjectives			Nouns	
additional	general	original	acquittal	proposal
adverbial	jovial	oval	arrival	recital
annual	legal	penal	betrayal	refusal
brutal	logical	personal	capital	rival
classical	magical	regal	denial	signal
clerical	mechanical	several		
comical	medical	trivial		
fatal	neutral			
fiscal	normal			

WARNING!

Do not confuse *capital*, a city, with *capitol*, a building.

THE AFFIX -*EL*

If you remember that -*el* is used less frequently than -*al* and if you memorize the spelling of the common words below, you will greatly reduce the possibility of misspelling words in which -*el* appears.

The affix -*el* originally diminished the meaning of a word to which it was attached. For example, tunnel once meant a small barrel or tun, and chapel meant a small church. Nowadays the original significance of -*el* is forgotten.

COMMON WORDS ENDING IN -*EL*

bushel	jewel	novel	satchel
cancel	kennel	nickel	shovel
channel	kernel	panel	swivel
flannel	model	parcel	travel
funnel	morsel	quarrel	trowel

THE AFFIX -LE

The affix -le is used far more frequently than -al or -el. The method below will help you to remember the words that end in -le.

1. Examine the following list carefully.

2. Form a mental image of each word.

3. Pronounce each word aloud, then write it down. Underline the le after you complete writing the word.

4. Pronounce the word again.

When you perform these steps, you are seeing, feeling, and hearing. In other words you are employing three senses to help you remember the correct spelling.

WARNING!

The affixes -el and -le are never used to make adjectives from nouns. *Nickel* and *little* are adjectives but they were not formed by adding an affix to a noun.

COMMON WORDS ENDING IN -LE

able	dribble	muscle	settle
ample	drizzle	muzzle	shuffle
angle	fable	myrtle	shackle
article	fickle	needle	shuttle
ankle	fiddle	nestle	sizzle
baffle	frizzle	nibble	sparkle
battle	gable	nuzzle	sprinkle
beetle	gentle	paddle	squabble
bottle	giggle	peaceable	strangle
brittle	gristle	people	subtle
buckle	grizzle	pestle	tackle
bundle	handle	pickle	thimble
bungle	huddle	possible	thistle
cattle	humble	prattle	treble
chuckle	hurdle	principle	tremble
circle	jangle	puzzle	trestle
couple	jingle	raffle	trickle
cripple	juggle	riddle	trifle
castle	jungle	ruffle	triple
corpuscle	knuckle	scribble	trouble
dangle	mantle	scruple	turtle
dazzle	miracle	scuffle	twinkle
double	muffle	scuttle	

EXERCISE 5

Select the word in each pair that is correctly spelled, and write it in the blank.

———————————— 1. a. brutel   b. brutal

———————————— 2. a. proposal   b. proposale

———————————— 3. a. flannel   b. flannal

———————————— 4. a. dangle   b. dangel

———————————— 5. a. drizzel   b. drizzle

———————————— 6. a. corpuscle   b. corpuscel

———————————— 7. a. fatal   b. fatel

———————————— 8. a. swivle   b. swivel

———————————— 9. a. tripel   b. triple

———————————— 10. a. signel   b. signal

———————————— 11. a. battle   b. battel

———————————— 12. a. quarrle   b. quarrel

———————————— 13. a. riddel   b. riddle

———————————— 14. a. mechanicle   b. mechanical

———————————— 15. a. angal   b. angle

———————————— 16. a. rival   b. rivle

———————————— 17. a. jewel   b. jewal

———————————— 18. a. nickel   b. nickle

———————————— 19. a. buckel   b. buckle

———————————— 20. a. fabel   b. fable

———————————— 21. a. thimble   b. thimbel

———————————— 22. a. capital   b. capitle

———————————— 23. a. knuckel   b. knuckle

———————————— 24. a. parcle   b. parcel

———————————— 25. a. regel   b. regal

Words Ending in -*ER* or -*OR*

The suffixes -*er* and -*or* mean *one who* or *that which*. For example, a *visitor* is *one who visits* and an *indicator* is *that which indicates*.

When should you use -*er* and when should you use -*or*?

Although there are many words with these suffixes, there is no rule governing their use.

Remember that most end in -*or*. Then study the list of -*er* words (below) and pay attention to those you use most often.

COMMON WORDS ENDING IN -*OR*, -*ER*

-OR			-ER	
actor	counselor	operator	advertiser	manager
administrator	editor	radiator	beginner	manufacturer
author	educator	refrigerator	bookkeeper	passenger
aviator	elevator	senator	computer	printer
bachelor	escalator	spectator	consumer	purchaser
collector	governor	sponsor	employer	receiver
commentator	indicator	supervisor	farmer	scanner
conductor	inventor		interpreter	treasurer
contractor	investigator		laborer	writer

Words Ending in -*AR*

A relatively small number of words end in -*ar*. The most common are listed below. If you study the list, this ending should never cause you trouble.

COMMON WORDS ENDING IN -*AR*

circular	dollar	grammar	familiar
calendar	regular	peculiar	liar
collar	singular	similar	popular

WARNING!

Don't confuse a *hangar*, a shelter for housing airplanes, and a *hanger*, which hangs clothes!

EXERCISE 6

Add the suffix -or, -er, *or* -ar *to each of the following words:*

1. gramm ____ ____

2. receiv ____ ____

3. conduct ____ ____

4. passeng ____ ____

5. govern ____ ____

6. scann ____ ____

7. operat ____ ____

8. doll ____ ____

9. supervis ____ ____

10. advertis ____ ____

Words Ending in -*ANCE*, -*ENCE*

There are no simple ways of learning when to add -*ance* or -*ence*. It is best to study each of the following lists, using the words as often as possible until you habitually spell them correctly.

COMMON -*ANCE*, -*ANCY*, -*ANT* WORDS

abundant	descendant	important	preponderant
abundance	elegance	inheritance	remembrance
acquaintance	elegant	irrelevancy	repentance
appearance	endurance	irrelevant	repentant
assistance	entrance	lieutenant	restaurant
assistant	entrant	maintenance	sergeant
balance	grievance	nuisance	significance
brilliance	guidance	observance	significant
brilliant	hindrance	observant	stimulant
clearance	ignorance	pendant	tenancy
countenance	ignorant	perseverance	tenant
defendant	importance	pleasant	tolerance

COMMON -*ENCE*, -*ENCY*, -*ENT* WORDS

absence	diligence	occurrence
absent	diligent	opponent
abstinence	divergence	patent
abstinent	divergent	patience
adherence	efficiency	patient
adherent	efficient	penitence
antecedent	eminence	penitent
apparent	eminent	permanence
audience	essence (essential)	permanent
coherence	equivalent	persistence
coherent	excellence	persistent
coincidence	excellent	pestilence
concurrence	existence	precedence
concurrent	existent	preference
conference	experience	presence
confidence	government	present
confident	impertinence	prominence
conscience	impertinent	prominent
consequence	imprudence	providence
consequent	imprudent	provident
competence	independence	reference
competent	independent	repellent
compliment (praise)	indulgence	reverence
convenience	indulgent	reverent
convenient	inference	residence
correspondence	influence (influential)	resident
correspondent	insistence	sentence
deference (deferential)	insolence	sufficient
dependence	insolent	superintendent
dependent	intelligence	tendency
difference	intelligent	violence
different	intermittent	violent
diffidence	magnificence	
diffident	magnificent	

Words Ending in -*ENSE*

There are only a few words ending in -*ense*.

WORDS ENDING IN -*ENSE*

defense	intense	pretense *or* pretence
dispense	license	sense
expense	nonsense	suspense
immense	offense *or* offence	tense
incense		

EXERCISE 7

Insert a *or* e *in the space indicated for the following words:*

1. complim _____ nt

2. remembr _____ nce

3. consist _____ nt

4. superintend _____ nt

5. depend _____ nt

6. exist _____ nce

7. descend _____ nt

8. acquaint _____ nce

9. griev _____ nce

10. perman _____ nt

11. magnific _____ nt

12. brilli _____ nce

13. compl _____ mentary

14. conveni _____ nce

15. abund _____ nce

16. guid _____ nce

17. consci _____ nce

18. coincid _____ nce

19. appar _____ nt

20. consequ _____ ntial

Words Ending in -*ARY*, -*ERY*

There are more than 300 words ending in -*ary*. There are fewer commonly used words ending in -*ery*.

COMMON WORDS ENDING IN -*ERY*

bakery	greenery	scenery
bravery	grocery	stationery
bribery	machinery	watery
cemetery	mastery	

Perhaps it may help you to remember that in cemetery only *e*'s are used. Recall that station*ery* is used to write a lett*er*.

COMMON WORDS ENDING IN -*ARY*

auxiliary	honorary	secretary
boundary	imaginary	secondary
centenary	infirmary	tertiary
dictionary	involuntary	tributary
elementary	library	vocabulary
evolutionary	revolutionary	

EXERCISE 8

Select the word in each pair that is correctly spelled, and write it in the blank.

_____ 1. a. boundery   b. boundary

_____ 2. a. revolutionary   b. revolutionery

_____ 3. a. cemetary   b. cemetery

_____ 4. a. imaginery   b. imaginary

_____ 5. a. tributery   b. tributary

_____ 6. a. corollary   b. corollery

_____ 7. a. coronery   b. coronary

_____ 8. a. solitary   b. solitery

_____ 9. a. militery   b. military

_____ 10. a. infirmary   b. infirmery

Words Ending in -ISE, -IZE

There are no hard and fast rules to differentiate between the words ending in *-ise* and *-ize*. Perhaps the best procedure would be to master the list of *-ise* words and then remember that all others are spelled *-ize*.

COMMON WORDS ENDING IN *-ISE, -IZE*

-ise

advertise	exercise
advise	franchise
arise	merchandise
chastise	revise
compromise	supervise
demise	surmise
despise	surprise
disguise	reprise
enterprise	

-ize

agonize	itemize
antagonize	legitimatize
authorize	localize
burglarize	modernize
capsize	neutralize
centralize	ostracize
characterize	patronize
demoralize	pulverize
dramatize	realize
emphasize	recognize
familiarize	specialize
fertilize	symbolize
generalize	tantalize
humanize	terrorize
hypnotize	visualize

WARNING!

There are only two common words ending in *-yze*:

analyze   paralyze

EXERCISE 9

Add the suffix -ise *or* -ize *to each of the following stems.*

1. agon _____

2. chast _____

3. exerc _____

4. surpr _____

5. visual _____

6. superv _____

7. modern _____

8. enterpr _____

9. fertil _____

10. general _____

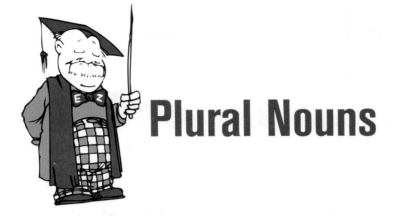

Plural Nouns

Read the statements below, focusing on the plural words in bold. Some of them raise tricky questions. Are the plurals correct in Option #1 or in Option #2?

Option #1:

Gloria **Mendes's sisters-in-law** all have very high **IQs**. Her **husband's** IQ is also extremely high. Gloria was surprised when none of them was sure how to spell **potatoes**—whether it ended in *os* or *es*.

Option #2:

Gloria **Mendes sister-in-laws** all have very high **IQ's**. Her **husbands** IQ is also extremely high. Gloria was surprised when none of them was sure how to spell **potatos**—whether it ended in *os* or *es*.

Alternative Option:

The sisters of the husband of Gloria Mendez are very intelligent. Her husband also has an extremely high IQ. Gloria was surprised when none of them was sure how to spell the plural of the word *potato*.

WHAT YOU WILL LEARN

In this chapter, you will learn the rules behind confusing plurals. Once you know these rules, it will be easy to see that all plurals in the Option #1 sentence are correct, and all plurals in the Option #2 sentence are incorrect. The Alternative Option has no misspellings because it avoids troublesome spellings altogether; however, as you can see, the first sentence is awkward and completely unnatural. It's much more complicated to rewrite to avoid difficult spellings than it is to learn the rules!

SECTIONS IN THIS CHAPTER

- Regular Plurals
- Nouns Ending in a Sibilant Sound
- Nouns Ending in Long $\overline{O}$
- Nouns Ending in -*F* or -*FE*
- Nouns Ending in -*Y*
- Special Situations

Regular Plurals

RULE 1

Most English nouns add -*s* to form the plural.

EXAMPLES   room + *s* = rooms
house + *s* = houses

Nouns Ending in a Sibilant Sound

RULE 2

Nouns ending in a sibilant sound (-*s*, -*ss*, -*sh*, soft -*ch*, -*x*, or -*z*) add -*es* to form the plural.

NOUNS ENDING IN A SIBILANT SOUND ADD -*ES* FOR PLURAL

Sibilant Sound	Plural Nouns
-*s*	bus + *es* = buses
	gas + *es* = gases
-*ss*	kiss + *es* = kisses
	class + *es* = classes
	business + *es* = businesses
-*sh*	rush + *es* = rushes
	leash + *es* = leashes
-*ch*	lunch + *es* = lunches
	bunch + *es* = bunches
	catch + *es* = catches
-*x*	box + *es* = boxes
	tax + *es* = taxes
-*z*	buzz + *es* = buzzes
	quiz + *es* = quizzes

Nouns Ending in Long Ō

A number of nouns ending in long ō add -*es* for the plural. Learn this entire list.

NOUNS ENDING IN LONG Ō WITH -*ES* PLURAL

cargo*es*	hero*es*	tomato*es*
desperado*es*	mango*es*	tornado*es*
echo*es*	mosquito*es*	torpedo*es*
embargo*es*	motto*es*	volcano*es*
go*es*	potato*es*	

A few nouns ending in ō, add only an -*s*. Remember them by groups.

NOUNS ENDING IN LONG Ō WITH -*S* PLURAL

Music		Miscellaneous	Circular Appearance
alto*s*		bronco*s*	dynamo*s*
soprano*s*	all are borrowed	studio*s*	cameo*s*
contralto*s*	from Italian	tattoo*s*	silo*s*
piano*s*		torso*s*	
solo*s*			

Nouns Ending in -*F* or -*FE*

RULE 3

Certain nouns ending in -*f* or -*fe* form the plural by changing *f* to *v* and adding -*s* or -*es*.

NOUNS CHANGING FINAL -*F* OR -*FE* TO -*V* AND
ADDING -*S* OR -*ES* FOR PLURAL

Common Nouns

calf	→	calves
elf	→	elves
knife	→	knives
leaf	→	leaves
life	→	lives
loaf	→	loaves
thief	→	thieves
wife	→	wives
wolf	→	wolves

All of the words above except *calf* may be learned in groups according to the sound of the vowel before the *f*.

Nouns with e̅e̅ Sound

| leaf | → | leaves |
| thief | → | thieves |

Nouns with ī Sound

knife	→	knives
life	→	lives
wife	→	wives

Nouns with el Sound

elf	→	elves
self	→	selves
shelf	→	shelves

NOUNS ENDING IN -*F* AND ADDING ONLY -*S* FOR PLURAL

-*ief*

belief	→	beliefs
brief	→	briefs
chief	→	chiefs
grief	→	griefs
handkerchief	→	handkerchiefs

-*oof*

hoof	→	hoofs (rarely hooves)
proof	→	proofs
roof	→	roofs

-*rf*

dwarf	→	dwarfs
scarf	→	scarfs (*or* scarves)
turf	→	turfs
wharf	→	wharfs (*or* wharves)

EXERCISE 1

Write plurals for the following words:

_____ 1. reproof

_____ 2. reprieve

_____ 3. sieve

_____ 4. halo

_____ 5. gulf

_____ 6. chief

_____ 7. albino

_____ 8. shelf

_____ 9. puff

_____ 10. bluff

_____ 11. slough

_____ 12. basso

_____ 13. mambo

_____ 14. surf

_____ 15. trough

_____ 16. stiletto

_____ 17. sheaf

_____ 18. radio

_____ 19. calf

_____ 20. loaf

Nouns Ending in -Y

RULE 4

Words ending in -y preceded by a *vowel* form their plural by adding -s.

ENDING IN -Y, PRECEDED BY A VOWEL, ADDING -S FOR PLURAL

day	→	days
boy	→	boys
monkey	→	monkeys
valley	→	valleys
volley	→	volleys

EXERCISE 2

Write the plurals of these words:

_____   1. holiday

_____   2. alley

_____   3. attorney

_____   4. buoy

_____   5. chimney

_____   6. donkey

_____   7. journey

_____   8. key

_____   9. pulley

_____   10. turkey

RULE 5

When the final -*y* is preceded by a *consonant* or *qu*, the -*y* changes to -*i* and -*es* is added to form the plural.

WORDS ENDING IN -*Y*, PRECEDED BY A CONSONANT, OR *QU*, CHANGING -*Y* TO -*I* AND ADDING -*ES* FOR PLURAL

academy	→	academ*ies*
ally	→	all*ies*
army	→	arm*ies*
caddy	→	cadd*ies*
cry	→	cr*ies*
soliloquy	→	soliloqu*ies*

Special Situations

COMPOUND NOUNS

RULE 6

Compound nouns add -*s* or -*es* to only the principal word to form the plural.

EXAMPLES   In the *in-law* series, the principal word is son, brother, etc.

brother*s*-in-law

mother*s*-in-law

NOTE:

A few compound words are practically single words and add the -*s* at the end. This explains such cases as:

spoonfuls	cupfuls
bowlfuls	handfuls

OLD ENGLISH PLURALS

A long time ago the English language had quite a list of words whose plurals ended not in *-s* but in *-en*. Only a few are left today, but they never give any trouble because they are learned in the very early grades of school. Other variations follow:

OLD ENGLISH PLURALS

General Words

child	→	child*en*
ox	→	ox*en*
foot	→	f*ee*t
tooth	→	t*ee*th
goose	→	g*ee*se
deer	→	deer
sheep	→	sheep
swine	→	swine

Animals

louse	→	l*ice*
mouse	→	m*ice*

The Sexes

man	→	m*e*n
woman	→	wom*e*n

NAMES OF PEOPLE

RULE 7

As a general rule, add *-s* to form the plural of names of people.

EXAMPLES   All the Johns in the school
All the Jennys in this class

LETTERS, SIGNS, FIGURES

RULE 8

Capital letters, numbers, and abbreviations form their plural by adding *s*.
Lower case letters use apostrophes to avoid confusion.

EXAMPLES   Cross your *t*'s and dot your *i*'s.
Mind your *P*s and *Q*s.
Underline the 3s in the line.
They have high IQs.

FOREIGN WORDS

Foreign words act differently when their plurals are formed. Many English words are
derived from Latin and Greek; study their unique plurals below.

1. Many **Latin** words ending in *-us* form their plural by changing the *-us* to *-i*. The
    most familiar of such words are

LATIN WORDS CHANGING FINAL *-US* TO *-I* FOR PLURAL

alumnus	→	alumn*i*
fungus	→	fung*i*
radius	→	radi*i*
bacillus	→	bacill*i*
terminus	→	termin*i*

2. Some Latin words ending in *-um* change to *a* to form the plural. A familiar word to
    us is *datum*, *data*.

LATIN WORDS CHANGING FINAL *-UM* TO *-A* FOR PLURAL

medium	→	media
addendum	→	addenda
bacterium	→	bacteria
curriculum	→	curricula
maximum	→	maxima
memorandum	→	memoranda
minimum	→	minima
stratum	→	strata

3. **Greek** has a group of nouns ending in *-is* singular, *-es* plural. A familiar case is *crisis, crises.*

GREEK WORDS CHANGING *-IS* TO *-ES* FOR PLURAL

analysis	→	analyses
antithesis	→	antitheses
axis	→	axes
ellipsis	→	ellipses
hypothesis	→	hypotheses
oasis	→	oases
parenthesis	→	parentheses
synopsis	→	synopses

4. The Greek language has given us a few words ending in *-on* singular, *-a* plural. These are from the ancient Greeks.

GREEK PLURALS

automaton	→	automata (mechanical figures working by themselves)
criterion	→	criteria (standard of judgment)

EXERCISE 3

Plurals of nouns.
Form the plurals of the following nouns:

_____   1. t

_____   2. deer

_____   3. anniversary

_____   4. wife

_____   5. kerchief

_____   6. 4

_____   7. court-martial

_____   8. lieutenant colonel

_____   9. bay

_____   10. tray

_____   11. flurry

_____   12. sulky

_____   13. kidney

_____   14. inequity

_____   15. satellite

_____   16. functionary

_____   17. avocado

_____   18. dynamo

EXERCISE 4

Have someone dictate the following passage containing many singular nouns for which you will write the plurals.

Brenda's mother sent her to the store to purchase some *grocery* (1)_____ for the long weekend. Among the *thing* (2)_____ on the list were: *tomato* (3)_____ , *potato* (4)_____ , and *avocado* (5)_____ . She also asked for several *quart* (6)_____ of soymilk, several *piece* (7)_____ of cake, and a pound of caramel-filled *chocolate* (8)_____ .

After making these and several other *purchase* (9)_____ , Brenda started to return home. As she walked through the *alley* (10)_____ along the way, she found a set of *key* (11)_____ , which she had lost several *day* (12)_____ before.

The Final -*y*

Why do you think that more than one *trolley* or *journey* would be *trolleys* and *journeys*, but more than one *ally* or *worry* would be *allies* and *worries*? Do you know what rule separates them and why the first two words ending in -*y* simply add an -*s* while the other two words drop the -*y* and end in -*ies*?

WHAT YOU WILL LEARN

In this chapter, you will learn rules for how words that end in -*y* change when they become plural or when a suffix is added.

SECTIONS IN THIS CHAPTER

- The -*Y* Preceded by a Vowel

- The -*Y* Preceded by a Consonant

The -*Y* Preceded by a Vowel

RULE 1

The final -*y* following a *vowel* remains *y* when suffixes are added.

These suffixes may be:

1. The letter -*s* to form the plural.

    EXAMPLES   attorney + *s* = attorney*s*
            chimney + *s* = chimney*s*
            donkey + *s* = donkey*s*
            medley + *s* = medley*s*
            pulley + *s* = pulley*s*
            trolley + *s* = trolley*s*
            valley + *s* = valley*s*
            volley + *s* = volley*s*

2. The suffix -*ing* or -*ed*

    EXAMPLES   allay + *ed*   = allay*ed*
            annoy + *ed* = annoy*ed*
            buy   *not applicable; irregular part tense: bought*
            allay + *ing* = allay*ing*
            annoy + *ing* = annoy*ing*
            buy + *ing*   = buy*ing*

3. The suffix -*er* meaning *one who*

    EXAMPLES   buy + *er* = buy*er*
            employ + *er* = employ*er*

4. The suffix -*ance*

    EXAMPLE   convey + *ance* = convey*ance*

5. The suffix -*al*

    EXAMPLE   portray + *al* = portray*al*

EXERCISE 1

Spell the following words correctly.

_____   1. *tourney* in plural

_____   2. Past tense of *allay*

_____   3. Past tense of *volley*

_____   4. *alley* in plural

_____   5. Past tense of *survey*

_____   6. Present participle of *portray*

_____   7. Past tense of *journey*

_____   8. Past tense of *relay*

_____   9. Plural of *delay*

_____   10. Past tense of *parlay*

The - *Y* Preceded by a Consonant

RULE 2

When a *consonant* precedes the -*y*, the *y* changes to *i* when suffixes are added.

Kinds of suffixes:

1. The plural of the noun formed with -*es*.

EXAMPLES   ally + *es*   =   all*ies*
enemy + *es* = enem*ies*
salary + *es* = salar*ies*
tragedy + *es* = traged*ies*

2. The verb form with *he*, *she*, or *it*, formed by adding *-es* or *-ed*.

EXAMPLES   carry + *es*   = carr*ies*
            dignify + *es*   = dignif*ies*
            marry + *es*   = marr*ies*
            carry + *ed*   = carr*ied*
            dignify + *ed*   = dignif*ied*

3. Making an adjective by adding *-ful*.

EXAMPLES   beauty + *ful*   = beaut*iful*
            mercy + *ful*   = merc*iful*
            pity + *ful*   = pit*iful*

4. Making a noun by adding *-ness*.

EXAMPLES   busy + *ness*   = bus*iness*
            cozy + *ness*   = coz*iness*
            icy + *ness*   = ic*iness*

5. Making an adverb by adding *-ly*.

EXAMPLES   airy + *ly*   = air*ily*
            angry + *ly*   = angr*ily*
            busy + *ly*   = bus*ily*
            clumsy + *ly*   = clums*ily*

WARNING!

There is only one case in which the *y* is retained. This is before *-ing*.

EXAMPLES   carry + *ing*   = carry*ing*
            copy + *ing*   = copy*ing*

EXERCISE 2

In the space to the left put the letter C *if the spelling is correct. If it is incorrect, write the proper spelling.*

_____   1. merciful

_____   2. beautiful

_____   3. cozily

_____   4. attornies

_____   5. valleys

_____   6. surveyor

_____   7. portraying

_____   8. pitying

_____   9. busied

_____   10. icyly

EXERCISE 3

Write the correct spelling of the following words all of which end in final y _before adding a suffix._

_____   1. pretty + ness

_____   2. petty + ness

_____   3. steady + ing

_____   4. ready + ed

_____   5. bully + s

_____   6. airy + ness

_____   7. pity + ed

_____   8. tally + ing

_____   9. buy + er

_____   10. duty + ful

_____   11. ready + ness

_____   12. carry + ed

_____   13. hurry + ing

_____	14. copy + er
_____	15. sloppy + ness
_____	16. lively + hood

REMEMBER!

When adding the present participle (-*ing*) to verbs ending in -*y*, do not change the *y*.

EXAMPLES

Word	+	*ing*		Present Participle
accompany	+	*ing*	=	accompany*ing*
bury	+	*ing*	=	bury*ing*
hurry	+	*ing*	=	hurry*ing*
study	+	*ing*	=	study*ing*
worry	+	*ing*	=	worry*ing*

The Final -*E*

The final -*e* poses more confusing suffix issues. When is the final *e* dropped and when is it retained? Why is the *e* dropped when we change from *shine* to *shining* and retained when *sense* becomes *senseless*? Which is correct—*dyeing* or *dying*?

WHAT YOU WILL LEARN

In this chapter, you will learn when to drop the final *e* and when to retain it. You'll also learn why *dyeing* and *dying* are both correct in the right contexts!

SECTIONS IN THIS CHAPTER
• Dropping the Final -*E*   • Retaining the Final -*E*   • Unusual Situations

Dropping the Final -*E*

FINAL -*E* RULE 1

Drop the final -*e* before a suffix beginning with a *vowel* (*a, e, i, o, u*).

SUFFIXES BEGINNING WITH A VOWEL

-able	-ence
-ed	-ance
-er	-ing
-est	-ous
-ity	

How to handle these suffixes.

1. Dropping the final *e* before -*er*.

   EXAMPLES large + *er* = larg*er*
   love + *er* = lov*er*
   give + *er* = giv*er*

2. Dropping the final *e* before -*est*.

   EXAMPLES large + *est* = larg*est*
   brave + *est* = brav*est*

3. Dropping the final *e* before -*able*.

   EXAMPLES move + *able* = mov*able*
   love + *able* = lov*able*
   imagine + *able* = imagin*able*
   advise + *able* = advis*able*
   desire + *able* = desir*able*

4. Dropping the final *e* before -*ing*.

   EXAMPLES come + *ing* = com*ing*
   receive + *ing* = receiv*ing*
   ache + *ing* = ach*ing*

NOTE!

When -*ing* is ADDED to words ending in -*ie*, the -*e* is dropped and the *i* changed to *y* to prevent two *i's* from coming together.

$$die + ing = dying$$
$$lie + ing = lying$$

Since many mistakes are made with the -*ing* words, the following list is provided. It contains some of your most useful words.

HANDLING -*ING*

whine	argue	advise
whin*ing*	argu*ing*	advis*ing*
write	surprise	dine
writ*ing*	surpris*ing*	din*ing*
shine	owe	lose
shin*ing*	ow*ing*	los*ing*
oblige	purchase	fascinate
oblig*ing*	purchas*ing*	fascinat-
judge	pursue	become
judg*ing*	pursu*ing*	becom*ing*
choose	tie	use
choos*ing*	ty*ing*	us*ing*

5. Dropping the final *e* before -*ous*.

   EXAMPLE The suffix -*ous* is frequently added to a verb to make an adjective that always has the meaning, *full of.*

   $$desire + ous = desirous$$

   EXAMPLE Sometimes the suffix -*ous* is added to a noun. Again an adjective results, also meaning, *full of.*

   $$pore + ous = porous \text{ full of pores}$$

6. Dropping the final *e* before -*ity*.

   EXAMPLE The suffix -*ity* may be added to an adjective to form a noun. The final *e* before the suffix disappears.

   $$extreme + ity = extremity$$

The same thing happens with these words:

HANDLING *-ITY*

austere	extreme	sincere
auster*ity*	extrem*ity*	sincer*ity*
dense	facile	immense
dens*ity*	facil*ity*	immens*ity*
opportune	grave	intense
opportun*ity*	grav*ity*	intens*ity*
scarce	passive	rare
scarc*ity*	passiv*ity*	rar*ity*

EXERCISE 1

Form new words by spelling the following:

_____   1.   revere + ing

_____   2.   love + ly

_____   3.   salvage + able

_____   4.   extreme + ly

_____   5.   pleasure + able

_____   6.   large + ly

_____   7.   nudge + ed

_____   8.   state + ed

_____   9.   vane + ity

_____   10.   fine + ed

_____   11.   dive + ing

_____   12.   shove + ed

_____ 13. devise + ing

_____ 14. deceive + ed

_____ 15. relieve + ing

_____ 16. procrastinate + ing

_____ 17. imagine + ed

_____ 18. besiege + ed

_____ 19. receive + ing

WARNING!

Verbs ending in *oe* (canoe) retain the *-e* to preserve the pronunciation.

canoeing   hoeing   tiptoeing

Dye and *singe* retain the *-e* to differentiate the word from *die* and *sing*.

dyeing (one's hair)   dying (absence of life)
singeing (burning)   singing (a song)

EXERCISE 2

Form the present participle (+ -ing) and the past participle (+ -ed) of the following verbs.

Word	Present Participle	Past Participle
1. benefit	_____	_____
2. commit	_____	_____
3. lure	_____	_____
4. refer	_____	_____
5. pine	_____	_____
6. elevate	_____	_____
7. propel	_____	_____

8.   fit   _____   _____

9.   recur   _____   _____

10. remit   _____   _____

11. open   _____   _____

12. club   _____   _____

13. plunge   _____   _____

14. singe   _____   _____

15. pursue   _____   _____

16. scare   _____   _____

17. throb   _____   _____

18. blog   _____   _____

19. use   _____   _____

20. whip   _____   _____

Retaining the Final -*E*

FINAL -*E* RULE 2

The final -*e* is retained when the suffix begins with a *consonant*.

SUFFIXES BEGINNING WITH A CONSONANT

-ness	-ful
-ment	-less

1. Adding the suffix -*ness*.

   Examine the following words that all belong in this class:

   ### HANDLING -*NESS*

complete complete*ness*	genuine genuine*ness*	acute acute*ness*
expensive expensive*ness*	large large*ness*	appropriate appropriate*ness*
coarse coarse*ness*	fierce fierce*ness*	vague vague*ness*
like like*ness*	polite polite*ness*	remote remote*ness*
rude rude*ness*	wide wide*ness*	

2. Adding the suffix -*ment*.

   Examine the following words that are all formed the same way:

   ### HANDLING -*MENT*

amuse amuse*ment*	enforce enforce*ment*	advance advance*ment*
arrange arrange*ment*	engage engage*ment*	advertise advertise*ment*
commence commence*ment*	excite excite*ment*	amaze amaze*ment*
move move*ment*	require require*ment*	manage manage*ment*
discourage discourage*ment*	achieve achieve*ment*	

WARNING: Some Exceptions

Abridgement, acknowledgement, and *judgement* are usually spelled
abridgment, acknowledgment, and *judgment.*

3. Adding the suffix -*ful*.

The following words belong to this division:

HANDLING -*FUL*

care	grace	remorse
care*ful*	grace*ful*	remorse*ful*
revenge	disgrace	hate
revenge*ful*	disgrace*ful*	hate*ful*
taste	resource	shame
taste*ful*	resource*ful*	shame*ful*

4. Adding the suffix -*less*.

Again the silent *e* is preserved because the suffix begins with the consonant *l*.

HANDLING -*LESS*

age	noise	voice
age*less*	noise*less*	voice*less*
care	sense	name
care*less*	sense*less*	name*less*
shame	shape	use
shame*less*	shape*less*	use*less*
change	cease	
change*less*	cease*less*	
grace	smoke	
grace*less*	smoke*less*	
guide	taste	
guide*less*	taste*less*	

WARNING: Some Exceptions

- *Due, true, whole*, drop the -*e* before -*ly*—*duly, truly, wholly*.
- Some words ending in -*e* drop the -*e* before -*ment* or -*ful*. *Argument* is an instance, as is *awful* (from awe).

Unusual Situations

FINAL -*E* RULE 3

Some words retain the final -*e* regardless of the suffix in order to retain pronunciation.

1. When the word ends in double -*ee*, the final -*e* is not dropped. This happens in order to retain the same pronunciation.

   EXAMPLES
   agree
   agree*able*
   agree*ing*
   agree*ment*

2. Words ending in -*oe* retain the final -*e*.

   EXAMPLES

canoe	shoe	tiptoe	woe
canoe*ing*	shoe*maker*	tiptoe*ing*	woe*ful*
	shoe*string*	tiptoe*d*	woebe*gone*
	shoe*ing*	tiptoe*s*	

3. Words ending in -*ce* or -*ge* will retain the final -*e* before a suffix beginning with a vowel. This is necessary to keep the soft pronunciation.

   EXAMPLES

notice	change	outrage
notice*able*	change*able*	outrage*ous*
service	courage	advantage
service*able*	courage*ous*	advantage*ous*

FINAL -*E* RULE 4

Certain words would lose their hard pronunciation of certain consonants unless a -*k* is added before a suffix beginning with *e, i,* or *y* (used as vowel).

EXAMPLES   *mimic + ing = mimicing*, which would not be pronounced with the hard c (= to *k*). Hence the *k* is inserted between the final *c* and the beginning vowel of the suffix. Note the following.

colic	→	coli**c**ky		
frolic	→	froli**c**king	→	froli**c**ked
mimic	→	mimi**c**king	→	mimi**c**ked
panic	→	pani**c**king	→	pani**c**ked
picnic	→	picni**c**king	→	picni**c**ked
traffic	→	traffi**c**king	→	traffi**c**ked

EXERCISE 3

Try your hand at spelling these words containing the final -e *and a suffix.*

1. agree   + ment   = _____

2. amuse   + ment   = _____

3. care   + ful   = _____

4. canoe   + ing   = _____

5. come   + ing   = _____

6. disagree   + able   = _____

7. engage   + ment   = _____

8. excite   + ment   = _____

9. immense   + ity   = _____

10. like   + ly   = _____

11. safe   + ty   = _____

12. sense   + less   = _____

13. shine   + ing   = _____

14. enlarge   + ment   = _____

15. entice   + ing   = _____

16. perceive   + ed   = _____

17. escape   + ing   = _____

18. discharge + ed   = _____

19. relieve   + ing   = _____

20. contrive   + ance   = _____

EXERCISE 4

Have someone read the following sentences to you and write them out. There will be many examples of dropping or retaining the final -e. See how many you spell correctly.

1. While they were *staring* at the stars, they saw something *stirring* in the bushes.

2. It takes much *planning* to build a house *preferred* by others.

3. The *cannery* used plenty of *cane* sugar with such fruits as *pineapples* and peaches.

4. By using *scraps* of food, the cook managed to *scrape* together a fair meal after the *scrapping* of the managers was over.

5. The little *moppet* sat *moping* in her little chair while the mother *mopped* up the food that was lying *sloppily* on the floor.

6. After Maria's parents *refused* to buy her the new computer game, she *fumed* and *fussed effusively* and finally stomped out of the room.

7. By *dotting* your *i*'s and *crossing* your *t*'s you can take a small step toward *better spelling*.

EXERCISE 5

Each of the following words has an error in the dropping or retention of final -e.
Make the correction in the space to the left.

_____   1. scarcly

_____   2. vengance

_____   3. truely

_____   4. tastey

_____   5. noticable

_____   6. changable

_____   7. perspireing

_____   8. retireing

_____   9. aweful

_____   10. wisedom

_____   11. assureance

_____   12. insureance

_____   13. outragous

_____   14. servicable

_____   15. couragous

_____   16. gorgous

_____   17. pronouncable

Doubling Final Consonants

Some words double the final consonants when adding a suffix, while others do not. Do you know when to double your consonants and when not to? Do you choose one over the other because it "looks right"—but you're not really sure? Once you learn these rules and understand why refe*rr*ing has two *r*'s while leve*l*ing has one *l*, you'll be well on your way to spelling with confidence.

WHAT YOU WILL LEARN

In this chapter, you will learn the answer to the question above—along with rules that will help you know for sure the next time you see those words. You'll learn four simple rules that will help you master this confusing issue.

SECTIONS IN THIS CHAPTER
• One-Syllable Words
• Words of More Than One Syllable
• Special Situations
• How Consonants Determine Meaning

One-Syllable Words

First, recall the meaning of the word *syllable*. A syllable is a unit of spoken language forming either a whole word (as *men*) or a division of a word (as *priv* in *priv•i•lege*).

For example:

run   *swim*   *hop*

These are one-syllable words. The following are two-syllable words:

con•fer   *pre•fer*   *trans•fer*

You notice that we have at least *two* syllables in each word. Now we can proceed to the rules. Notice what happens to one-syllable words when we add *-ing*.

ru*nn*ing   swi*mm*ing   ho*pp*ing

The final consonant (*n, m, p*) has been doubled before a suffix beginning with a vowel. We could have added the suffix *-er*.

ru*nn*er   swi*mm*er   ho*pp*er

RULE 1

When a one-syllable word ends in one vowel then one consonant, that consonant is doubled before a suffix beginning with a vowel.

Important Note: Rule 1 applies to *one-syllable words ending in one vowel then one consonant*. Remember that this is not a rule applying to all one-syllable words.

ONE-SYLLABLE WORDS DOUBLING CONSONANT BEFORE SUFFIX BEGINNING WITH VOWEL

Word		+ *er*		+ *ing*
hit	→	hi*tt*er	→	hi*tt*ing
spin	→	spi*nn*er	→	spi*nn*ing
wrap	→	wra*pp*er	→	wra*pp*ing
trim	→	tri*mm*er	→	tri*mm*ing

WARNING: Some Exceptions

This rule is nearly perfect, but it is a little flawed. Notice the word *flawed* (ends in one syllable and one consonant, followed by a suffix that begins with a vowel). Exceptions to the rule include *gnaw* (*gnawing*, *gnawed*), *flaw* (*flawed*), *thaw* (*thawing*, *thawed*), and *awe* (*awed*). Do you notice one final consonant in common? We do not double the final consonant, *w*.

EXERCISE 1

Combine the following words with the suffixes beside them.

Word	Suffix	
1. fill	ed	_____
2. file	ed	_____
3. cramp	ing	_____
4. hop	ing	_____
5. let	ing	_____
6. trip	ing	_____
7. run	er	_____
8. blog	er	_____
9. drum	ing	_____
10. scrub	ed	_____

Words of More Than One Syllable

RULE 2

Many words that are two or more syllables follow the same guidelines as Rule 1, meaning that when the *word ends in one vowel and one consonant*, that *consonant is doubled before a suffix beginning with a vowel*. However, this rule *only* applies to words of two or more syllables *when the accent is on the last syllable*.

occ•ur´   ad•mit´   per•mit´

If the final syllable has no accent, there will be no doubling of the consonant. Thus, *benefit* will not double the *t*, because the accent is on the first syllable.

be´•ne•fit•ing   tra´•vel•ed

Study the suffixes to the following words. Each word satisfies three conditions.

1. It is more than one syllable.

2. The last syllable has the accent.

3. The last syllable ends in *one* vowel and a *single* consonant.

TWO-SYLLABLE WORDS DOUBLING CONSONANT BEFORE SUFFIX BEGINNING WITH VOWEL

Word		+ *ing*		+ *ed*		+ Other Suffix
abhor	→	abhorring	→	abhorred	→	abhorrence
admit	→	admitting	→	admitted	→	admittance
allot	→	allotting	→	allotted	→	allottance
annul	→	annulling	→	annulled	→	annulment (one *l* because the suffix begins with a consonant)
dispel	→	dispelling	→	dispelled		
excel	→	excelling	→	excelled		
occur	→	occurring	→	occurred	→	occurrence
omit	→	omitting	→	omitted		
permit	→	permitting	→	permitted		
rebel	→	rebelling	→	rebelled	→	rebellion
recur	→	recurring	→	recurred	→	recurrence
regret	→	regretting	→	regretted		
transfer	→	transferring	→	transferred		
defer	→	deferring	→	deferred	→	deference
refer	→	referring	→	referred	→	reference
confer	→	conferring	→	conferred	→	conference
equip	→	equipping	→	equipped	→	equipment

WARNING: Pronunciation Changes

All of the words in the previous examples double the last consonant in every instance *except* for the last four under the "Other Suffix" column. Look at each word and consider why the double consonant rule explained in Rule 2 does not apply. Notice how the accent is on the last syllable of *defer, deferring,* and *deferred; refer, referring,* and *referred; confer, conferring,* and *conferred;* and *equip, equipping,* and *equipped;* but the pronunciation changes in the words *defer*ence, *ref*erence, and *con*ference to the first syllable.)

Exceptions: Of course, there are always exceptions. Exce*ll*ence maintains two *l*'s even though the stress moves to the first syllable (ex-*cel*, exce*ll*ing, exce*ll*ed, exce*ll*ence).

Special Situations

RULE 3

When adding *-ness* to a word, use *nn* if the original word ends in *n*.

EXAMPLES
mean + *ness* = mean*ness*
plain + *ness* = plain*ness*
thin + *ness* = thin*ness*

RULE 4

Words ending in *-ful* have a single *l* unless *-ly* is added.

EXAMPLES
careful + *ly* = carefu*lly*
beautiful + *ly* = beautifu*lly*
dutiful + *ly* = dutifu*lly*
wonderful + *ly* = wonderfu*lly*

hopeful + *ly* = hopefu*lly*
useful + *ly* = usefu*lly*
youthful + *ly* = youthfu*lly*

How Consonants Determine Meaning

Now for a few pairs of words with different meanings, depending upon the doubling of the consonants.

bar   →   He *barred* the door.
bare   →   He *bared* his arm.

pin   →   Mary *pinned* her dress.
pine   →   Mary *pined* away.

plan   →   They *planned* a happy life.
plane   →   The carpenter *planed* the wood.

scrap   →   The two dogs *scrapped*.
scrape   →   Lila *scraped* her knee.

wag   →   The puppy *wagged* her tail.
wage   →   He *waged* a bitter war.

Notice how the meaning is determined by the single or double consonant and why correct spelling is so important to convey your meaning.

EXERCISE 2

Write correctly the words formed as the exercise indicates. Hint: Say the word out loud if you need to hear where the stress is.

_____	1. infer + ing
_____	2. interfer + ence
_____	3. shop + ing
_____	4. disapprove + al
_____	5. nine + teen
_____	6. hit + ing
_____	7. singe + ing
_____	8. fame + ous

_____ 9. control + ing

_____ 10. repel + ent

_____ 11. desire + ing

_____ 12. tire + less

_____ 13. true + ly

_____ 14. swim + er

_____ 15. trim + er

_____ 16. occur + ence

_____ 17. move + able

_____ 18. commit + ed

_____ 19. equip + ment

_____ 20. excel + ing

_____ 21. admit + ing

_____ 22. admit + ance

_____ 23. reboot + ing

_____ 24. plot + ing

_____ 25. edit + ing

EXERCISE 3

Write the present participle (+ ing) _and_ past participle (+ ed) _of the following verbs._
Some will double the final consonant; others will not. When in doubt, refer to the rules
on doubling final consonants.

Word	Present Participle	Past Participle
1. adapt	_____	_____
2. cramp	_____	_____
3. design	_____	_____

4. conceal _____   _____

5. congeal _____   _____

6. blot _____   _____

7. stop _____   _____

8. crush _____   _____

9. excel _____   _____

10. defer _____   _____

11. envelop _____   _____

12. extol _____   _____

13. flutter _____   _____

14. happen _____   _____

15. hum _____   _____

16. level _____   _____

17. quarrel _____   _____

18. rub _____   _____

19. signal _____   _____

20. retreat _____   _____

EXERCISE 4

Fill in the missing word using the suffix given in parentheses. Each missing word appears earlier in the sentence in a different form. In some instances, the final consonant of the original word will be doubled.

EXAMPLE   (able) A venture that earns profit is <u>profitable</u>.

1. (-ing) Let's *begin* at the _____.

2. (-y) You would describe someone who has *wit* as being _____.

3. (-er) One who *designs* is a _____.

4. (-ical) Someone who *quizzes* with lots of questions is _____.

5. (-er) You might use a hair _____ to *dry* your hair.

6. (-able) A place that's suitable to *inhabit* is called _____.

7. (-er) One who *reads* a lot of books is an avid _____.

8. (-er) Someone who writes a *blog* is a _____.

9. (-al) When you are waiting for a loan to be *approved*, you are waiting for _____.

10. (-ing) When you *clean*, you are _____.

11. (-ing) When you *scrub*, you are _____.

12. (-ment) When work is *assigned*, it is an _____.

EXERCISE 5

Add the indicated ending to each of the following words.

_____ 1. tearful + ly

_____ 2. careful + ly

_____ 3. open + ness

_____ 4. dutiful + ly

_____ 5. bountiful + ly

_____ 6. common + ness

_____ 7. mimic + ed

_____ 8. picnic + ing

_____ 9. mimic + ing

_____ 10. panic + y

English as a Second Language

Spelling in English is difficult because one sound may be written many different ways. You cannot rely on phonetics to help you. In addition, it is easy to confuse words that have only slight differences in the way they are spelled. For many ESL students, vowels are the most difficult part of spelling English. In this section, you will see the way various English vowel sounds are commonly spelled. For each vowel sound, we give both the most common spelling or spellings and also additional spellings that are used less frequently.

The sound symbols used here are based on the pronunciation keys used in most dictionaries. You do not need to memorize these symbols. They are just here to help you recognize the sound that goes with the spelling. Sample words are included for the spellings of each sound.

After each set of sounds you will find an exercise to help you review.

WHAT YOU WILL LEARN

You will learn to distinguish sounds that are easily confused, an understanding that is essential for better spelling.

SECTION IN THIS CHAPTER

- A Guide to Pronunciation and Spelling

A Guide to Pronunciation and Spelling

Ĭ AS IN *FIT* AND Ē AS IN *FEET*

The short vowel ĭ is most often spelled simply *i* or *y*. However, there are a number of other possible, though less common, spellings.

Ĭ AS IN *FIT*

Most Common Spellings	
i	as in chip, finish, fix, include, kick, lip, mint, pig, pill, pit, ring, spinach, split, which, will, win
y	as in antonym, hymn, larynx, myth, physical, syntax

Additional Spellings	
e	as in eclipse, ecology, economy, emerge, emit, England, English
ee	as in been
o	as in women
ui	as in built, guild, guinea pig

The ē sound, similar to the Spanish *i*, has several common spellings in English, and a few less common ones. Like other long vowels in English, it is usually represented by a double vowel or by a pair of vowels.

Ē AS IN *FEET*

Most Common Spellings	
ee	as in eerie, deep, keen, meet, see
ea	as in bean, each, tea, teach, wheat
ie	as in chief, priest, relieve, series

Additional Spellings	
e	as in concede, eternal, scenic
ei	as in neither, receive
eo	as in people
ey	as in key
i	as in fatigue, machine, ravine

EXERCISE 1

Complete each word with the correct letter or letters.

1. A sh _____ p is a furry white animal that says "ba-a-a."

2. A sh _____ p is a large boat.

3. Something that doesn't cost much money is ch _____ p.

4. Do you like to eat potato ch _____ ps while you watch television?

5. Don't l _____ ve yet. Stay a little longer.

6. Where do you l _____ ve?

7. It's cold in here. Let's turn on the h _____ t.

8. The batter h _____ t the ball.

9. When do you go to sl _____ p at night?

10. Be careful not to sl _____ p and fall on the ice.

Ĕ AS IN *SET* AND Ĭ AS IN *SIT*

This is the same short *ĭ* sound you reviewed in the previous section. The short *ĕ* sound is spelled most often with the letter *e*. However, sometimes it is spelled with the combination *ea*, and there are a few other variations that are occasionally used.

Ĕ AS IN *SET*

Most Common Spellings

e	as in belt, bet, elementary, elephant, fellow, hello, lend, penny, rest, seldom, self, seven, whether, yes

Additional Spellings

ea	as in bread, breakfast, head, instead, pleasure, spread
a	as in many, anything
ai	as in said
ay	as in says
ie	as in friend
ue	as in guess, guest

EXERCISE 2

Complete each word with the correct letter or letters.

1. Jenny and I made a b _____ t on who was going to win the World Cup.

2. Linda b _____ t her tongue while she was eating her dinner.

3. Fill out the form with a l _____ d pencil.

4. Albert forgot to put the l _____ d on the pot.

5. You don't have to stand. There is room for you to s _____ t down.

6. Can you help me s _____ t the table for dinner?

7. You speak English very w _____ ll.

8. W _____ ll you help me with my homework?

9. Kim has to f _____ ll out an application for a job.

10. The little boy f _____ ll down when he was roller blading.

Ā AS IN *LATE* AND Ĕ AS IN *LET*

The *ā* sound is most often spelled *a*, *ai*, or *ay*. The *a* spelling is usually followed by a consonant and a silent *e*. The *ay* spelling commonly comes at the end of a word.

Ā AS IN *LATE*

Most Common Spellings	
a	as in *able*, *age*, *ape*, *ate*, *aviator*, *bake*, *brave*, *fable*, *flake*, *game*, *grape*, *labor*, *lazy*, *plate*, *rave*, *spade*, *wake*, *waste*
ai	as in *braille*, *brain*, *complain*, *explain*, *jail*, *mail*, *plain*, *stain*, *straight*, *waist*
ay	as in *bay*, *gay*, *hay*, *layer*, *may*, *mayor*, *player*, *pray*, *spray*, *stay*, *way*

Additional Spellings	
ea	as in *great*, *break*
ei	as in *eight*, *neighbor*, *reign*, *reindeer*
ey	as in *they*, *prey*

EXERCISE 3

Complete each word with the correct letter or letters.

1. Many species m _____ te in the spring.

2. I m _____ t my friend at the mall yesterday.

3. The patient has a severe p _____ n in his abdomen.

4. Could you lend me a p _____ n to write down the phone number?

5. When I was a little girl, I used to wear my hair in br _____ ds.

6. Would you like some butter on your br _____ d?

7. If you drop the glass, you will br _____ k it.

8. She always has orange juice for br _____ kfast.

9. If you leave the g _____ te open, the dog will run into the street.

10. Please g _____ t some bottled water at the supermarket on your way home.

Ī AS IN *MY* AND *Ā* AS IN *MAY*

The most common spelling for *ī* is the letter *i*. Like the *ā* sound, it is often followed by a consonant and a silent *e*, and it can also be followed by a silent *g* or *gh*. The *ī* sound is sometimes spelled *y*, especially when it comes at the end of a word. Both the *i* and the *y* can be followed by a silent *e* at the end of a word.

Ī AS IN *MY*
Most Common Spellings

i	as in b*i*te, bl*i*nd, br*i*be, d*i*ner, dr*i*ve, f*i*ght, fl*i*ght, gr*i*nd, h*i*ve, l*i*on, m*i*ght, m*i*ne, m*i*ld, n*i*ne, qu*i*te, r*i*de, s*i*ght, s*i*gh, s*i*gn, t*i*ght, t*i*re, wh*i*le, wh*i*te, w*i*ld
y	as in b*y*, dr*y*, fr*y*, ps*y*chology, sp*y*, st*y*le, t*y*pe, tr*y*, wh*y*
ie	as in d*ie*, l*ie*, t*ie*
ye	as in d*ye*, r*ye*

Additional Spellings

ai	as in *ai*sle
ei	as in h*ei*ght
uy	as in b*uy*

EXERCISE 4

Complete each word with the correct letter or letters.

1. How h _____ gh is that mountain?

2. H _____ is for horses.

3. The ship is moored in the b _____ .

4. The post office is right b _____ the supermarket.

5. Go to the post office to b _____ the stamps.

6. Are you going to p _____ with cash or a credit card?

7. It's as American as apple p _____ .

8. She has beautiful red hair. I can't believe she's going to d _____ it black.

9. What d _____ will they arrive?

10. Every year, thousands of people d _____ of heart disease.

Ă AS IN *MAN* AND Ā AS IN *MAIN*

The *ă* sound is almost always spelled *a*. This makes it one of the easiest vowel sounds to put in writing. Notice that the *ă* sound is often followed by a consonant, but never by a single consonant followed by a silent *e*. The silent *e* is used only when the vowel sound is *ā*.

Ă AS IN *MAN*
Most Common Spellings
a   as in ant, bad, black, bran, can, cat, gram, graph, grass, happy, jam, kangaroo, lamp, mash, matter, splash, tap
Additional Spellings
ai   as in plaid *au*   as in laugh, aunt

EXERCISE 5

Complete each word with the correct letter or letters.

1. Oat br _____ n cereal has become very popular.

2. You can figure it out. Use your br _____ n.

3. When you are ready, just t _____ p on the door.

4. The police tied yellow t _____ pe around the scene.

5. The turkey was brought in on a silver pl _____ tter.

6. He certainly put enough food on his pl _____ te.

7. Those black creatures flying around the belfry are b _____ ts.

8. He has to decide whether to fish or cut b _____ t.

9. We need more information. This study doesn't provide enough d _____ ta.

10. One d _____ te every American schoolchild knows is Independence Day.

Ă AS IN *CAT*, Ŏ AS IN *COT*, AND Ŭ AS IN *CUT*

The short vowels ŏ and ŭ, like the short ă, are almost always spelled with the single letter representing the vowel. If you can recognize these vowel sounds, you will be able to spell them without too much trouble.

Ŏ AS IN *COT*

Most Common Spellings
o   as in b**o**dy, fl**o**ck, g**o**t, h**o**p, kn**o**t, l**o**g, n**o**t, pl**o**t, sp**o**t, tr**o**t

Additional Spellings
a   as in wh**a**t, w**a**sp

Ŭ AS IN *CUT*

Most Common Spellings
u   as in b**u**tter, cr**u**mb, fl**u**b, g**u**n, m**u**tt, r**u**n, st**u**mble, s**u**pper, tr**u**nk

Additional Spellings
ou   as in c**ou**sin, d**ou**ble
o   as in **o**ven, w**o**nder

EXERCISE 6

Complete each word with the correct letter or letters.

1. After the B _____ ttle of Waterloo, Napoleon's reign was over.

2. We ordered a b _____ ttle of wine with dinner.

3. The tiny little gn _____ ts that fly around on a summer evening can drive you crazy.

4. I have to untangle the cord. It's all tied up in kn _____ ts.

5. Almonds are my favorite n _____ ts.

6. His first play received terrible reviews, and was a total fl _____ p.

7. The baby birds are trying to fl _____ p their wings.

8. A slang word for a policeman is c _____ p.

9. You can wear a c _____ p on your head.

10. You drink coffee from a c _____ p.

REVIEW EXERCISE A—
Ĭ, Ī, Ĕ, Ē, Ă, Ā, Ŏ, Ŭ

Complete each word with the correct letter or letters.

1. My team can b _____ t your team.

2. Would you be willing to b _____ t on that?

3. I would, b _____ t I don't have any money.

4. You just know your team can't possibly w _____ n.

5. Don't wh _____ ne just because you lost.

6. He missed the m _____ n point of the argument.

7. All U.S. presidents, so far, have been m _____ n.

8. José is a good m _____ n.

9. I'll take either one. They s _____ m to be exactly the s _____ me.

10. Where have you b _____ n all this time?

ŎŎ AS IN *LOOK* AND Ŏ AS IN *LOCK*

The short double *oŏ* sound is almost always spelled with a double *oo*, usually followed by a single consonant. The only problem for spelling is that you must remember to use the double letter and not confuse this sound with the short *ŏ*, usually spelled with a single *o*.

ŎŎ AS IN *LOOK*
Most Common Spellings
oo   as in f*oo*t, b*oo*k, h*oo*k, w*oo*d, cr*oo*k, c*oo*k
Additional Spellings
u   as in b*u*ll, p*u*t
ou   as in c*ou*ld, sh*ou*ld, w*ou*ld

EXERCISE 7

Complete each word with the correct letter or letters.

1. I love to read a good b ——— k.

2. My neighbors have a swing on their b ——— ck porch.

3. I'd enjoy fishing better if I didn't have to put the worm on the h ——— k.

4. He needed money, so he h ——— cked his trumpet at the pawn shop.

5. It was hot, so we went wading in the br ——— k.

6. The little girl was building a tower with her bl ——— cks.

Â AS IN *CARE*, Ô AS IN *CORE*, Û AS IN *CUR*

The *â* is usually spelled *a* or *ai*; the *û* sound is usually spelled with a *u*. Both are usually followed by an *r*. The *ô* sound, usually spelled *o*, has more variations in the consonants that can follow it.

Â AS IN *CARE*

Most Common Spellings

a   as in *a*rea, b*a*re, d*a*ring, gl*a*re, sh*a*re, squ*a*re, w*a*res, st*a*re

Additional Spellings

ai   as in fl*ai*r, p*ai*r, *ai*r, st*ai*r
ea   as in p*ea*r, t*ea*r (meaning "rip"), w*ea*r
e   as in wh*e*re

Ô AS IN *CORE*

Most Common Spellings

o   as in b*o*rn, c*o*rd, l*o*ng, m*o*rning, *o*r, *o*re, sw*o*re, t*o*rch

Additional Spellings

a   as in h*a*lter, t*a*ll, w*a*lk, w*a*rm
au   as in *au*dition, c*au*ght, c*au*ldron, c*au*se, h*au*nt
aw   as in h*aw*k, s*aw*, y*aw*n
ou   as in b*ou*ght, f*ou*r

Û AS IN *CUR*

Most Common Spellings

u   as in b*u*rger, c*u*rl, f*u*r, st*u*rdy, s*u*rface, t*u*rkey, t*u*rn

Additional Spellings

e   as in p*e*rmanent, sw*e*rve
ea   as in *ea*rn
i   as in sh*i*rt, st*i*r, wh*i*rl
o   as in w*o*rld, w*o*rm

EXERCISE 8

Complete each word with the correct letter or letters.

1. They are forecasting f _____ r weather for the weekend—warm and sunny.

2. This is a present f _____ r you.

3. Animal rights activists object when people wear f _____ r coats.

4. I have to go to the hardware st _____ re.

5. It's considered rude to st _____ re at people.

6. That shirt is t _____ rn.

7. T _____ rn right at the next corner.

8. Where w _____ re you? I couldn't find you anywhere.

9. Miners dig for _____ re.

10. Would you like this one _____ r that one?

Ä AS IN *CARD* AND Ô AS IN *CORD*

The *ä* sound is also frequently followed by an *r*, but *not* always. It is usually spelled *a*.

Ä AS IN *CARD*
Most Common Spellings
a   as in are, arch, arm, calm, far, harsh, scarf, tarnish, yarn
Additional Spellings
ea   as in heart

EXERCISE 9

Complete each word with the correct letter or letters.

1. You can walk from here. It isn't f _____ r.

2. Did you want three apples or f _____ r?

3. The farmer put the animals in the b _____ rn at night.

4. He has always lived in the house where he was b _____ rn.

5. It was a bad accident, and it left him with a sc _____ r on his cheek.

6. Is the ball game over already? What was the sc _____ re?

7. People used to dry, or p _____ rch, the corn to store it for the winter.

8. In the summer we like to sit on the front p _____ rch and watch the world go by.

9. He pursued his goal with great _____ rdor and enthusiasm.

10. Will the meeting please come to _____ rder?

Ō AS IN *ROTE* AND Ō̄Ō AS IN *ROOT*

The long single ō is most commonly spelled *o* or *oa*. When it is spelled *o*, it is often followed by a single consonant and a silent *e*. This is the same pattern you saw for the long *ā* sound. The long double ō̄ō, which sounds like the Spanish *u*, is most commonly spelled *oo*, *ou*, or *u*. However, for both of these sounds a number of additional spellings are possible.

Ō AS IN *ROTE*

Most Common Spellings

o	as in b*o*ne, c*o*zy, h*o*le, j*o*ke, n*o*te, *o*pen, *o*ver, p*o*ny, r*o*se, s*o*lo, wh*o*le
oa	as in b*oa*t, c*oa*l, l*oa*n, m*oa*n, r*oa*st, t*oa*st
oe	as in d*oe*, f*oe*, t*oe*

Additional Spellings

ou	as in b*ou*lder
ough	as in th*ough*
ow	as in b*ow*, fl*ow*, sh*ow*
ew	as in s*ew*

Ō̄Ō AS IN *ROOT*

Most Common Spellings

oo	as in bl*oo*m, b*oo*n, ch*oo*se, c*oo*l, h*oo*t, l*oo*ny, n*oo*se, r*oo*ster, t*oo*, z*oo*m

Additional Spellings

o	as in d*o*, t*o*, tw*o*
ou	as in gh*ou*l, r*ou*te, y*ou*
ough	as in thr*ough*
oe	as in sh*oe*
u	as in r*u*de
ue	as in bl*ue*, tr*ue*
ui	as in cr*ui*se
ew	as in cr*ew*, kn*ew*

EXERCISE 10

Complete each word with the correct letter or letters.

1. C _____ l mines are usually found in mountainous areas.

2. It gets c _____ l in the evening. You should bring a sweater.

3. I wouldn't touch that with a ten-foot p _____ le.

4. She swims ten laps in the p _____ l every day.

5. Of course you can stay with us. We have plenty of r _____ m.

6. When I'm in a new city, I like to just r _____ m around the streets.

7. As a general r _____ le, it's a good idea not to open e-mail attachments from someone you don't know.

8. The actor considered that r _____ le the high point of his career.

9. It's always easier to do a job when you have the right t _____ ls.

10. You have to pay a t _____ ll on all the highways.

OI AS IN *FOIL* AND *OU* AS IN *FOUL*

The *oi* sound, spelled either *oi* or *oy*, always uses the *oy* spelling at the end of a word. The *ou* sound, spelled either *ou* or *ow*, usually uses the *ow* spelling at the end of a word.

OI AS IN *FOIL*

Most Common Spellings

oi	as in b*oi*l, ch*oi*ce, cl*oi*ster, j*oi*nt, l*oi*n
oy	as in ann*oy*, b*oy*, t*oy*

OU AS IN *FOUL*

Most Common Spellings

ou	as in b*ou*ndary, c*ou*nt, l*ou*d, *ou*t, s*ou*nd
ow	as in b*ow*, br*ow*n, c*ow*, cr*ow*d, h*ow*

Additional Spellings

ough	as in b*ough*

EXERCISE 11

Complete each word with the correct letter or letters.

1. Smoking is not all _____ ed anywhere in the building.

2. He called her name al _____ d, and everyone turned to look.

3. Pewter is an all _____ of tin and lead.

4. If you strike _____ l in your backyard, you'll be rich.

5. In the evening, you can hear an _____ l hoot.

6. Don't make so much n _____ se. You'll wake everyone up.

7. N _____ is the time for us to take action!

8. This ticket will be v _____ d if you don't use it by the date stamped on the back.

9. He v _____ ed to be true, but, he was unfaithful.

10. Use n _____ ns and verbs when you write. Av _____ d too many adjectives.

REVIEW EXERCISE B–
ŎŎ, Ŏ, Â, Ô, Û, Ä, Ō, OŌ, OI, OU

Complete each word with the correct letter or letters.

1. My father always c _____ rves the turkey on Thanksgiving.

2. Drive slowly. There are lots of c _____ rves on this road.

3. Put on your c _____ t before you go out in the cold.

4. We put an extra c _____ t in the room for the baby to sleep on.

5. We c _____ t quite a few fish in the lake last year.

6. The g _____ se laid an egg.

7. She g _____ s to school with me.

8. Smoking is n _____ t allowed here.

9. She always writes a thank-you n _____ te when someone gives her a present.

10. By aftern _____ n, n _____ ne of the snow was left. The sun had melted it.

UNACCENTED SYLLABLES

Unaccented, or barely accented, vowels present a special problem for spelling. The sound is something like **uh**, but this sound can be represented by any of the vowels or even by a combination of vowels. This is a problem even for native English speakers, who often have trouble deciding, for example, if a word should end *-ence* or *-ance*. Pronunciation will not offer any help here.

UNACCENTED SYLLABLES	
a	as in *a*lone
ai	as in cert*ai*n
e	as in both*e*r
i	as in happ*i*ly
io	as in intent*io*n
o	as in cal*o*rie
u	as in min*u*s

EXERCISE 12

Complete each word with the correct letter or letters.

1. N _____ cessity is the mother of invention.

2. The parents and children had a very emot _____ ion _____ l reunion.

3. The province declared its independ _____ nce, and a civil war began.

4. In hot weather, everyone p _____ rspires.

5. He went to college for a lib _____ r _____ l arts degree.

SILENT LETTERS

In English, there are a number of letters that are sometimes written but not pronounced. We have already mentioned the silent *e*, which comes after a single consonant and changes the pronunciation of the preceding vowel. For example, the addition of a silent *e* changes the short *ă* in hat to the long *ā* in hate.

In addition, there are a number of consonants that are often not pronounced, such as *g* and *k* when they come before an *n*. Following is a list of the most common silent letters.

SILENT LETTERS

c	as in *s*cience, *s*cissors
d	as in We*d*nesday
g	as in *g*naw, *g*nat, si*g*n, rei*g*n
h	as in *h*eir, *h*onor, *h*our, shep*h*erd
k	as in *k*nee, *k*night, *k*nife, *k*nock, *k*now
l	as in a*l*mond, ca*l*f, ca*l*m, fo*l*k, ha*l*f, so*l*der, ta*l*k, wa*l*k, yo*l*k
n	as in condem*n*, dam*n*, hym*n*, solem*n*
p	as in corp*s*, cu*p*board, *p*neumonia, *p*sychology, ras*p*berry
t	as in fas*t*en, glis*t*en, has*t*en, hus*t*le, lis*t*en, of*t*en, nes*t*le, this*t*le

EXERCISE 13

Complete each word with the correct letter or letters.

1. You can cut the string with a _____ nife or with a pair of s _____ issors.

2. Ca _____ m down and try to ta _____ k slowly.

3. He's seeing a _____ sychiatrist who is willing to lis _____ en to his problems.

4. The _____ eir to the throne will rei _____ n over the country.

5. The condem _____ ed man ate a hearty dinner.

The Hyphen

English is a language rich in compound words. Sometimes two nouns are combined as in *secretary-treasurer* because the new term combines the functions of both. The hyphen here shows that you are talking about one man or woman. Many compound words are adjectives formed from various parts of speech. For example, to say that a *car is of low price* sounds archaic. Instead, we write *low-priced* car.

In describing a suit that you could wear at once after you had bought it, you could write: *a suit that was already made*, or the much shorter, *ready-made* suit.

Many hyphenated words eventually become so familiar that they are written as one word. Certain magazines, such as *Time* and *Newsweek*, frequently write as single words those words that texts and dictionaries still hyphenate. However, the trend is away from the use of hyphens, often combining compound words that were previously hyphenated, such as *citywide*, *countdown*, *stickup*, and *healthcare*.

WHAT YOU WILL LEARN

In this chapter, you will learn when to hyphenate and when not to hyphenate.

SECTIONS IN THIS CHAPTER

- Compound Adjectives
- Compound Nouns
- Compound Numbers and Fractions
- Compounds with Certain Particles
- Used for Clarity
- Used to Divide Words

Compound Adjectives

WHEN TO HYPHENATE

There are eight types of such hyphenated adjectives.

1. Noun or adjective + participle

   EXAMPLES   *fire-fighting* apparatus (noun + participle)
   bad-looking apples (adjective + participle)

2. Noun + adjective

   EXAMPLES   *good-natured* man
   feel-good movie

3. Compound numbers between 21 and 99

   EXAMPLES   *twenty-fifth* person
   the three hundred and *seventy-fifth* person

4. Number + nouns

   EXAMPLES   the *five-year* plan
   thirty-cent candies
   twelve *two-year-olds*

5. Short adverbs (*best, far, ill, long, much, well*) + participle

   EXAMPLES   *best-known* author
   far-fetched theory
   ill-gotten gains
   long-needed vacation
   well-founded argument

6. Adjectives of nationality

   EXAMPLES   *Franco-Prussian* War
   Anglo-Saxon
   Asian-American

7. Two nouns forming an adjective

   EXAMPLES   a *father-son* event
   a *brother-sister* act

8. Verb plus other elements forming an adjective

   EXAMPLES   the *would-be* actor
   the *wait-and-see* plan for peace
   a *hit-and-run* driver

WHEN *NOT* TO HYPHENATE

1. When the adjective follows the noun

   EXAMPLES *She was an executive well known for her honesty.*
   He was a man ill fitted for the job.

2. When two independent adjectives precede the noun and are not combined

   EXAMPLES *Jack wore his old blue sweater.*
   But: *Jack wore his sky-blue sweater* (only one adjective).
   She carried the tired, old dog.

3. When an adverb modifies an adjective

   EXAMPLES *He was a highly paid executive.*
   This was a nicely kept room.
   It was a newly born calf.

4. When a comparative or superlative form is one of the two modifiers

   EXAMPLES *There was no kinder hearted person in the room.*
   The lowest priced car was the compact.
   But: *A low-priced car was desired.*

5. When the compound modifier is a proper noun of two words

   EXAMPLES *Thomas Mann was a Nobel Prize winner.*
   He was the South American representative in the Security Council.

6. When one word in the compound modifier has an apostrophe

   EXAMPLES *Last year's earnings were strong.*
   The third century's literature was most religious.
   The seventh day's fast was broken.

EXERCISE 1

Indicate at the left whether the following words are properly hyphenated. Place a C *if correct and an* X *if wrong.*

_____ 1. well-fed cattle

_____ 2. redcheeked youngster

_____ 3. tenday reducing diet

_____ 4. a three-month delay

——————————————— 5. the twenty-second victim

——————————————— 6. poorly lit interior

——————————————— 7. state-wide elections

——————————————— 8. eighty-dollar seats

——————————————— 9. a seven-day wonder

——————————————— 10. the kind-hearted teacher

——————————————— 11. hornrimmed spectacles

——————————————— 12. the legend of the saber toothed tiger

——————————————— 13. a well kept garden

——————————————— 14. his ill-fated story

——————————————— 15. an actor who is well-known

——————————————— 16. a first class performance

——————————————— 17. the silver plated fork

——————————————— 18. the sky-blue water

——————————————— 19. England's far-flung empire

——————————————— 20. the far-off hills

Compound Nouns

By using the hyphen with two or more familiar words, new words have been added to our vocabulary.

1. Use the hyphen when two normally distinct functions are united in one person or thing.

 secretary-treasurer   } *united*
writer-designer   } functions

However, *do not* hyphenate double terms that represent a single office:

EXAMPLES   Major General
Secretary of Defense
Lieutenant Commander   *single*
General Manager   *office*
Executive Assistant
Manager Trainee

2. Use the hyphen when two nouns form a new noun. Usually the first acts with the force of an adjective.

EXAMPLES   *light-year*
foot-pound
nation-state

3. Sometimes a noun will be combined with another part of speech to form an entirely new noun.

EXAMPLES   *son-in-law*
jack-in-the-box
know-it-all

4. A verb may be combined with some other part of speech to make a noun.

EXAMPLES   *know-how*
a do-nothing   verb plus object helps make new nouns
a cure-all
a know-nothing

a flare-up   *play-off*
a stand-in   *drive-in*   verb plus preposition helps make new nouns
a go-between   *shake-up*

Compound Numbers and Fractions

1. Use the hyphen in numbers from twenty-one to ninety-nine.

2. In fractions use the hyphen when the fraction is used as an adjective.

EXAMPLE   *The recipe needs three and one-half cups of flour and two and one-eighth cups of soymilk.*

WARNING!

Do not use the hyphen when the fraction is not a single adjective.

EXAMPLES   The chairperson asked *one third* of the group to stay.
He drank *one half* of the cup quickly.

Compounds with Certain Particles

1. All compounds with *self-* use the hyphen.

   EXAMPLES   *self-sacrifice*
   self-interest
   self-help book

2. Compounds with *all-* use the hyphen.

   EXAMPLES   *all-important*
   all-purpose
   all-inclusive

3. Most compounds with *half-* use the hyphen.

   EXAMPLES   *half-moon*
   half-truth

   There are some exceptions to this rule.

   EXAMPLES   *halfway*
   halfhearted

4. Most compounds with *cross-* use the hyphen.

   EXAMPLES   *cross-examine*
   cross-reference

   There are exceptions to this rule.
   EXAMPLES   *crosscut*
   crossbreed

5. With some exceptions, words with *high-, low-,* and *full-* use the hyphen.

   EXAMPLES   *high-class*
   low-grade
   full-fledged

CAUTION!

Do *not* hyphenate the reflexives such as *yourself, himself, herself,* or *self* in such adjectives as *selfless*.

6. The prefix *re-* takes the hyphen when it means *again*, especially if necessary to prevent confusion.

   EXAMPLES   *re-form* the squad
   re-cover the pot

NOTE!

- Note the difference between *reform* the prisoner and *re-form* the broken line of infantry.
- To eliminate the hyphen in *re-cover* might lead to mispronunciation or misunderstanding.

7. Occasionally a hyphen is used with prefixes ending in the same vowel that begins the next word.

EXAMPLES   *co-owner*
pre-engineered

In general, however, those words are written as one word, without a hyphen.

EXAMPLES   *cooperate*
preeminent

8. Use a hyphen with some words beginning with *anti*.

EXAMPLES   *anti-Semitism*
anti-imperialism

However, the trend today is to combine words that begin with *anti*.

EXAMPLES   *antioxidant*
antiperspirant

9. Use a hyphen when a prefix is added to a word beginning with a capital letter.

EXAMPLES   *mid-Atlantic*
pro-British

10. Use a hyphen with titles that are preceded by *vice-* or *ex-*, or are followed by *-elect*.

EXAMPLES   *Vice-President*
President-elect
ex-Governor

WARNING!

Remember that many words begin as two words, become hyphenated, then become one word. Always use a current dictionary if you're not certain!

Used for Clarity

Use a hyphen to avoid confusion of meaning. Look at the following sentence.

She is an old-furniture buyer for an antique store.

Without the hyphen, we would appear to be describing her as *an old buyer*. With the hyphen, it is clear that she buys old furniture.

WORDS THAT ARE NEVER HYPHENATED

background	outline
downstairs	pastime
farewell	railroad
headline	semicolon
inasmuch	together
keyboard	warehouse
midday	yourself
nevertheless	

WORDS THAT ARE ALWAYS HYPHENATED

brother-in-law	son-in-law
daughter-in-law	aide-de-camp
father-in-law	man-of-war
mother-in-law	runner-up
sister-in-law	jack-o'-lantern

Used to Divide Words

The hyphen is also used to divide a word at the end of a line of text. The word must be divided according to syllables. If you are unsure of where to break a word, consult the dictionary or the "10,000 Word Ready Reference Spelling List" at the back of this book. Most computer software programs have auto-hyphenate settings.

WORDS ALWAYS WRITTEN SEPARATELY

any day	by the way	every way	in order
by and by	each other	every time	in spite
by the bye	en route	in fact	no one

WARNING!

Do not confuse *already*, an adverb expressing time, with *all ready*, an adjective meaning fully prepared.

 EXAMPLES   The members of the team were *all ready* to go.
He had *already* left.

EXERCISE 2

Spell the following words correctly by inserting the hyphen where it belongs. If the word is correctly spelled, write C in the space to the left.

_____   1. sisterinlaw

_____   2. man of war

_____   3. aidedecamp

_____   4. runon sentence

_____   5. down-stairs

_____   6. anti war rally

_____   7. ex-husband

_____   8. re-emerge

_____   9. self-centered person

_____   10. one quarter of the population

_____   11. runnerup

_____   12. drivein theater

_____   13. secretary-treasurer

_____   14.   Lieutenant General

_____   15.   tradein

_____   16.   fire-fighting engine

_____   17.   pro-European policy

_____   18.   builtin arch

_____   19.   The final play-off

_____   20.   broken-down houses

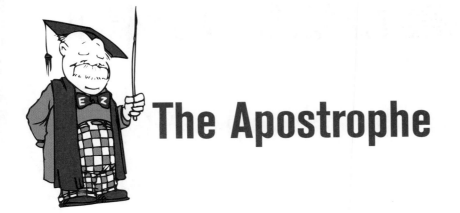

The Apostrophe

The apostrophe is a little mark of great significance. For instance, it allows us to form contractions (such as *isn't* and *aren't*), and it shows possession with clarity and conciseness so that the *book belonging to the student* can simply be the *student's book*. The apostrophe has many good uses, and proper placement is important.

WHAT YOU WILL LEARN

In this chapter, you will learn when and how to use apostrophes correctly. A few confusions are common. For instance, you might wonder when to use *whose* and when it should be *who's*, whether to write *the house of Jim Roberts* or *Jim Roberts' house* or *Jim Roberts's house*. In this chapter, you'll find out!

SECTIONS IN THIS CHAPTER
• Show Contraction
• Show Possession
• Indicate Double Ownership

Show Contraction

1. Use the apostrophe to indicate a lost vowel.

EXAMPLES
do n*ot* = don't
can n*ot* = can't
could n*ot* = couldn't
we *a*re = we're
you *a*re = you're
they *a*re = they're
he *i*s = he's
she *i*s = she's
it *i*s = it's

Show Possession

TO SHOW POSSESSION: COMMON NOUNS

1. Most frequently the apostrophe is used to show possession. A *singular noun* not ending in -*s* adds *'s*.

EXAMPLES
The hat of the girl = the girl's hat
The rights of the man = the man's rights

2. Add *'s* to a *singular noun* that ends in -*s* or an s-sound if a new syllable is formed by pronouncing the possessive.

EXAMPLES
The hair of the actress = the actress's hair
The daughter of the boss = the boss's daughter

3. To show possession with a *plural noun*, add *'s* if the noun does not end in *s*.

EXAMPLES
men's clothing
women's hats
children's shoes

4. If the *plural noun* ends in -*s* (as most nouns do), add only the apostrophe.

EXAMPLES
the doctors' fees
the dentists' conference
the teachers' demands

TO SHOW POSSESSION: PROPER NOUNS

1. To show possession of a *singular proper noun* not ending in -*s*, add *'s*.

| EXAMPLES | Mr. Mann's library
Sarah Smith's dog
Dr. Levitt's office

2. When the *proper noun* ends in -*s* and has only one syllable, add *'s*.

| EXAMPLES | Alger Hiss's case
Rudolf Hess's escape

3. When the *proper noun* ending in -*s* has two or more syllables, add only the apostrophe.

| EXAMPLES | Kate Dickens' classes
Roger Williams' expulsion

TO SHOW POSSESSION: COMPOUND NOUNS

1. The apostrophe is used only after the last noun in the compound.

| EXAMPLES | my mother-in-law's house
the man-of-war's sting

TO SHOW POSSESSION: INDEFINITE PRONOUNS

1. Use the same rules for indefinite pronouns as those above for common nouns.

| EXAMPLES | One's honor is at stake. (*singular*)
The others' phones were on while ours were off. (*plural*)

TO SHOW POSSESSION: PERSONAL PRONOUNS

1. Personal pronouns *never* use the apostrophe for their possessive case.

| EXAMPLE | his, hers, its, ours, theirs

2. Be especially careful with *whose*. What is the difference between:

Whose house is this?
and
Who's there?

NOTE!

In some cases, the apostrophe may be used to avoid repetition of *s* sound.

EXAMPLE   for mildness' sake

Indicate Double Ownership

1. When you wish to indicate *ownership by two or more* persons, use the apostrophe *only* for the last.

EXAMPLES   Lewis and Clark's expedition
Jim and Andrea's business
Smith, Kline and French's clients

2. If you are talking about *separate ownership*, use the apostrophe after each noun.

EXAMPLE   The president's and secretary of state's reports
This means there were two reports, one by each officer.

NOTE!

The apostrophe means "belonging to whatever immediately precedes it," *except* when it is used to indicate a lost vowel.

EXAMPLES   children's—belonging to children
men's—belonging to men
boss's—belonging to a single boss
bosses'—belonging to more than one boss

EXERCISE 1

Rewrite the following phrases, using the apostrophe to show possession:

_____   1. The doll of the young girl

_____   2. The votes of the members

_____   3. The styles of the ladies

_____   4. The paws of the cats

_____   5. The decorations of the sailors

_____   6. The laptop of the professor

_____   7. A shoe of a woman

_____   8. The voice of the soprano

_____   9. The tail of the dog

EXERCISE 2

Circle the two words in each sentence that can form a contraction, and write the contraction in the blank space.

1. _____   They do not vote often.

2. _____   We have not lost hope.

3. _____   The designers could not agree on the color.

4. _____   You are always late.

5. _____   They can not always win.

6. _____   It is too late to go now.

7. _____   Let us wait a little longer.

8. _____   We would not take "no" for an answer.

Capital Letters

The poet E.E. Cummings chose not to begin his sentences with capital letters, and he signed his name ee cummings. For less artistic reasons, many business people now seek to save a few seconds by not using capital letters in rushed text messages, but no one questions their ability to capitalize a letter appropriately. The time to break the rules is when you know them, understand the impact and implications of breaking them, and have a solid reputation for knowing what is correct.

WHAT YOU WILL LEARN

Knowing when to capitalize and when not to is as important as any other rule in spelling. In this chapter, you will learn the rules of capitalization.

SECTIONS IN THIS CHAPTER

- Basic Principles
- Proper Nouns
- Books, Plays, Music

Basic Principles

WHAT TO BEGIN WITH A CAPITAL LETTER

1. The first word of a sentence.

2. The first word of a quoted sentence.

3. The first word, and important words, in titles of books, songs, movies, and plays.

4. Proper nouns.

5. The pronoun *I*.

6. The first word of a salutation and complimentary closing of a letter.

Proper Nouns

WHEN TO CAPITALIZE

Proper Names
Sioux City
Eastern District High School
State Legislature
United Nations

Definite Place Names
Madison Avenue
Central Park

Family Relationships
Aunt Jane
Uncle Bill (but when preceded by a
possessive: my uncle Bill)

**Substitute for Person's Name
(especially in direct address)**
"Hurry up, Dad!"
"Yes, Mom, I'm hurrying!"
Dear Editor:
Dear Customer Service Dept.:

Definite Events
May Day
War of 1870

Races, Languages, Religions
German
Hindu
French
Caucasian
Mongolian
Judaism

Titles
Uncle Don
Dr. Jones

Organization Names
Verizon Wireless
Whole Foods
California Pizza Kitchen
Famous Footwear

Deity (and Words Associated with Deity)
God
Christ
Buddha
Scriptures

Trade Names
Build-a-Bear stores
Comcast Digital Voice customers

WARNING!

Capitalize only the part of the *trade name* that differentiates it from all other brands.

NOTE:

Capitalize the word *Internet*!

WHEN *NOT* TO CAPITALIZE

Words That Are Not a Specific Name
our high school
the cold stream

Point of the Compass
four degrees north

The Names of the Seasons
spring
summer
autumn
winter

Studies Other than Languages
chemistry
biology
economics

A Title After a Modifier
my uncle
a doctor
my father

Books, Plays, Music

REMEMBER THIS RULE IN CAPITALIZING A TITLE!

Don't cap the "CAPs." The last "CAP" stands for:

C—conjunctions (and, but, or, for, nor)
A—articles (the, a, an)
P—prepositions (of, to, for, from, in)

(Only cap one of these "CAPs" if it is the first word of a title.)

EXAMPLES   Book: *Alice in Wonderland*
Play: *Death of a Salesman*
Music: *Let It Be*

EXERCISE

Try your hand at capitalizing the words that need capitals.

1. We stopped at the hotel westover.

2. The new toyota trucks are well advertised.

3. We celebrate decoration day.

4. the north side high school

5. We saw the lion king.

6. They sang irish folk songs.

7. In english courts, the bible is kissed.

8. Walt Disney's "uncle Scrooge" comic books used to be very popular.

9. They walked along fifth avenue.

10. Many people ask for washington coffee.

11. Our vacation to britain lasted three weeks.

12. Bard college is in new york.

13. the taming of the shrew is a play written by shakespeare.

14. My courses in college include mathematics, english, and french.

15. Last spring we visited aunt emily who lives out west.

Spelling Abbreviations

This chapter includes some of the most commonly used words and abbreviations—from days of the week to measurement terms.

WHAT YOU WILL LEARN

In this chapter, you will learn abbreviations, titles, and business terms, beginning with words we use every day—the days of the week.

SECTIONS IN THIS CHAPTER
• Date and Time
• Business Terms
• Personal Titles
• Measurement Terms

EXERCISE 1

Answer the following questions to double check your spellings and abbreviations:

1. The day after Tuesday is _____.

2. The abbreviation for Tuesday is _____.

3. The abbreviation for March is _____.

4. The month after January is _____.

5. The abbreviation for April is _____.

NOTE:

The trickiest day to spell is Wednesday and the trickiest month is February. If you answered #1 in the exercise with the correct spelling of *Wednesday* and #4 with the correct spelling of *February*, congratulations! If you got these wrong, pay special attention to learning them. They will, without a doubt, continue to come up regularly!

Date and Time

DAY, MONTH, TIME

DAYS OF THE WEEK

Abbreviation	Weekday
Sun.	Sunday
Mon.	Monday
Tues.	Tuesday
Wed.	Wednesday
Thurs.	Thursday
Fri.	Friday
Sat.	Saturday

MONTHS OF THE YEAR

Abbreviation	Month
Jan.	January
Feb.	February
Mar.	March
Apr.	April
Aug.	August
Sept.	September
Oct.	October
Nov.	November
Dec.	December

TIME

Abbreviation	Time
AD	anno Domini (Latin for "In the year of the Lord")
BC	before Christ
AM, A.M., a.m.	ante meridiem (Latin for "before noon")
PM, P.M., p.m.	post meridiem (Latin for "after noon")
EST	eastern standard time
CDT	central daylight time
MST	mountain standard time
PDT	pacific daylight time

Business Terms

ABBREVIATION	TERM
acct.	account
ans.	answer
assn.	association
Ave.	avenue
bldg.	building
Blvd.	boulevard
bros.	brothers
COD	collect on delivery
dept.	department
Esq.	esquire
etc.	and so forth
FOB	freight on board
Inc.	incorporated
Jr.	junior
Ltd.	limited
mfg.	manufacturing

(continued)

Mts.	mountains
No.	number
PO	post office
PS	postscript (written after the letter)
RR	railroad
RSVP	reply, if you please (French: répondez s'il vous plaît)
Sr.	senior
SS	steamship
St.	street

NOTE:

Most abbreviations *do not* use periods when upper-cased letters are used and *do* use periods when lower-cased letters are used.

Personal Titles

ABBREVIATION	TITLE
Asst.	Assistant
Capt.	Captain
Com.	commander
	commissioner
	commission
	committee
DDS	Doctor of Dental Surgery
Dr.	Doctor
Gov.	Governor
Hon.	Honorable
Lt.	Lieutenant
M.D.	Doctor of Medicine
Mr.	Mister
Mrs.	Married woman's title
Ms.	Woman's title (married or unmarried)
PhD	Doctor of Philosophy
Pres.	President
Prof.	Professor
Rev.	Reverend
RN	Registered Nurse
Supt.	Superintendent
Sec. or Secy.	Secretary
Treas.	Treasurer

Measurement Terms

STANDARD MEASUREMENT

Abbreviation	Term
in.	inch
ft.	foot
yd.	yard
oz.	ounce
lb.	pound
bu.	bushel
doz.	dozen
hr.	hour
yr.	year

METRIC MEASUREMENT

Abbreviation	Term
l	liter
mg	milligram
kg	kilogram
cm	centimeter
mm	millimeter
km	kilometer

EXERCISE 2

In the space to the left, put the correct abbreviations of the following words:

_____ 1. Secretary

_____ 2. Treasurer

_____ 3. Collect on Delivery

_____ 4. Before noon

_____ 5. Junior

_____   6. dozen

_____   7. August

_____   8. Doctor of Medicine

_____   9. Honorable

_____   10. year

_____   11. Saturday

_____   12. Rural Free Delivery

_____   13. Reply if you please

_____   14. Esquire

_____   15. department

_____   16. pound

_____   17. Governor

_____   18. Dentist

_____   19. Reverend

_____   20. Boulevard

EXERCISE 3

Write the words for which the following abbreviations are given:

_____   1. PhD

_____   2. Ave.

_____   3. in.

_____   4. etc.

_____   5. no.

_____   6. Bros.

_____   7. PS

_____   8. RR

_____   9. Sept.

_____   10. FOB

_____   11. Prof.

_____   12. Asst.

_____   13. EST

_____   14. Gov.

_____   15. Wed.

_____   16. Asst.

_____   17. SS

_____   18. St.

_____   19. recd.

_____   20. dept.

_____   21. MD

_____   22. Treas.

_____   23. Sat.

_____   24. Hon.

_____   25. Rev.

_____   26. Sec.

_____   27. DDS

_____   28. Capt.

_____   29. Mar.

_____   30. PM

More Homonyms and Homophones and Other Confusing Word Pairs

Back in Chapter 2, you learned about homonyms and homophones. Here, you will have lists of homonyms and homophones and other commonly confused words, along with several practice exercises. If you're not sure about the difference between *libel* and *liable* or *whether* and *weather*, you're *liable* to appreciate the knowledge you'll gain from this chapter!

WHAT YOU WILL LEARN

In this chapter, you will learn the difference between many confusing word pairs. Learning to distinguish these from one another will build your skills immensely and help you with the kinds of spelling errors that spell-checkers cannot always check.

SECTIONS IN THIS CHAPTER
• Homonyms and Homophones
• Other Confusing Word Pairs

Homonyms and Homophones

Key

n. = noun
v. = verb
adj. = adjective
pp. = past participle
adv. = adverb
pro. = pronoun
prep. = preposition

aisle, n.   a narrow passage
   The bride walked down the **aisle**.

isle, n.   an island
   Poets sometimes write about the Golden **Isles**.

already, adv.   by this time
   We had **already** eaten our lunch.

all ready, adj.   all are ready
   We were **all ready** to leave.

altar, n.   a tablelike structure used for religious purposes in a church or out of doors
   The bride and groom walked to the **altar**.

alter, v.   to make a change
   Plastic surgeons can **alter** features.

altogether, adv.   entirely
   I **altogether** disapprove of such behavior.

all together, adj.   all in one place
   The students were **all together** at the assembly.

berth, n.   a place to sleep
   We ordered a **berth** on the train.

birth, n.   act of being born
   The **birth** of the prince caused much joy.

bloc, n.   a combination of persons with a common purpose
   The radicals voted as a **bloc** in the legislature.

block, n.   a solid piece of material
   He put his fountain on a **block** of concrete.

boarder, n.   one who is provided with meals and lodging
   The **boarder** paid his rent to his landlady.

border, n.   a boundary
   The **border** between the U.S. and Canada is not fortified.

born, pp.   that which has been given birth
  The baby was **born** at dawn.

borne, pp.   carried
  The countess was **borne** in her sedan chair.

brake, n.   an instrument to stop something
  Because the **brake** was broken, the car rushed downhill.

break, v.   to smash, cause to fall apart
  Be careful not to **break** these rare glasses.

bridal, adj.   pertaining to a wedding
  The **bridal** gown was made of taffeta.

bridle, n.   part of a harness
  The horse pulled at his **bridle**.

bridle, v.   to restrain
  Some gossips need to **bridle** their tongues.

canvas, n.   a kind of rough cloth
  Sue's favorite bag is made of **canvas**.

canvass, v.   to solicit
  Election workers went out to **canvass** the neighborhood.

capital, n.   a major city of a state or nation; also, something of extreme
           importance; also, stock of wealth
  Albany is the **capital** of New York.
  Kidnapping in some states is a **capital** offense.
  Liberia welcomes foreign **capital**.

capitol, n.   a building
  In Washington the **capitol** is popular with visitors.

chord, n.   a pleasant combination of tones
  The pianist electrified his audience with his opening **chords**.

cord, n.   a rope
  Can you get me some **cord** to tie these books?

cord, n.   a unit to measure fuel wood
  He chopped three **cords** of wood today.

coarse, adj.   vulgar
  Such **coarse** language cannot be permitted.

course, n.   a way to be followed
  In this emergency, only one **course** was indicated.
  John took the academic **course** in high school.

complement, n. or v.   something that completes another
> The wine was an excellent **complement** to the meal.

compliment, n. or v.   something said in praise
> The supervisor **complimented** her team for a job well done.

correspondence, n.   letters exchanged
> The **correspondence** between the two adversaries was lively.

correspondents, n.   those communicating by letter
> He had numerous **correspondents** to whom he wrote often.

EXERCISE 1

Underline the correct word in parentheses.

1. This story cannot (alter, altar) the situation.

2. Most food (born, borne) illnesses are caused by bacteria or parasites.

3. If you put your foot on the (break, brake) you will stop the car.

4. Many sincere people oppose (capital, capitol) punishment.

5. The center (aisle, isle) of the theater was very wide.

6. When the search party arrived, the fire had (all ready, already) died out.

7. Many friends and relatives attended the (bridle, bridal) ceremony.

8. The old bridge was (altogether, all together) dangerous.

9. When the test day came, we were (all ready, already).

10. Some people don't like to use (capitol, capital) letters when texting.

council, n.   a deliberative body
> The city **council** was called into special session.

counsel, n.   advice; also an attorney
> My **counsel** in this case is to avoid temperature extremes.
> The defendant's **counsel** made a stirring plea.

councilor, n.   one who is a member of a council
   The newly elected **councilor** was given an ovation.

counselor, n.   an advisor, usually legal
   In America we use the expression **counselor**, whereas in Britain it is solicitor or barrister.

core, n.   a center of fruit
   The **core** of my apple was rotten.

corps, n.   a unit of people
   General Smith commanded the Second Army **Corps**.

descent, n.   a going down
   The flight's **descent** was smooth.

dissent, n.   a disagreement
   Justice Holmes' **dissents** were famous.

desert, v.   to leave behind
   It is a terrible crime to **desert** one's child.

dessert, n.   sweets after a meal
   We had sliced peaches for **dessert**.

dual, adj.   double
   Dr. Jekyll and Mr. Hyde were the **dual** personalities of one man.

duel, n.   combat of two men
   Hamilton was killed in the **duel** with Burr.

feint, v.   to make a pretense of
   The boxer **feinted** with his left, then struck with his right.

faint, v.   to lose consciousness
   We nearly **fainted** from hunger.

flair, n.   instinctive attraction to
   The model had a **flair** for style.

flare, v.   to shine with a sudden light
   A match **flared** in the darkness.

fowl, n.   a bird of any kind
   Chicken is a type of **fowl**.

foul, adj.   offensive to the senses
   The air in the dungeon was **foul**.

gate, n.   a means of entrance or exit
   The rusty **gate** was ajar.

gait, n.   a manner of walking
   The old man's **gait** was slow and uncertain.

heir, n.   one who inherits property
  The eldest son was the **heir** to his father's estate.

air, n.   atmosphere
  The mountain **air** was chilly.

horde, n.   a crowd or throng
  A **horde** of barbarians once sacked Rome.

hoard, n. a hidden supply
  The miser added the coin to his **hoard**.

hostel, n.   an inn
  The young cyclists stayed overnight at a **hostel**.

hostile, adj.   unfriendly
  The lawyer cross-examined the **hostile** witness.

instance, n.   example
  The lawyer gave **instance** after **instance** of good behavior.

instants, n.   plural, meaning moments
  Pain was stopped for several **instants** before the operation was continued.

its, pro.   The possessive case of it
  The organization doubled **its** membership this year.

it's, abbreviated form of **it is**
  It's too late to go to any restaurant now.

led, v.   the past tense of **lead**
  The new manager **led** the meeting.

lead, n.   (lĕd) a metal
  Lead pipes are no longer used for drinking water.

libel, n.   a defamatory statement
  The politician sued the newspaper for **libel**.

liable, adj.   likely
  The sidewalk is so icy that you're **liable** to fall.

EXERCISE 2

Underline the correct word in parentheses.

1. England called its Privy (Council, Counsel) into session.

2. It takes a 40° angle to (compliment, complement) an angle of 50° to make a right angle.

3. To get out of the swamp, there was only one (course, coarse) to follow.

4. The (desert, dessert) at the end of the banquet was delicious.

5. (It's, Its) amazing how much you can find on the Internet.

6. The legislature passed the bill without any (dissent, descent).

7. The teacher (lead, led) his class outside.

8. The witness refused to answer any question without advice from his (counsel, council).

9. Joe ate his apple down to the (corps, core).

10. The judge said that he had a (dual, duel) responsibility.

miner, n.   one who extracts minerals from the earth
　　Mark Twain frequently wrote about **miners** in the Old West.

minor, adj., n.   unimportant; below legal age
　　This injury to the skin was a **minor** one.
　　Alcoholic beverages may not be sold to **minors**.

peace, n.   a state of quiet; freedom from war
　　The U.N. tries hard to keep the **peace**.

piece, n.   a portion
　　Would you like a **piece** of cake?

pedal, n.   a foot lever
　　The bicycle seat was so high that the child's foot could not reach the **pedal**.

peddle, v.   to travel with items for sale
　　He earned a small income by **peddling** vegetables.

plain, adj., n.   *as an adjective,* simple, unadorned
In this small town we live in **plain** houses.
as a noun, a flat area of land
Many pioneers perished while crossing this **plain**.

plane, n.   an airplane; a tool; a flat surface
The **plane** made a forced landing.
To smooth the surface, the carpenter used a **plane**.

principal, adj., n.   *as an adjective,* main, important
These were the **principal** points in the CEO's speech.
as a noun, the head official in a school
A high school **principal** must be a good administrator.

principle, n.   a statement of a rule in conduct or in science or mathematics
Archimedes discovered the **principle** of buoyancy in liquids.
A candidate for high office should be a person of **principle**.

raise, v.   to increase salary
My boss gave me a **raise**.

raze, v.   to destroy to the ground
The building was **razed** because it was old and unsafe.

review, n.   a reexamination
The teacher conducted a **review** before the test.

revue, n.   a theatrical production of songs, skits, and dances
The dramatic society wanted to present a **revue**.

shear, v.   to cut or clip
With sharp scissors, the tailor was able to **shear** the cloth.

sheer, adj.   straight up and down without a break
The **sheer** precipice was a hundred feet high.

sight, n.   something that is seen
The skyline of New York is an impressive **sight**.

site, n.   location of a planned building
The architect studied the **site** carefully.

soar, v.   to fly high
The hawk **soared** high in the sky.

sore, adj.   painful
Unaccustomed to exercise, his muscles were **sore**.

stationary, adj.   fixed, attached
The old-fashioned schoolroom had **stationary** desks and chairs.

stationery, n.   paper used in correspondence
Maya designs beautiful **stationery** on her computer.

straight, adj.   direct
> The path leading to the house was **straight**.

strait, n.   a waterway
> The captain steered the ship through the **strait**.

tail, n.   the end of a body of an animal
> The cat's **tail** is black with a white tip.

tale, n.   a narrative
> The children's book told a happy **tale**.

taut, adj.   tightly drawn
> The lines that held the sails were **taut**.

taught, v.   instructed
> The students were **taught** the elements of algebra.

team, n.   group on one side
> Our hockey **team** was the best in the league.

teem, v.   to be filled to overflowing
> The mountain lake **teemed** with fish.

there, adv.   an adverb of place
> He placed the package **there**.

their, pro.   a possessive pronoun
> The students brought **their** laptops.

they're pro. + v.   contraction of they are
> "**They're** here," the children shouted.

to, prep.   *preposition with a verb to make an infinitive*
> **To** err is human; **to** forgive, divine.
> > *preposition with noun or pronoun*
> Please take this book **to** him.

too, adv.   also, more than enough
> > We arrived late for dinner **too**.
> The software was **too** expensive.

two, numeral, the number 2
> He had **two** letters of recommendation.

vain, adj.   conceited
> The **vain** actor started his own fan club.

vane, n.   weathercock
> The farmer glanced at the **vane** to see the wind's direction.

vein, n.   blood vessel
> The chef dropped her knife and accidentally punctured a **vein**.

veracious, adj.   truthful
>   The jury believed that the witness's report was **veracious**.

voracious, adj.   having a huge appetite
>   Most large animals are **voracious**.

vial, n.   a small vessel for liquids
>   The druggist gave the customer a **vial** of medicine.

vile, adj.   morally despicable
>   The judge said the criminal's offense was **vile**.

waist, n.   middle section of the body; a garment
>   Tonya has a narrow **waist**.
>   The bridal gown's **waist** was made of lace.

waste, v., n.   to squander; material that is squandered
>   To **waste** food is almost a crime when so many starve.
>   Many manufacturers dispose of industrial **waste** through incineration.

week, n.   a period of seven days
>   There are four **weeks** in a month.

weak, adj.   lacking strength
>   The beggar was **weak** and frail from lack of food.

weight, n.   the amount that an object registers on a scale
>   The child's **weight** was below normal.

wait, n.   a period of waiting
>   The commuters had a long **wait** for the train.

who's, personal pronoun; a contraction of *who is*
>   "**Who's** there?" she asked.

whose, possessive of *who*
>   **Whose** coat is this?

your, possessive of *you*
>   This is **your** lucky day.

you're, a contraction of *you are*
>   "**You're** elected," declared the chairman.

EXERCISE 3

Underline the correct word in parentheses.

1. An appendectomy can hardly be considered (minor, miner) surgery.

2. He was a great admirer of (peace, piece) by friendly negotiation.

3. Because of motor difficulties the (plane, plain) had to make a forced landing on the (plane, plain).

4. The (principle, principal) causes of the disagreement should be easy to resolve.

5. The young girl placed the belt around her (waste, waist).

6. The graduates threw (their, there) caps into the air.

7. This pressure was (to, too, two) much to bear.

8. It is not necessary to use expensive (stationery, stationary) on minor occasions.

9. We could never discover (whose, who's) MP3 player it was.

10. "(They're, their) here," exclaimed the teacher.

Other Confusing Word Pairs

There are many other word pairs that are often confused because they sound almost alike, such as *illusion* and *allusion*. Strictly speaking, such pairs are not homonyms or homophones. However, they cause spelling difficulties and for that reason are listed and defined below. So, too, are words that resemble one another so closely in spelling that they are a frequent source of trouble, as *moral* and *morale*, and *dairy* and *diary*.

advice, n.   counsel
> We asked the teacher for **advice**.

advise, v.   to give counsel
> Our parents are ready to **advise** us.

affect, v.   to influence
> The heartwarming story **affected** readers.

effect, v.   to bring about a result
> By his skill and knowledge, the doctor **effected** a cure.

ally, v.   to join with
>England can usually be expected to **ally** herself with the United States.

ally, n.   one who joins with another
>France was our **ally** in World War II.

alley, n.   a narrow thoroughfare
>The cat disappeared down the **alley**.

allusion, n.   a reference to
>The judge made an **allusion** to an old ruling.

illusion, n.   a deception
>Magicians create **illusions**.

angel, n.   a supernatural being
>Disputes about **angels** are found in medieval thought.

angle, n.   corner; point of view
>Advertisers are always looking for a new **angle**.

ascent, n.   act of mounting upward
>The **ascent** of Mount Everest is hazardous.

assent, n.   agreement
>The father gave his **assent** to his daughter's marriage.

beside, prep.   by the side of
>The bride stood **beside** her husband.

besides, adv.   in addition to
>**Besides** a bonus, he received a raise.

breath, n.   an exhalation
>The **breath** froze in the cold air.

breathe, v.   to take in or let out breath
>The doctor asked the patient to **breathe** in deeply.

cloths, n.   bits of cloth
>I carry soft **cloths** to clean my computer screen.

clothes, n.   covering for the human body
>Rita bought new **clothes** for her trip.

complacent, adj.   self-satisfied
>When he received the prize he had a **complacent** smile.

complaisant, adj.   inclined to please or oblige
>He was so **complaisant** that people liked to deal with him.

consul, n.   an official in one country representing another
>The Russian **consul** in the United States represents his country's interests.

counsel, n.   an attorney
>The **counsel** for the defense entered a plea of guilty.

corporal, adj.   relating to the body
    Teachers no longer use **corporal** punishment.

corporeal, adj.   relating to physical rather than immaterial
    Ghosts do not have a **corporeal** existence.

credible, adj.   believable
    The witness made her story **credible**.

creditable, adj.   praiseworthy
    The soldier's action was **creditable**.

device, n.   a contrivance
    The inventor showed his new **device**.

devise, v.   to make a contrivance
    The inventor **devised** a new means of producing electricity.

elicit, v.   to bring out
    By patiently questioning, the investigator **elicited** the truth.

illicit, adj.   unlawful
    The moonshiners operated an **illicit** distillery.

emigrant, n.   one who leaves a country for another
    America welcomes **emigrants** from many lands.

immigrant, n.   one who comes to another country after leaving his own
    Forty million **immigrants** brought many resources to America.

formally, adv.   done in a formal or regular manner
    The couple dressed **formally** for the show.

formerly, adv.   earlier
    Formerly, young employees had to wait a long time for promotion.

ingenious, adj.   clever, tricky
    The device for operating the ship was **ingenious**.

ingenuous, adj.   open, frank, innocent
    The **ingenuous** story won over the jury.

later, adv.   comparative degree of late
    It's **later** than you think.

latter, adv.   of two things, the one mentioned second
    Of the two desserts, ice cream or sherbet, I chose the **latter**.

EXERCISE 4

Underline the correct word in parentheses.

1. He likes to wear brightly colored (clothes, cloths).

2. This development in art comes in a (later, latter) period in history.

3. Refugees in Hong Kong rushed to the American (consul, counsel) for safety.

4. Before signing this contract, you should get legal (advice, advise).

5. He placed the boxes (beside, besides) the wall.

6. During the early part of this century, many (immigrants, emigrants) from England went to Australia.

7. All those who attended the banquet were (formerly, formally) attired.

8. The young child had an (ingenious, ingenuous) smile.

9. The United States has been an (ally, alley) of England.

10. The orator's speech was full of literary (illusions, allusions).

loose, adj.   free, unattached
   The screw was **loose**.

lose, v.   to miss from one's possession
   I **lose** my keys all the time!

moral, adj., n.   pertaining to the good and proper
   We live by **moral** law as well as the court's law.

morale, n.   state of well-being of a person or group
   The **morale** of our team was high.

personal, adj.   pertaining to a person or individual
   Our quarrel in the office was not due to a business but to a **personal** argument.

personnel, n.   the body of persons employed in some service
   Because he had a deep understanding of people, he was appointed **personnel** manager.

quiet, adj., n.   free from noise
> In hospital areas, **quiet** must be preserved.

quite, adj.   entirely, completely
> Our customers are **quite** happy with our online service department.

respectfully, adv.   showing deference
> Cara spoke **respectfully** to her new boss.

respectively, adv.   in the order given
> The manager spoke to the bookkeeper, salesperson, and administrative assistant **respectively**.

than, a conjunction; usually introduces a comparison
> Gold is heavier **than** silver.

then, adv.   an adverb that indicates a time
> We'll see you **then**.

EXERCISE 5

Underline the correct word in parentheses.

1. The new bonus structure raised the (moral, morale) of our sales team.

2. Such demands are (quiet, quite) impossible to meet.

3. Problems of (personal, personnel) always arise where there are many employees.

4. The (loose, lose) stone caused the boy to slip.

5. Love is more powerful (then, than) hate.

6. I was (formally, formerly) dressed for the occasion.

7. Where did you (lose, loose) the money?

8. Every fable has a (moral, morale).

9. The tree-shaded street was (quite, quiet) deserted.

10. Rather (than, then) take a risk, he put his money in a bank.

Word Building

When learning an instrument, the monotony of scale exercises can be tiresome. Without these scales, however, no virtuoso would ever develop. Spelling, too, has its scales and exercises. They may seem just as boring as the musical exercises, but they are similarly valuable.

Study the following word families. Sometimes you will forget the spelling of one of these words. If you can remember its relatives, you will not have to consult the dictionary. A little time spent with these now will mean time saved later.

WHAT YOU WILL LEARN

In this chapter, you will gain additional practice with suffixes and become familiar with word families, which will give you greater perspective on spelling individual words.

SECTION IN THIS CHAPTER

- Word Families

Word Families

WORDS AND VARIATIONS

Word	Related Words		
abolish	abolished	abolishing	abolition
accomplish	accomplished	accomplishing	accomplishment
account	accounted	accounting	accountant
acknowledge	acknowledged	acknowledging	acknowledgment
advise	advised	advising	adviser (or advisor)
allude	alluded	alluding	allusion
almost	always	already	altogether
appear	appeared	appearing	appearance
arrange	arranged	arranging	arrangement
arrive	arrived	arriving	arrival
assist	assisted	assisting	assistance
begin	began	beginning	beginner
believe	believed	believing	believer
busy	busied	busying	business
change	changed	changing	changeable
choose	chose	choosing	chosen
complete	completed	completely	completion
confide	confident	confidence	confidentially
conscience	conscientious	subconscious	unconscious
consider	considered	considerable	consideration
continue	continued	continuation	continually
control	controlling	controller	controllable
critic	critical	criticize	criticism
deceive	deceit	deception	deceiver
decide	decided	decision	deciding
define	definite	definition	definitely
describe	descriptive	describing	description
desire	desirous	desiring	desirable
embarrass	embarrassed	embarrassing	embarrassment
endure	endured	endurable	endurance
equip	equipped	equipping	equipment
every	everybody	everywhere	everyone
exceed	exceeded	exceeding	exceedingly
excel	excelled	excellent	excellence
excite	exciting	excitement	excitable
exist	existed	existing	existence
experience	experienced	experiencing	experiment
extend	extended	extensive	extension
impress	impressed	impressive	impression
intend	intended	intensive	intension
interfere	interfered	interfering	interference
interrupt	interrupted	interrupting	interruption

Word	Related Words		
obey	obe*dient*	obe*dience*	obe*isance*
occasion	occasion*ed*	occasion*al*	occasion*ally*
peace	peace*ful*	peace*able*	peace*ably*
permit	permit*ted*	permi*ssible*	permi*ssion*
persist	persist*ed*	persist*ent*	persist*ence*
pity	pit*ied*	pity*ing*	pit*iable*
possess	possess*ed*	possess*ive*	possess*ion*
practice	practic*al*	practic*ed*	practic*able*
prefer	prefer*red*	prefer*ring*	prefer*ence*
recognize	recogniz*ed*	recogni*tion*	recogniz*able*
separate	separa*tion*	*in*separ*able*	separate*ly*
sincere	sincer*ity*	*in*sincere	sincere*ly*
surprise	surprise*d*	surpris*ingly*	surpris*ing*

EXERCISE

Indicate by the letter C if the following words are correctly spelled. Correct all errors in the space to the left.

_____ 1. arranger

_____ 2. choosers

_____ 3. difinative

_____ 4. preferential

_____ 5. inseparable

_____ 6. hypocritical

_____ 7. undefineable

_____ 8. undesireable

_____ 9. pityless

_____ 10. unaccountable

_____ 11. unchangeable

_____ 12. incompletely

_____ 13. disarrange

_____ 14. confiding

_____ 15. confidential

_____ 16. indecisive

_____ 17. non-existant

_____ 18. preferrable

_____ 19. experiential

_____ 20. unendureable

_____ 21. necessarly

_____ 22. transferred

_____ 23. cancel

_____ 24. changable

_____ 25. judgement

_____ 26. accomadate

_____ 27. gaurantee

_____ 28. reciepts

_____ 29. secretary

_____ 30. business

_____ 31. choosen

_____ 32. posessed

_____ 33. reconized

_____ 34. sincereity

_____ 35. existance

_____ 36. embarassed

_____ 37. excellent

_____ 38. exciteable

_____ 39. prefered

_____ 40. ocassion

20

Most Frequently Misspelled Words

This chapter includes two lists of words that have been found to be the most frequently misspelled. The first are general, everyday words. We call them the "One Hundred Pests." The second list was compiled by a study that found the most commonly misspelled words in business. Did you know that two of the most commonly misspelled words in business are *misspelled* and *business*?

WHAT YOU WILL LEARN

In this chapter, you will learn whether the most commonly misspelled words are some of the ones that have been difficult for you. You may also notice how many you've already learned! You will also find a list of professions following "Business Terms," as many of these are also commonly misspelled.

SECTIONS IN THIS CHAPTER
• One Hundred Pests
• Business Terms
• Commonly Misspelled Professions

One Hundred Pests

ONE HUNDRED COMMONLY MISSPELLED WORDS

ache	doctor	jeopardy	raise	Tuesday
acne	does	journalist	read	two
again	done	judgment	ready	
always	don't			very
among		knew	said	
ancestors	early	know	says	wear
announce	easy		separate	Wednesday
answer	enough	laid	shoes	week
	every	loose	since	where
been		lose	some	whether
beginning	February		straight	which
believe	forty	making	sugar	whole
blue	friend	many	sure	women
break		meant		won't
built	grammar	minute	tear	would
business	guess	much	their	write
busy			there	writing
buy	half	neighbor	they're	wrote
	having	neither	though	
can't	hear		through	
choose	heard	often	tired	
color	here		tonight	
coming	hoarse	piece	trouble	
cough	hour		truly	
could				
country	instead			

Business Terms

The words that follow are those that are most commonly misspelled in business correspondence. If you want to improve your business effectiveness, study these words closely until you can spell every one correctly.

The list was compiled by the National Office Management Association after a comprehensive study of 10,652 letters collected from business concerns and government agencies located throughout the country.

The words are not strange or unusual. They appear frequently in business letters. Many of them appear on other pages of this book. Mastery of this list will protect you against the spelling mistakes committed by many business men and women.

COMMONLY MISSPELLED BUSINESS TERMS

A
accept
accommodate
accountant
accumulate
acknowledgment
acquainted
acquire
acquisition
acquitted
actually
additionally
address
adjustable
administration
advances
advertisement
advisability
advise
affects
affidavit
affirmative
agency
aggravate
allotment
allowance
all right
alphabetic
aluminum
analysis
analyze
anniversary
announcement
anticipating
anxiety
apology
apparatus
appearance
applicant
appraisal
appropriation
approval
argument
arrears
arrival
articles
assessable
assignment
assistance

associate
assured
attached
attorney
attempt
attendance
attractive
auditor
available
aviation

B
baggage
balance
bankruptcy
banquet
barrel
barter
becoming
beneficiary
benefited
biased
bookkeeping
borrower
brief
broadcast
brokerage
budget
bulletin
bureau
business

C
calculator
calendar
campaign
canceled
candidate
capacity
capitalization
carrier
cartage
carton
certificate
circular
clearance
coincidence
collapsible
collateral

collision
column
combination
combustible
commerce
commission
committee
commodity
community
companies
comparative
compel
compensation
competent
complaint
complimentary
concession
condemn
conference
confirmation
congestion
conscientious
consequence
considerable
consignee
consolidated
construction
consumer
container
contemplating
contemporary
contingent
convenience
conveyance
cooperate
corporation
corroborate
corrugated
counterfeit
coupon
courteous
credentials
creditor
curiosity
currency
customer
cylinder

COMMONLY MISSPELLED BUSINESS TERMS *(continued)*

D
decision
defendant
deferred
deficit
definite
defray
demonstration
depreciation
description
desperate
destination
deteriorate
determination
develop
dictionary
director
disappear
disappoint
disastrous
disbursements
discernible
discontinued
discrepancy
discuss
dispatch
dissatisfaction
dissolution
distinction
distinguish
distributor
dividend
document
doubt
duplicate
durable

E
earliest
earnest
easier
economic
eighth
elevator
eligible
embarrass
emergency
enormous
enterprise
envelope

equally
equipped
especially
estimate
essentially
eventually
evidence
exaggerate
examination
exasperate
excellent
except
exchange
executive
exhibition
existence
expedite
explanation
extension

F
facilitate
February
financier
foreclosure
forehead
forfeit
formally
formerly
forty
franchise
fundamental
furniture
futile

G
generally
genuine
government
grammar

H
handkerchief
hastily
hazard
height
hoping
hosiery
humorous

I
illegible
immediately
impracticable
inasmuch
inconsistent
inconvenience
incorporated
incredible
increment
indelible
indemnity
indispensable
inducement
industrial
inevitable
inferred
inflation
infringement
initiate
inquiry
insolvency
inspection
instance
institution
instructor
insurance
integrity
intelligence
interpretation
inventory
investigate
invoice
involved
itemized
itinerary
its
it's

J
jobber
journal

K
knowledge

L
laboratory
latter
leased

COMMONLY MISSPELLED BUSINESS TERMS *(continued)*

ledger
legitimate
leisure
liabilities
library
license
likable (*or* likeable)
liquidation
literature
lucrative
luxury

M
machinery
maintenance
management
manila
manufacturer
margin
material
maturity
mechanical
medicine
memorandum
mercantile
merchandise
merge
middleman
miniature
miscellaneous
misrepresent
misspelled
moistener
monopoly
mortgage
movie
municipal

N
necessary
ninth
notary
noticeable
notwithstanding
nowadays

O
obliging
observation

obsolete
obstacle
occasionally
occurred
omission
oneself
opportunity
optimism
option
ordinance
organization
outrageous
overdraw
overhead
oxygen

P
pamphlet
parallel
parenthesis
parliament
particularly
pavilion
peaceable
peculiarities
pecuniary
percent
perforation
performance
permanent
permissible
perpendicular
perseverance
personal
personnel
persuade
perusal
petition
petroleum
physical
physician
plaintiff
plausible
policy
practically
precedence
precise
preface
preference

prescription
presence
presidency
prestige
primitive
principal
principle
privilege
procedure
process
professional
prominence
promissory
pronunciation
prospectus
psychology

Q
qualification
quantity
questionnaire
quotation

R
readjustment
really
reasonable
rebate
receipt
recognize
recommend
reconstruction
reference
regardless
register
reimburse
reinforcement
relations
remedied
remittance
representative
requisition
resign
respectfully
respectively
responsible
restaurant
ridiculous
rural

COMMONLY MISSPELLED BUSINESS TERMS (continued)

S
sacrifice
salary
salutation
sanitary
satisfactory
schedule
scissors
secretarial
security
seize
separate
several
significance
similar
simultaneous
sincerely
sociable
society
solemn
solvent
sometimes
source
southern
souvenir
specialize
specify
spectacular
speculate
statement
stationary

stationery
statistics
straightened
strenuous
strictly
sublet
subsidize
substantial
substitute
subtle
successful
suggestion
summary
superfluous
superintendent
surplus
surprise
susceptible
syllable
syndicate
systematize

T
tangible
tariff
tendency
testimonials
tickler
together
transferred
transparent

treasurer
triplicate
Tuesday
turnover
typewriter
typical
typographical

U
unanimous
university
unmistakable
utilities
utilize

V
verification
vicinity
visible
volume
voucher

W
waive
warrant
Wednesday
whatever
wholesale
wholly
women

NOTE:

As the list was compiled several years ago, it does not include computer and other new technological terms, which you will find elsewhere in this book. The only alteration made to this list is the removal of words that are no longer common. It's been quite a while since business people wrote about *mimeographs* and *carbon*!

Commonly Misspelled Professions

A
Accountant
Administrator
Anchorman
Anesthetist
Animator
Archaeologist
Architect
Athlete
Attorney
Auditor

B
Bookkeeper

C
Carpenter
Cashier
Chauffeur
Consultant

D
Dietitian

E
Engineer

H
Horticulturist

L
Lecturer

M
Manicurist
Mathematician
Mediator
Meteorologist
Musician

O
Oceanographer

P
Paralegal
Pharmacist
Physician
Physicist

Professor
Programmer
Psychiatrist
Psychologist

R
Receptionist
Rehabilitation counselor

S
Statistician
Surveyor
Systems Analyst

T
Technician

U
Upholsterer

V
Veterinarian

21

Computer Terms

Computers have their own "languages," and new technology is emerging at rapid speeds. Developers, as well as end-users, continue to expand our computer-related vocabulary, and an increasing number of technical terms have entered our common usage. As vocabulary evolves with technology, new words enter; others become obsolete. Daisy wheel typewriters and records stored on microfiche have given way to computers and a multitude of storage devices.

WHAT YOU WILL LEARN

In this chapter, you will learn the spellings of common computer-related terms. While you will find a brief section about computer acronyms, you will not find a list of them here. Although these have their place (and you can easily find long lists of acronyms), our focus here is on the spellings of complete words.

SECTIONS IN THIS CHAPTER

- Computer Acronyms
- One Word or Two?
- Computer-age Generated Words
- Common Computer Words

Computer Acronyms

We have already addressed acronyms, which are common in computer terms. We may be familiar with many of these acronyms, or even use them daily without knowing the words they represent. This is exactly why acronyms are especially useful with computer and technological terms. We do not need to know that DSL is a "digital subscriber line" to get connected to the Internet. Other terms, such as instant messenger (IM), are simply shortened for convenience. Some examples follow:

FTP   File Transfer Protocol
DVD   Digital Versatile Disc (formerly Digital Video Disc)
DSL   Digital Subscriber Line
MAC   Macintosh Computer
HTML   Hypertext Markup Language
URL   Uniform Resource Locator
PDA   Personal Digital Assistant
CD   Compact Disc
IM   Instant Messaging
WYSIWYG (pronounced wisiwig): What You See Is What You Get

Language shortcuts are being created and refined all the time through e-mail and instant messaging. While these are commonly used online, too often people assume everyone knows them. These language shortcuts are evolving slang and are not necessary to learn, but they are a growing subset of slang language. If you do sometimes use them, be careful to avoid their use in business and with those who may not know the newest online slang.

Back in Chapter 4, you saw several examples, including LOL (laughing out loud), BRB (be right back), and CU (see you).

One Word or Two?

Web site, website
Web page, webpage
e-mail, email
Webcam
Webcast
Webmaster

Web site and web page have come to be primarily defined as website and webpage. These are examples of words that have changed over time. *Webmaster* is one word. The words webcam and webcast are also each one word. While some people write *email* as one word, *e-mail* is still the more commonly listed choice.

Computer-age Generated Words

Many words are developed by those in the technical field long before they come to common usage. The term "bit" was coined by the statistician John Tukey in 1949. He was looking for a shortened form of "Binary Digit." According to Tukey, he had considered "bigit" or "binit," but abbreviation evolved over lunch to become the bite-sized word "bit."

If you recall homonyms and homophones, *bit* (small bit of computer information) would be a homonym for *bit* as in small bite. From the word *bit*, new words have been created to refer to the technology. (*Byte* and *nybble* are homophones for *bite* and *nibble*.) Of course, mega is a standard prefix for something large (and one million *bytes* would be a *megabyte*).

Bit: a shortened term for Binary Digit
Byte: a sequence of bits
Nybble: a small byte
Megabyte: one million bytes

Common Computer Words

Most of the following phrases are in common use. Study only the words that concern you. Because the goal here is spelling and not in-depth computer knowledge, we provide the most basic terms and ask that you focus on words that might be part of your vocabulary.

Adware
Affiliate
Application
Bandwidth
Baud Rate
Bluetooth
Blog
Blogger
Broadband
Compatibility
Computerized
Configuration
Connection
Cursor
Cyberbullying
Database

Debug
Decode
Digital
Disc (also Disk)
Download
Downloadable
E-commerce
Electronic
E-mail/Email
Emoticon
Ethernet
Expandable
Gigabyte
Glitch
Graphics
Hard drive

Hardware	Peripheral
Hyperlink	Pixel
Hypertext	Pixilated
Inkjet	Processor
Interactive	Programmer
Interface	Retrieval
Internet	Server
Laptop	Spam (unsolicited bulk e-mails)
Laser	Spell-check, Spell-checker
Macintosh	Software
Matrix	Suite
Megabyte	Surfer
Megapixel	Synchronize
Microprocessor	Telecommuting
Modem	Template
Monitor	Terminal
Multimedia	Upload
Multitasking	Webcam
Network	Webcast
Newsgroup	Webmaster
Output	Website

EXERCISE

From each group select the correctly spelled word and place the letter before it in the space at the left.

1. (a) didgital   (b) digitle   (c) digital   (d) digatal

2. (a) retrieval   (b) retreival   (c) retrievle   (d) retreeval

3. (a) acronim   (b) acranym   (c) acarnym   (d) acronym

4. (a) retrieval   (b) retreival   (c) retreivle   (d) retrievel

5. (a) access   (b) acess   (c) acces   (d) acesse

6. (a) compatability   (b) compatibility
      (c) commpatability   (d) compattability

_____ 7. (a) periferal (b) peripheral (c) peripherle (d) peripharal

_____ 8. (a) inter-face (b) inter face (c) interface (d) intraface

_____ 9. (a) interractive (b) inneractive (c) interactive (d) enteractive

_____ 10. (a) nybble (b) nibbel (c) nible (d) nibel

_____ 11. (a) expandable (b) expandible (c) expandabel (d) expandibel

_____ 12. (a) softwere (b) sofware (c) softwear (d) software

_____ 13. (a) programer (b) programmar (c) programmer (d) programar

_____ 14. (a) processer (b) proceser (c) processor (d) procesor

_____ 15. (a) tele-comuting (b) telecomuting
                        (c) telecommuting (d) tele-commuting

_____ 16. (a) Mackintosh (b) Macintosh (c) McIntosh (d) Macentosh

_____ 17. (a) mailmerge (b) mail-merge (c) male merge (d) mail merge

More Commonly Misspelled Words

Thank goodness we don't have to know how to spell a food before we can eat it! Many of the foods we eat every day pose spelling confusions. Some people scrawl the middle of the word *banana* because they're never quite sure whether it has one *n* or two. Have you ever felt frustrated by being unsure of the spellings of words you write over and over on shopping lists? Maybe you think you'll look them up later then forget until the next time. Now is the time to learn those pesky words once and for all!

WHAT YOU WILL LEARN

In this chapter, you will learn to spell some of the difficult words that we encounter on a regular basis—words related to food, household, community, and schools. If these lists don't include related words that you find difficult, take the extra few moments to look them up and add them to the lists.

SECTIONS IN THIS CHAPTER:

- Foods and Food-related Words
- Household, Community, and School Words

Foods and Food-related Words

Appetizer	Dessert	Restaurant
Artichoke	Dough	Sauté
Arugula	Doughnut	Seitan
Asparagus	Eggplant	Sesame
Avocado	Enchilada	Sorbet
Banana	Flavoring	Spaghetti
Barley	Gourmet	Sundae
Broccoli	Hors d'oeuvre/Hors d'oeuvres	Tabbouleh
Barbeque	Lasagna	Teriyaki
Cabbage	Lettuce	Tomato/Tomatoes
Caramel	Macaroni	Tortilla
Casserole	Nachos	Truffles
Cauliflower	Noodles	Vanilla
Celery	Papaya	Vegan
Chestnut	Parmesan	Vegetable
Chili	Pineapple	Vegetarian
Chocolate	Pistachios	Watermelon
Croissant	Potato/Potatoes	Wok
Cuisine	Pumpkin	
Culinary	Raspberry	

EXERCISE 1

Circle the correctly spelled word in the parentheses for each sentence below.

1. Vincent stopped eating meat and became a (vegeterian, vegetarian).

2. Sandra is a (vegen, vegan). She eats no animal or dairy products.

3. Milla loves (pumpkin, pumkin) pie when it's cold outside.

4. My favorite jelly is (raspberry, rasberry).

5. Nick is having sweet (potatoes, potatos) and (brocolli, broccoli) for lunch.

6. My neighbor grows (avocados, avacadoes).

7. Penny loves (bananna, banana) bread.

8. Do you prefer (chocolate, choclate) or (vanilla, vannila)?

Household, Community, and School Words

Household	Community	School
Apartment	Cooperative	Admissions
Basement	Councilperson	Guidance counselor
Ceiling	Governor	Instructor
Colander	Mayor	Kindergarten
Condominium	Nonprofit	Principal
Cupboard	Politics	Professor
Dehumidifier	Resources	Schedule
Efficiency	Revitalization	Syllabus
Food Processor	Township	
Furnace	Volunteer	
Humidifier		
Neighborhood		
Refrigerator		
Scissors		
Vacuum		

EXERCISE 2

Circle the correctly spelled words below.

1. vacum, vacuum

2. kindergarden, kindergarten

3. admitions, admissions

4. refridgerator, refrigerator

5. condominium, condominnium

6. counselperson, councilperson

7. efficiency, efficency

8. cieling, ceiling

Medical and Health Terms

The expansion of medical research and services and growing interest in nutrition and alternative treatments has made many medical and health terms commonplace. In this chapter, some of the most common abbreviations and terms related to disease, treatment, and health are briefly defined. In some cases, areas of common spelling difficulties are italicized.

WHAT YOU WILL LEARN

In this chapter, you will learn the proper spelling of common terms in the areas of medicine, nutrition, and health.

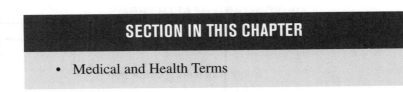

SECTION IN THIS CHAPTER

- Medical and Health Terms

Medical and Health Terms

MEDICAL ABBREVIATIONS

Abbreviation	Term/Definition
AIDS	Acquired Immunodeficiency Syndrome
CATSCAN (CT Scan)	Computerized Axial Tomography Scan
	A radiological diagnostic technique in which a series of x-rays are computerized to show a scan (picture) of the body
Chol.	Cholesterol
DOA	Dead on arrival
ECG or EKG	Electrocardiogram
EEG	Electroencephalogram
HIV	Human Immunodeficiency Virus
HMO	Health Maintenance Organization
IUD	Intrauterine device
IV	Intravenously
LPN	Licensed Practical Nurse
MRI	Magnetic Resonance Imaging
PCP	Pencyclidine
PCP	Primary Care Physician
PT	Physical Therapist
RN	Registered Nurse
RPH	Registered Pharmacist

MEDICAL AND HEALTH TERMS

Term	Definition
A	
abrasion	Superficial tearing of the skin
abscess	Localized buildup of pus
acne	Inflammation of oil glands
acupressure	Treating acupuncture points without needles
acupuncture	Puncture of skin by needle to relieve pain
allergy	Hypersensitive reaction to certain substances
allopathic	Traditional Western medicine
alternative	Different from the traditional course of action
alternative health practitioners	There is a vast array of alternative professionals, including: acupuncturist, herbalist, holistic practitioner, homeopath, hypnotherapist, naturopath
ambulance	Vehicle equipped for transportation of ill or wounded to hospital
ambulatory	Able to walk about
amnesia	Loss of memory
analgesic	Substance providing relief from pain
anesthesia	Loss of sensation or feeling
aneurysm	Abnormal widening of vein or artery
antibiotic	Antibacterial substance
antioxidant	Substance that protects body cells from the damaging effects of oxidation

MEDICAL AND HEALTH TERMS *(continued)*

Term	Definition
*a*orta	Artery carrying blood from the heart
arter*io*sclerosis	Hardening of the arteries
arthr*itis*	Acute or chronic joint inflammation
*ayurv*edic	Ancient Hindu science of health and medicine

B

Term	Definition
be*nign*	Harmless
biofeedback	Monitoring function, such as heart rate or blood pressure; using that feedback for health
biop*sy*	Examination of small sample of tissue
bo*ny*	Relating to bone

C

Term	Definition
cal*cify*	To make stony by deposit of calcium salts
calor*ie*	Measure of energy (heat) in nutrition
cap*illary*	Thin-walled blood vessel
carbo*hyd*rate	A biological compound that is a source of food and energy
carcinogenic	Cancer-causing substance
car*ci*noma	Type of cancer
car*ies*	Tooth or bone decay
cartil*age*	Type of connective tissue
chiropractor	Spine specialist
*cho*lesterol	Fatty substance found in blood
co*ag*ulant	That which produces clotting
col*icky*	Pertaining to paroxysmal pain
com*plem*entary	One treatment that works alongside another
convale*scent*	Recovering from illness
cuti*cle*	Dead skin at base of fingernail or toenail
c*y*st	Abnormal fluid or gas-fllled cavity

D

Term	Definition
diaphra*gm*	Large muscle between chest and abdomen
dia*rrhea*	Loose or watery stools
diet*ary*	Related to diet

E

Term	Definition
e*cz*ema	Skin rash characterized by itching
emb*ryo*	Fetus in first 8 weeks after conception
en*ema*	Fluid injected through rectum to lower bowel
epi*lepsy*	Disease of nervous system characterized by convulsive seizures

G

Term	Definition
gl*au*coma	Disease of the eye caused by increased pressure within the eye
gyn*e*cologist	Specialist in women's diseases

H

Term	Definition
hemo*rrh*age	Abnormal bleeding caused by rupture or tear of a blood vessel

MEDICAL AND HEALTH TERMS *(continued)*

Term	Definition
he*pat*itis	Inflammation of the liver
herbal	Made from herbs
holistic	Taking into account the whole body and mind
hom*eo*pathy	An alternative, natural therapy
hom*eo*st*as*is	Internal balance
hyg*ie*ne	Science of health preservation
hypnosis	Trancelike state
hypo*ch*ondriac	One who is excessively anxious about supposed ill health
h*y*sterectomy	Surgical removal of uterus

I

*iatro*genic	Illness caused by medical intervention
indigest*i*ble	Not easily digested
infec*tious*	Capable of being easily diffused or spread
i*n*oculate	To inject a substance into the skin or tissues
intra*venous*	Into or within a vein

J

jug*u*lar	Relating to a large vein in the neck

K

ki*n*etic	Pertaining to motion

L

l*a*rynx	Voicebox
le*u*kemia	Malignant disease of the white blood cells
l*ymph*	Transparent yellowish fluid containing cellular elements

M

mas*tect*omy	Surgical removal of breast
mens*trua*tion	Monthly discharge of blood and tissue from the uterus
metabolism	Processing of a substance within the body
mi*graine*	Periodic severe headaches
mu*cus*	Viscous fluid produced by certain glands in the body

N

nau*sea*	Desire to vomit
neural*gia*	Sharp pain produced by nerve stimulation
n*e*uritis	Inflammation of nerve
nutr*ie*nt	Source of nourishment in food
nutr*ition*	Nourishment in food

O

obstetri*cian*	Specialist in pregnancy and childbirth
*ophthal*mologist	Specialist in diseases of the eye
op*iate*	Opium-like narcotic
opti*cian*	Eye doctor
osteo*porosis*	Disease in which bones become abnormally thin and brittle

MEDICAL AND HEALTH TERMS *(continued)*

Term	Definition
P	
paraplegic	One who is paralyzed from the waist down
pediatrician	Specialist in treating children
pharmaceutical	Drug treatment
phlebitis	Inflammation of a vein
phlegm	Mucus produced by the lungs
phobia	Abnormal fear
pneumonia	Inflammation of lung tissue
podiatrist	Foot doctor
preventive, preventative	Measures or substances taken to prevent disease
prophylaxis	Prevention of disease
psychiatry	Branch of medical science dealing with mental health
R	
rabies	Hydrophobia
regimen	A systematic course of treatment
remedy	Treatment to remove pain or treat disease
S	
saccharin	Sugar substitute
saliva	Secretion of salivary glands
sickle cell anemia	Hereditary form of malformation of red blood cells
syringe	Device for injecting liquids
T	
therapeutic	Method or substance used or practiced to cure or relieve symptoms of disease
thoracic	Pertaining to the chest
tonsillectomy	Surgical removal of tonsils
tourniquet	Device for stopping bleeding
toxicity	State of being poisonous
U	
ulcerous	Pertaining to loss of tissue
uremia	Accumulation of toxic substances caused by certain kidney diseases
urinary	Pertaining to urine
V	
vaccination	Inoculation to stimulate immunity to disease
vaccine	Altered microorganisms that stimulate immunity
vertebra	Roundish bone in spinal column
viable	Capable of survival
viral	Pertaining to a virus
W	
whooping cough	Children's disease characterized by violent, paroxysmal cough

EXERCISE

From each group select the correctly spelled word and place the letter before it in the space at the left.

_____   1. (a) diarhea   (b) diahea   (c) dierrhea   (d) diarrhea

_____   2. (a) innoculate (b) inocculate (c) inocullate (d) inoculate

_____   3. (a) anisthesia (b) anesthesia (c) anessthesia (d) annesthesia

_____   4. (a) calory   (b) calorie   (c) calore   (d) callorie

_____   5. (a) hemorrhage   (b) hemorhage
                      (c) hemmorhage   (d) hemorrage

_____   6. (a) rabes   (b) rabies   (c) rabeis   (d) rabbies

_____   7. (a) tonsilectomy   (b) tonsilecimy
                      (c) tonsillectimy   (d) tonsillectomy

_____   8. (a) abscess   (b) absess   (c) abses   (d) absces

_____   9. (a) capillary   (b) capilary   (c) cappilary   (d) capillery

_____ 10. (a) colicy   (b) colicky   (c) collicky   (d) collichy

_____ 11. (a) larnyx   (b) larinx   (c) larynx   (d) larinks

_____ 12. (a) arterosclerosis   (b) artiriosclerosis
                      (c) arteriosclerosis   (d) arterioslerosis

_____ 13. (a) indigestable   (b) indigestible
                      (c) indegestible   (d) indegistible

_____ 14. (a) diafram   (b) diaphram   (c) diraphragm (d) diaphragm

_____ 15. (a) sacharin   (b) saccarin   (c) saccharin   (d) saccharrin

24

Achievement Tests

Achievement Test 1

Score _____

CHAPTERS 1–4

Indicate by writing T *or* F *to the left whether the following statements about English spelling are true or false. (Answers begin on page 237.)*

_____ 1. English spelling is difficult because it is not phonetic.

_____ 2. At one time in the history of English the endings in *through, thorough, plough* were pronounced.

_____ 3. The letter *p* in *ptomaine, pterodactyl,* and *ptarmigan* is pronounced in Modern English.

_____ 4. New words are invented by scholars.

_____ 5. Such words as *birth—berth, air—heir* are called antonyms.

_____ 6. Many poor spellers do not hear words correctly.

_____ 7. *Media* is the plural of *medium.*

_____ 8. There are no rules in spelling that are worth learning.

_____ 9. The most reliable source of information for spelling is the dictionary.

_____ 10. Acronyms are useless you know what they stand for.

_____ 11. The sounds of English vowels have not changed through the centuries.

_____ 12. When a word must be divided at the end of a line, the hyphen should always come after a vowel.

_____ 13. To become a better speller you must read everything very slowly.

_____ 14. Many good spellers can tell that a word is misspelled by its appearance (or configuration).

_____ 15. All good spellers inherit this ability.

_____ 16. Sometimes you can discover your own spelling devices to help you.

_____ 17. A good way to recall the spelling of *stationary* is to think of *station*.

_____ 18. Computer spell-checkers should be used, but not relied on.

_____ 19. The words *theater* and *theatre* are examples of *antonyms*.

_____ 20. There is little value in compiling your own list of misspelled words.

_____ 21. In learning how to spell the word *superintendent* it is advisable to pronounce each syllable distinctly.

_____ 22. In learning how to spell a new word it is helpful to write it several times correctly.

_____ 23. The trouble with English spelling is that there are no rules.

_____ 24. Computer spellcheckers can recognize homonyms.

_____ 25. There is no difference in pronunciation between *trough* and *through*.

_____ 26. *Tough* and *rough* are homonyms.

_____ 27. *Through* and *true* have the same final sound.

_____ 28. The final sound in *knight* and *tight* is pronounced *īt*.

_____ 29. Many English words derived from ancient Greek have silent letters as in *psyllium* and *pseudonym*.

_____ 30. Words like *privilege* and *government* are frequently misspelled by omitting a letter.

_____ 31. Careful observation will help you to become a better speller.

_____ 32. It is possible to train your eyes to recognize misspelled words by their appearance.

_____ 33. You can remember the correct spelling of the word *principle* by associating it with *rule*.

_____ 34. The words *hair* and *heir* are pronounced the same.

_____ 35. Though "practice makes perfect," many professional writers are sometimes plagued by misspellings.

_____ 36. English words are spelled exactly as they sound.

_____ 37. The best way to study spelling is to memorize all the words you need.

_____ 38. Because there are the letters *gh* in *night* and *sight*, they should be pronounced.

_____ 39. A person writing *litature* instead of *literature* has probably not heard the word correctly.

_____ 40. Because the *b* in *debt* is silent, the *b* in *debit* should also be silent.

Achievement Test 2

Score _____

CHAPTER 6

Underscore the word spelled correctly in the parentheses.

1. The agent signed the (receipt, reciept) for the rent.

2. It was a great (relief, releif) to go home at last.

3. Mary gave a loud (shriek, shreik) and ran.

4. The marines refused to (yeild, yield) their positions.

5. He was a perfect (fiend, feind) in his behavior.

6. His (acheivement, achievement) was remarkable.

7. Once we have lost our reputation, it is difficult to (retreive, retrieve) it.

8.   It takes a good (freind, friend) to make one.

9.   That pizza has too many (calaries, calories)!

10.   He was (chief, cheif) of the whole island.

11.   We were (receiveing, receiving) visitors all day.

12.   It is difficult to (deceive, decieve) people all the time.

13.   Strenuous efforts are required to (achieve, acheive) a scholarship.

14.   Astronomers can now (percieve, perceive) stars that are quite small.

15.   Our (neighbors, nieghbors) to the south were angry at our behavior.

16.   He has a (mischievious, mischievous) smile. I wonder what he was up to.

17.   LOL is an (acronym, acranym) for laughing out loud.

18.   Although the (ceiling, cieling) was low, he bought the house.

Achievement Test 3

Score _____

CHAPTERS 7–8

In the following sentences the italic words are sometimes correctly spelled, sometimes misspelled. In the spaces to the left, place C if the spelling is correct. Write the correct spelling for all misspelled words.

_____   1.   Our lighter team was at a *dissadvantage*.

_____   2.   Park all *disabled* cars here.

_____   3.   Any *mistatement* of fact will be punished.

_____   4.   The man could not *reccollect* the date of the accident.

_____   5.   The doctor *recommended* rest.

_____   6.   This procedure was an *inovation*.

_____   7.   Let's *rennovate* your apartment.

_____   8.   Many ingredients in packaged foods are *unatural*.

_____ 9. This apartment had been *unoccupied* for a month.

_____ 10. Congress tried to *overide* the veto.

_____ 11. The sergeant was *dimoted*.

_____ 12. Sugar will easily *disolve* in water.

_____ 13. As a lawyer, Clarence Darrow was *preminent*.

_____ 14. One should always have some *anteseptic* handy for unexpected cuts.

_____ 15. His behavior under fire was *degrading*.

Select the correct choice of the two in parentheses:

_____ 16. By crossing the state border they ran into difficulty with the (intra-state, interstate) commission.

_____ 17. Do not (interrupt, interupt).

_____ 18. At the end of his letter he added a (poscript, postscript).

_____ 19. Many (suburban, subburban) communities are growing.

_____ 20. When the lights blew out we called the (superrintendent, superintendent).

_____ 21. Quite a few hotels here welcome (transient, transent) guests.

_____ 22. The judge ruled that this evidence was not (admissible, admissable).

_____ 23. Such arguments are (laughible, laughable).

_____ 24. It was (unthinkable, unthinkible) that he could lose the game.

_____ 25. Sonya is (eligible, eligable) to collect unemployment benefits.

_____ 26. England has always been (invincible, invincable) in a crisis.

_____ 27. (Legible, legable) handwriting is a delight for the reader.

_____ 28. Make yourself (comfortable, comfortible).

_____ 29. Many foods are (perishible, perishable) unless properly refrigerated.

_____ 30. Evidence of the disease was not yet (demonstrable, demonstrible).

In the following sentences the italic words are sometimes correctly spelled, sometimes misspelled. In the spaces to the left, place C if the spelling is correct. Write the correct spelling for all misspelled words.

_____ 31. The debater made a *mistake*.

_____ 32. I don't *reccolect* what happened.

_____ 33. *Professional* ball players earn high salaries.

_____ 34. His sleight of hand was *unoticeable*.

_____ 35. That player is vastly *overated*.

_____ 36. The word *anticedent* is used in both grammar and mathematics.

_____ 37. Iodine is still a popular *antiseptic*.

_____ 38. "Don't *interrupt* me," she exclaimed.

_____ 39. Lincoln was not very happy when several states *seseded* from the Union.

_____ 40. The doctor diagnosed the disease as a *preforated* ulcer.

_____ 41. We must look at things in their proper *prespective*.

_____ 42. Let us *proceed* with the meeting.

_____ 43. A *percocious* child can learn to play chess well.

_____ 44. This water is hardly *drinkible*.

_____ 45. Some mountains are *inaccessable*.

_____ 46. The *combustible* materials were placed in fire-proof bins.

_____ 47. Sasha is *eligable* for a promotion.

_____ 48. Backup systems make data *retrieval* easy.

_____ 49. "Such language is *detestable*," said the teacher.

_____ 50. He was an old *acquaintence*.

_____ 51. The face of the *defendent* became pale as the verdict was read.

_____ 52. Sometimes little things turn out to have great *significence*.

_____ 53. The mechanics overhauled the airplane motor in a *hanger*.

_____ 54. The *collar* of his shirt was frayed.

_____ 55. The business advertised in a local newspaper for an experienced *operator*.

_____ 56. Most department store customers prefer to use an *escalator* rather than the elevator or stairs.

_____ 57. The *radiater* of the car started to overheat.

_____ 58. Readers who disagree with a newspaper's editorial position should write a letter to the *editor*.

_____ 59. One of the duties of a *superviser* is to train employees.

_____ 60. The *purchaser* is protected by a money-back guarantee.

Achievement Test 4

Score _____

CHAPTERS 9–11

Underline the word spelled correctly in the parentheses.

1. All the (buffaloes, buffalos) were killed in this territory.

2. The president sent through his two (vetoes, vetos) to Congress.

3. The (tomatoes, tomatos) had ripened.

4. We examined six (pianos, pianoes) before we selected one.

5. Cowboys learn how to do many stunts with their (lassoes, lassos).

6. The newspaper is a struggling (media, medium).

7. All the (leafs, leaves) fell down.

8. Many old (beliefs, believes) must be disregarded.

9. Leah is a (vegetarian, vegitarian).

10. This farm still made use of (oxes, oxen).

11. Hailstones fell down several (chimneys, chimnies).

12. In this machine, there were many levers and (pulleys, pullies).

13. The players took several practice (volleys, vollies) before the game.

14. The (salaries, salarys) of her employees were frequently raised.

15. The Greeks composed the greatest dramatic (tragedeys, tragedies).

16. The judge pronounced his sentence (angrily, angryly).

17. It is advisable to be (mercyful, merciful).

18. The band played several (medleys, medlies).

19. The appointment is (Tusday, Tuesday).

20. Good posture always (dignifies, dignifys) the person.

21. My father reminded us that we would be (dineing, dining) at six.

22. It was the loveliest sight (imagineable, imaginable).

23. (Judging, Judgeing) from the attendance, the play was a hit.

24. The end of the novel was (surpriseing, surprising).

25. Thoreau was (writeing, writing) a great deal while staying at Walden Pond.

26. The wounded dog was (whining, whineing) all night long.

27. All those (desireous, desirous) of success must work hard.

28. The (density, denseity) of the atmosphere is being studied.

29. The lecturer spoke clearly and (sincerely, sincerly).

30. Certain traits sometimes run in (families, familys).

31. We both like (dining, dineing) out frequently.

32. This trail is not for the birds but for (donkeys, donkies).

33. Much (encouragment, encouragement) was required before the baby took his first steps.

34. They achieved (unimagineable, unimaginable) success.

35. This line had the fewest (casualties, casualtys).

36. We noticed that all the ants seemed (busily, busyly) engaged in building a new home.

37. Jascha Heifetz was (accompanied, accompanyed) by an accomplished pianist.

38. When Erin ran late, her mother was (worried, worryed).

39. Reynolds frequently (portrayed, portraied) the English nobility of the 18th century.

40. His insights frequently seemed touched with (sublimity, sublimeity).

41. Such actions at this time seem (inadvisable, inadviseable).

42. She came close to (singing, singeing) her hair on the stove.

43. In business writing, (vagueness, vaguness) can easily cause miscommunication.

44. We learn more by listening than (argueing, arguing).

45. It was a (lovely, lovly) wedding.

46. Such (couragous, courageous) action was rarely seen.

47. Dinner was (tastless, tasteless).

48. Working long on the (contriveance, contrivance) made him a bit fanatic about it.

49. (Anniversaries, anniversarys) should be celebrated properly.

50. Lead is a dangerous (toxin, toxen).

51. The printer corrected the (proofs, prooves) of the new book.

52. My friend liked all his (brothers-in-law, brother-in-laws).

53. The castle was (beseiged, besieged) for ten days.

54. Mary's (likeness, likness) was obvious in the portrait.

55. After many lessons, they learned to dance (gracfully, gracefully).

56. This celebration was (truly, truely) magnificent.

57. The comic made his living by (mimicing, mimicking) others.

58. The little girl fell asleep counting (sheeps, sheep).

59. All the (alumni, alumnuses) of Fairweather College returned on Founder's Day.

60. Before the American public high schools, there were many (academies, academys).

61. It is very difficult to discover a single (curricula, curriculum) that can satisfy all people.

62. Ehrlich stained many (bacilli, bacilluses) in his career.

Achievement Test 5

Score _____

CHAPTERS 12–15

Underline the word spelled correctly in the parentheses.

1. He wanted to buy a (low-priced, low priced) car.

2. This author was (best known, best-known) for his characterization.

3. She was the (thirty-first, thirty first) queen to be chosen.

4. This hypothesis was a little (far-fetched, far fetched).

5. The puppy was (newly-born, newly born).

6. It was the (highest priced, highest-priced) dress in the store.

7. It was a successful (pre-election, preelection) bet.

8. To get this loan, you must have a (coowner, co-owner).

9. They cheered the (exgovernor, ex-governor).

10. (Vice-Admiral, Vice Admiral) Rooney was promoted.

11. The doctors (conferred, confered) for two hours.

12. We had no (preference, preferrence) in this matter.

13. After many trials, he was (transferred, transfered) to another prison.

14. The girl quickly tore the (wrapings, wrappings) from the package.

15. Many new bills are thrown into the legislative (hoper, hopper).

16. Back then, Mulvaney was the best (hitter, hiter) in the league.

17. Marva served turkey, with all the (trimings, trimmings), on Thanksgiving.

18. The XYZ Company had a (controlling, controling) interest in the firm.

19. Our graduates (excelled, exceled) over all others at Yale.

20. The prisoner never (regretted, regreted) his misdeeds.

21. The house had a (low-ceiling, low ceiling).

22. (One half, one-half) of the audience left at the end of the first act.

23. All night the tune kept (dining, dinning) in her head.

24. The actress wore a (low cut, low-cut) gown at the awards ceremony.

25. The employer demanded several (references, referrences).

26. We are all (hoping, hopping) for permanent peace.

27. Such freak accidents seldom (occured, occurred).

28. The culprit wore a (hangdog, hang-dog) look.

29. America, at that time, had (unparalleled, unparaleled) prosperity.

30. It was the (twenty ninth, twenty-ninth) celebration of the ending of the war.

31. The (pre-dawn, predawn) flight was a success.

32. My cousin was the (high scorer, high-scorer) in the game.

33. My mother always (prefered, preferred) to save rather than spend everything.

34. The (ex policeman, ex-policeman) was found guilty of perjury.

35. The judge and the attorneys (conferred, confered) for three hours.

36. The athlete (chined, chinned) thirty times on the horizontal bar.

37. You have to be (proactive, pro-active) to run a home-based business.

38. The poor little bird (flaped, flapped) her wings feebly and then remained still.

39. The (red-cheeked, red cheeked) child seemed shy.

40. Carl is (eighty eight, eighty-eight) years old.

41. Media often uses (sub-liminal, subliminal) advertising.

42. The man seemed (regretful, regrettful) of his actions.

43. This digital book reader seems to be the (lowest priced, lowest-priced) on the Internet.

44. I love (spagetti, spaghetti).

45. His appearance at the trial was (well-timed, well timed).

46. He was (hiting, hitting) well in that game.

47. This computer is (running, runing) on the latest operating system.

48. Many guards (patroled, patrolled) the prison on the day of the execution.

49. Passengers should be (already, all ready) at 10 P.M.

50. A (run-on, run on) sentence contains more than enough for one complete sentence.

51. We greeted the (senator-elect, senator elect).

52. Rescue boats went back and forth in the (mid Atlantic, mid-Atlantic) area.

53. Her praises were (extoled, extolled) for her amazing performance.

54. Many words are commonly misspelled in (busness, business).

55. After a little encouragement the guitarist (regaled, regalled) the picnickers with many songs.

56. Vera won first prize, but Stuart was (runner up, runner-up).

57. Kristin takes (spining, spinning) classes at her gym.

58. A few parts of the story were (omitted, omited) by the defendant.

59. The boy (scraped, scrapped) his knee when he fell.

60. Periods of prosperity have (recurred, recured) with regularity in this state.

61. Their marriage was (annuled, annulled) by mutual consent.

62. Jack is a computer (programer, programmer).

63. The crowd (paniced, panicked) after the accident.

64. South America (rebeled, rebelled) against the mother country.

65. Judge Harmon (deferred, defered) sentence until Friday.

Achievement Test 6

Score _____

CHAPTERS 16–17

Underline the word spelled correctly in the parentheses.

1. Many college freshmen (don't, dont) know how to study.

2. This salesman specialized in (mens', men's) shoes.

3. It was (his, his') greatest victory.

4. (Who'se, Who's) there?

5. Dot all the (i's, is) and cross the (ts, t's).

6. "(Youve, You've) won your battle," said the trainer.

7. The shopper specialized in (lady's, ladies') shoes.

8. This was my (brother-in-law's, brother's-in-law's) house.

9. Kira works in the (children's, childrens') ward.

10. This (couldn't, could'nt) have happened to a nicer person.

11. It was once more a conflict between (East, east) and (West, west).

12. The young artists admired the works of (grandma Moses, Grandma Moses).

13. He specialized in the (hindu, Hindu) languages.

14. My uncle belonged to the (elks, Elks).

15. Their wedding song was ("Dance Me To The End Of Love," "Dance Me to the End of Love").

16. A classic novel is (*A Tale of two Cities*, *A Tale of Two Cities*).

17. They traveled (North, north) for twenty miles.

18. On (Columbus Day, Columbus day), many stores have sales.

19. One of the greatest musical hits of all time is (*My fair Lady*, *My Fair Lady*).

20. He was recently elected to the (house of representatives, House of Representatives).

21. The (boy's, boys') mother was proud of his talent.

22. (They're, theyr'e) meeting us for dinner.

23. The conference passed a resolution against all high (doctor's, doctors') fees.

24. The numerous (teacher's, teachers') contributions were finally rewarded.

25. Count all the (7's, 7s) in this line!

26. We enjoyed (Penn and Teller's, Penn's and Teller's) humor.

27. The sale took place in the (women's, womens') hosiery department.

28. "I never want to touch a penny of (their's, theirs)," she said.

29. All the (ts, t's) in this word are left uncrossed.

30. He admired his (lawyer's, lawyers') integrity.

31. The Ivy League colleges are situated mostly in the (east, East).

32. After studying (french, French) literature, he began to appreciate Molière.

33. Higher (Mathematics, mathematics) fascinated Einstein at an early age.

34. (Governor, governor) Rockefeller attempted to balance the state budget.

35. Many couples meet through (Internet, internet) dating services.

36. The fiftieth state in the Union is (hawaii, Hawaii).

37. Anne Morrow Lindbergh wrote *North to the* (*Orient, orient*).

38. There are one hundred members of the U.S. (Senate, senate).

39. On (arbor day, Arbor Day) an interesting ceremony took place.

40. Of all the novels Brad read in high school, (*Of Mice and Men, Of mice and Men*) was his favorite.

41. Great praise has come recently to (admiral, Admiral) Rickover.

42. A famous personality years ago was (uncle Floyd, Uncle Floyd).

43. This store had good bargains in (boys', boy's) shoes.

44. These cold winters make me think of moving (south, South).

Achievement Test 7

Score _____

CHAPTER 19

Select the correctly spelled word from the two in parentheses.

1. Teachers frequently give good (advice, advise) to their students.

2. England and the U.S. have long been (alleys, allies).

3. There is nothing as beautiful as a happy bride walking down the (isle, aisle).

4. My parents said that they were (already, all ready).

5. Frequently one can have an optical (illusion, allusion) after eyestrain.

6. The judge refused to (altar, alter) his decision.

7. (Altogether, All together) there were twelve cents in his pocket.

8. The casket was (borne, born) on the shoulders of the pallbearers.

9. There were several smiling (angles, angels) in this artist's depiction of heaven.

10. We ordered an upper (berth, birth) on the train to Chicago.

11. My father was almost (besides, beside) himself with grief.

12. (Break, Brake) the news gently.

13. Jade lost her (breath, breathe) on the treadmill.

14. The cowboy grasped the horse by the (bridal, bridle).

15. Ward leaders tried to (canvass, canvas) the district.

16. In Washington we visited the beautiful (Capital, Capitol).

17. The angry principal began to (censure, censor) the students for misbehavior.

18. He could chop several (cords, chords) of wood each day.

19. Miles buys all of his (cloths, clothes) online.

20. In college, my brother took the premedical (course, coarse).

21. Don't forget to (complement, compliment) him on his good grades.

22. Zach is applying for a job as an (advice, advise) columnist.

23. The cook removed the (corps, core) of the apple.

24. Scientists are often (incredulous, incredible) of new theories.

25. Many authors kept (diaries, dairies) when they were young.

26. Justice Oliver Wendell Holmes frequently would (dissent, descent) from his colleagues.

27. After the meal, we had a delicious (dessert, dissert).

28. Da Vinci invented a (devise, device) to hurl cannonballs.

29. Hamilton and Burr fought a (duel, dual) in New Jersey.

30. This spot was (formally, formerly) a cemetery.

31. For several (instance, instants) he remained quiet.

32. Through an (ingenious, ingenuous) trick, the magician escaped.

33. Actors like to receive (complements, compliments) on their performances.

34. The (boarder, border) never paid his rent on time.

35. The Dutch (consul, counsel) in New York helped us to obtain a visa.

36. The new president was (formally, formerly) inaugurated.

37. Praise raises (morale, moral).

38. A graduate of Harvard was the (personal, personnel) manager of the store.

39. Avogadro's (principal, principle) led to many other important discoveries.

40. This company advertises a fine quality of (stationery, stationary).

41. Some say social networking is a (waste, waist) of valuable time.

42. New inventions (supersede, supercede) old customs.

43. It was an (excedingly, exceedingly) hot day.

44. Lucas (succeeds, suceeds) in school because he has a great teacher.

45. The parade (proceded, proceeded) without further interruption.

46. The magician created an optical (allusion, illusion) for us.

47. The West will not (accede, acede) to these demands.

48. After the waters (receeded, receded), we returned to our home.

49. The (corps, corpse) was taken to the morgue.

50. The bird spread (it's, its) wings.

51. "It's (later, latter) than you think," the motivational speaker said.

52. Four yellow-robed monks (led, lead) the way yesterday.

53. Jackie didn't know (whether, weather) or not to go to the conference.

54. Several (lose, loose) shingles fell down.

55. Liquor is not permitted to be sold to (minors, miners).

56. A world at (peace, piece) is a world of security.

57. It was as (plane, plain) as the nose on his face.

58. After the hike, the girls were (quite, quiet) tired.

Answer Key

25

For Chapters 3–23

CHAPTER 3
EXERCISE 1 *Page 19.*

1. su • pər • ʹsil • ē • əs
2. ʹhyü • mər
3. ʹli • kwəd
4. ʹin • tri • kə • sē
5. in • ʹtim • ə • dāt
6. nä • ʹēv
7. ʹgüb • ə(r) • nə • ʹtor • ē • əl
8. ʹfar • si • kəl
9. der • əd • ən(t)s
10. ri • ʹvyü

EXERCISE 2 *Page 20.*

1. edutainment
2. mentee
3. beatlesque
4. webinar
5. regift
6. taxflation

CHAPTER 4
EXERCISE 1 *Page 26.*

Answers will vary.

EXERCISE 2 *Pages 26–27.*

1. believe
2. cemetery
3. principal
4. grammar
5. compliment
6. stationary
7. useful
8. resentful
9. artful
10. mnemonic

EXERCISE 3 *Page 27.*

Answers will vary.

CHAPTER 5
EXERCISE 1 *Page 35.*

1. bo•nan•za
2. re•fresh
3. fa•tigue
4. pun•ish•ment
5. or•deal
6. rum•mage
7. miss•ing
8. gas•o•line
9. ex•ca•vate
10. ty•ran•ni•cal

EXERCISE 2 *Page 37.*

1. grammar
2. separate
3. usually
4. C
5. calendar
6. C
7. C
8. editor
9. C
10. C
11. C
12. tailor
13. cafeteria
14. government
15. C
16. C
17. description
18. equivalent
19. conqueror
20. successor

EXERCISE 3 *Page 38.*

1. hundred
2. modern

3. perspiration
4. western
5. relevant
6. cavalry
7. children
8. jewelry
9. larynx
10. pattern

CHAPTER 6
EXERCISE 1 *Page 40.*

No answers are needed for this exercise because the correct spellings are given.

EXERCISE 2 *Page 41.*

1. aggrieve
2. brief
3. friend
4. grieve
5. frontier
6. mischief
7. shield
8. shriek
9. wield
10. species
11. relieve
12. leisure
13. handkerchief
14. receipt
15. seize
16. perceive
17. grief
18. niece
19. conceive

EXERCISE 3 *Page 43.*

The answers to this exercise are incorporated in the sentences.

EXERCISE 4 *Page 44.*
The answers to this exercise are found in the passage.

CHAPTER 7
EXERCISE 1 *Page 48.*
1. dissolve
2. dissimilar
3. misspell
4. disappear
5. mistake

EXERCISE 2 *Page 48.*
circumscribe—draw limits
transcribe—write a copy
subscribe—sign one's name
describe—represent by words
prescribe—dictate directions

EXERCISE 3 *Page 49.*
1. misstep
2. misunderstood
3. dissimilar
4. restart
5. substandard
6. transatlantic
7. premarital
8. antiestablishment
9. circumnavigates
10. postoperative

EXERCISE 4 *Pages 50–51.*
1. persecuted
2. proceed
3. precocious
4. perspective
5. prescribe
6. perforated
7. produce
8. persist
9. perpetual
10. propose

CHAPTER 8
EXERCISE 1 *Pages 55–56.*
The answers are contained in the exercise.

EXERCISE 2 *Page 56.*
The answers are contained in the exercise.

EXERCISE 3 *Pages 57–58.*
1. accidentally
2. critically
3. elementally
4. equally
5. exceptionally
6. finally
7. generally
8. incidentally
9. intentionally
10. radically
11. logically
12. mathematically
13. practically
14. professionally
15. really
16. typically
17. usually
18. verbally
19. globally

EXERCISE 4 *Pages 59–60.*
1. advantageous
2. courageous
3. perilous

4. mountainous
5. famous
6. desirous
7. mischievous
8. adventurous
9. bounteous
10. dangerous
11. grievous
12. humorous
13. outrageous
14. libelous
15. poisonous

EXERCISE 5 *Page 63.*

1. b
2. a
3. a
4. a
5. b
6. a
7. a
8. b
9. b
10. b
11. a
12. b
13. b
14. b
15. b
16. a
17. a
18. a
19. b
20. b
21. a
22. a
23. b
24. b
25. b

EXERCISE 6 *Page 65.*

1. grammar
2. receiver
3. conductor
4. passenger
5. governor
6. scanner
7. operator
8. dollar
9. supervisor
10. advertiser

EXERCISE 7 *Page 67.*

1. compliment
2. remembrance
3. consistent
4. superintendent
5. dependent
6. existence
7. descendant
8. acquaintance
9. grievance
10. permanent
11. magnificent
12. brilliance
13. complimentary or complementary, depending upon meaning
14. convenience
15. abundance
16. guidance
17. conscience
18. coincidence
19. apparent
20. consequential

EXERCISE 8 *Pages 68–69.*

1. b
2. a
3. b
4. b
5. b
6. a
7. b
8. a
9. b
10. a

EXERCISE 9 *Page 70.*

1. agonize
2. chastise
3. exercise
4. surprise
5. visualize
6. supervise
7. modernize
8. enterprise
9. fertilize
10. generalize

CHAPTER 9
EXERCISE 1 *Page 75.*

1. reproofs
2. reprieves
3. sieves
4. halos or haloes
5. gulfs
6. chiefs
7. albinos
8. shelves
9. puffs
10. bluffs
11. sloughs

12. bassos or bassi (Italian)
13. mambos
14. surfs
15. troughs
16. stilettos or stilettoes
17. sheaves
18. radios
19. calves
20. loaves

EXERCISE 2 *Page 76.*

1. holidays
2. alleys
3. attorneys
4. buoys
5. chimneys
6. donkeys
7. journeys
8. keys
9. pulleys
10. turkeys

EXERCISE 3 *Pages 80–81.*

1. t's
2. deer
3. anniversaries
4. wives
5. kerchiefs
6. 4s
7. courts•martial
8. lieutenant colonels
9. bays
10. trays
11. flurries
12. sulkies
13. kidneys
14. inequities

15. satellites
16. functionaries
17. avocados
18. dynamos

EXERCISE 4 *Page 81.*

1. groceries
2. things
3. tomatoes
4. potatoes
5. avocados
6. quarts
7. pieces
8. chocolates
9. purchases
10. alleys
11. keys
12. days

CHAPTER 10
EXERCISE 1 *Page 85.*

1. tourneys
2. allayed
3. volleyed
4. alleys
5. surveyed
6. portraying
7. journeyed
8. relayed
9. delays
10. parlayed

EXERCISE 2 *Pages 86–87.*

1. C
2. C
3. C
4. attorneys

5. C
6. C
7. C
8. C
9. C
10. icily

EXERCISE 3 *Pages 87–88.*

1. prettiness
2. pettiness
3. steadying
4. readied
5. bullies
6. airiness
7. pitied
8. tallying
9. buyer
10. dutiful
11. readiness
12. carried
13. hurrying
14. copier
15. sloppiness
16. livelihood

CHAPTER 11
EXERCISE 1 *Pages 92–93.*

1. revering
2. lovely
3. salvageable
4. extremely
5. pleasurable
6. largely
7. nudged
8. stated
9. vanity
10. fined

11. diving
12. shoved
13. devising
14. deceived
15. relieving
16. procrastinating
17. imagined
18. besieged
19. receiving

EXERCISE 2 *Pages 93–94.*

1. benefit	benefiting	benefited
2. commit	committing	committed
3. lure	luring	lured
4. refer	referring	referred
5. pine	pining	pined
6. elevate	elevating	elevated
7. propel	propelling	propelled
8. fit	fitting	fitted
9. recur	recurring	recurred
10. remit	remitting	remitted
11. open	opening	opened
12. club	clubbing	clubbed
13. plunge	plunging	plunged
14. singe	singeing	singed
15. pursue	pursuing	pursued
16. scare	scaring	scared
17. throb	throbbing	throbbed
18. blog	blogging	blogged
19. use	using	used
20. whip	whipping	whipped

EXERCISE 3 *Pages 98–99.*

1. agreement
2. amusement
3. careful
4. canoeing
5. coming
6. disagreeable

7. engagement
8. excitement
9. immensity
10. likely
11. safety
12. senseless
13. shining
14. enlargement
15. enticing
16. perceived
17. escaping
18. discharged
19. relieving
20. contrivance

EXERCISE 4 *Page 99.*

The answers to this exercise are contained in the sentences among the words italicized.

EXERCISE 5 *Page 100.*

1. scarcely
2. vengeance
3. truly
4. tasty
5. noticeable
6. changeable
7. perspiring
8. retiring
9. awful
10. wisdom
11. assurance
12. insurance
13. outrageous
14. serviceable
15. courageous
16. gorgeous
17. pronounceable

CHAPTER 12
EXERCISE 1 *Page 103.*

1. filled
2. filed
3. cramping
4. hopping
5. letting
6. tripping
7. runner
8. blogger
9. drumming
10. scrubbed

EXERCISE 2 *Pages 106–107.*

1. inferring
2. interference
3. shopping
4. disapproval
5. nineteen
6. hitting
7. singeing
8. famous
9. controlling
10. repellent
11. desiring
12. tireless
13. truly
14. swimmer
15. trimmer
16. occurrence
17. movable
18. committed
19. equipment
20. excelling
21. admitting
22. admittance
23. rebooting
24. plotting
25. editing

EXERCISE 3 *Pages 107–108.*

1. adapt | adapting | adapted
2. cramp | cramping | cramped
3. design | designing | designed
4. conceal | concealing | concealed
5. congeal | congealing | congealed
6. blot | blotting | blotted
7. stop | stopping | stopped
8. crush | crushing | crushed
9. excel | excelling | excelled
10. defer | deferring | deferred
11. envelop | enveloping | enveloped
12. extol | extolling | extolled
13. flutter | fluttering | fluttered
14. happen | happening | happened
15. hum | humming | hummed
16. level | leveling | leveled
17. quarrel | quarreling | quarreled
18. rub | rubbing | rubbed
19. signal | signaling | signaled
20. retreat | retreating | retreated

EXERCISE 4 *Pages 108–109.*

1. beginning
2. witty
3. designer
4. quizzical
5. dryer
6. inhabitable
7. reader
8. blogger
9. approval
10. cleaning
11. scrubbing
12. assignment

EXERCISE 5 *Page 109.*

1. tearfully
2. carefully
3. openness
4. dutifully
5. bountifully
6. commonness
7. mimicked
8. picnicking
9. mimicking
10. panicky

CHAPTER 13
EXERCISE 1 *Page 113.*

1. sheep
2. ship
3. cheap
4. chips
5. leave
6. live
7. heat
8. hit
9. sleep
10. slip

EXERCISE 2 *Page 114.*

1. bet
2. bit
3. lead
4. lid
5. sit
6. set
7. well
8. will
9. fill
10. fell

EXERCISE 3 *Page 115.*

1. mate
2. met
3. pain
4. pen
5. braids
6. bread
7. break
8. breakfast
9. gate
10. get

EXERCISE 4 *Page 116.*

1. high
2. hay
3. bay
4. by
5. buy
6. pay
7. pie
8. dye
9. day
10. die

EXERCISE 5 *Page 117.*

1. bran
2. brain
3. tap
4. tape
5. platter
6. plate
7. bats
8. bait
9. data
10. date

EXERCISE 6 *Page 118.*

1. Battle
2. bottle
3. gnats
4. knots
5. nuts
6. flop
7. flap
8. cop
9. cap
10. cup

REVIEW EXERCISE A
Pages 118–119.

1. beat
2. bet
3. but
4. win
5. whine
6. main
7. men
8. man
9. seem, same
10. been

EXERCISE 7 *Page 119.*

1. book
2. back
3. hook
4. hocked
5. brook
6. blocks

EXERCISE 8 *Pages 120–121.*

1. fair
2. for
3. fur
4. store

5. stare
6. torn
7. turn
8. were
9. ore
10. or

EXERCISE 9 *Page 121.*

1. far
2. four
3. barn
4. born
5. scar
6. score
7. parch
8. porch
9. ardor
10. order

EXERCISE 10 *Pages 122–123.*

1. coal
2. cool
3. pole
4. pool
5. room
6. roam
7. rule
8. role
9. tools
10. toll

EXERCISE 11 *Pages 123–124.*

1. allowed
2. aloud
3. alloy
4. oil
5. owl
6. noise

7. now

8. void

9. vowed

10. nouns, avoid

REVIEW EXERCISE B *Page 124.*

1. carves

2. curves

3. coat

4. cot

5. caught

6. goose

7. goes

8. not

9. note

10. afternoon, none

EXERCISE 12 *Page 125.*

1. Necessity

2. emotional

3. independence

4. perspires

5. liberal

EXERCISE 13 *Page 126.*

1. knife, scissors

2. calm, talk

3. psychiatrist, listen

4. heir, reign

5. condemned

CHAPTER 14
EXERCISE 1 *Pages 131–132.*

1. C

2. X

3. X

4. C

5. C

6. C

7. C

8. C

9. C

10. C

11. X

12. X

13. X

14. C

15. X

16. X

17. X

18. C

19. C

20. C

EXERCISE 2 *Pages 137–138.*

1. sister-in-law

2. man-of-war

3. aide-de-camp

4. run-on

5. downstairs

6. antiwar

7. C

8. C

9. C

10. C

11. runner-up

12. drive-in

13. C

14. C

15. trade-in

16. C

17. C

18. built-in

19. C

20. C

CHAPTER 15
EXERCISE 1 *Pages 142–143.*
1. The young girl's doll
2. The members' votes
3. The ladies' styles
4. The cats' paws
5. The sailors' decorations
6. The professor's laptop
7. The woman's shoe
8. The soprano's voice
9. The dog's tail

EXERCISE 2 *Page 143.*
1. don't
2. haven't
3. couldn't
4. You're
5. can't
6. It's
7. Let's
8. wouldn't

CHAPTER 16
EXERCISE *Page 148.*
1. Hotel Westover
2. Toyota
3. Decoration Day
4. North Side High School
5. *The Lion King*
6. Irish
7. English, Bible
8. Uncle
9. Fifth Avenue
10. Washington coffee
11. Britain
12. Bard College, New York
13. *The Taming of the Shrew*, Shakespeare
14. English, French
15. Aunt Emily, West

CHAPTER 17
EXERCISE 1 *Page 150.*
1. Wednesday
2. Tues.
3. Mar.
4. February
5. Apr.

EXERCISE 2 *Pages 153–154.*
1. Sec. or Secy.
2. Treas.
3. COD
4. A.M., AM, or a.m.
5. Jr.
6. doz.
7. Aug.
8. MD
9. Hon.
10. yr.
11. Sat.
12. RFD
13. RSVP
14. Esq.
15. dept.
16. lb.
17. Gov.
18. DDS
19. Rev.
20. Blvd.

EXERCISE 3 *Pages 154–155.*
1. Doctor of Philosophy
2. Avenue
3. inch

4. et cetera (and so forth)

5. number

6. brothers

7. postscript

8. railroad

9. September

10. Freight on Board

11. Professor

12. assistant

13. Eastern Standard Time

14. governor

15. Wednesday

16. assistant

17. steamship

18. Street

19. received

20. department

21. Doctor of Medicine

22. treasurer

23. Saturday

24. Honorable

25. Reverend

26. Secretary

27. Doctor of Dental Surgery

28. Captain

29. March

30. post meridiem (after noon)

CHAPTER 18
EXERCISE 1 *Page 162*.

1. alter

2. borne

3. brake

4. capital

5. aisle

6. already

7. bridal

8. altogether

9. all ready

10. capital

EXERCISE 2 *Page 165*.

1. Council

2. complement

3. course

4. dessert

5. It's

6. dissent

7. led

8. counsel

9. core

10. dual

EXERCISE 3 *Page 169*.

1. minor

2. peace

3. plane—plain

4. principal

5. waist

6. their

7. too

8. stationery

9. whose

10. They're

EXERCISE 4 *Page 172*.

1. clothes

2. later

3. consul

4. advice

5. beside

6. emigrants

7. formally

8. ingenuous

9. ally

10. allusions

EXERCISE 5 *Page 173*.

1. morale
2. quite
3. personnel
4. loose
5. than
6. formally
7. lose
8. moral
9. quite
10. than

CHAPTER 19
EXERCISE *Pages 177–178*.

1. C
2. C
3. definitive
4. C
5. C
6. C
7. undefinable
8. undesirable
9. pitiless
10. C
11. C
12. C
13. C
14. C
15. C
16. C
17. non-existent
18. preferable
19. C
20. unendurable
21. necessarily
22. C
23. C
24. changeable
25. judgment or judgement
26. accommodate
27. guarantee
28. receipts
29. C
30. C
31. chosen
32. possessed
33. recognized
34. sincerity
35. existence
36. embarrassed
37. C
38. excitable
39. preferred
40. occasion

CHAPTER 21
EXERCISE *Pages 190–191*.

1. c
2. a
3. d
4. a
5. a
6. b
7. b
8. c
9. c
10. a
11. a
12. d
13. c
14. c
15. c
16. b
17. d

CHAPTER 22
EXERCISE 1 *Page 194.*

1. vegetarian
2. vegan
3. pumpkin
4. raspberry
5. potatoes, broccoli
6. avocados
7. banana
8. chocolate, vanilla

EXERCISE 2 *Page 195.*

1. vacuum
2. kindergarten
3. admissions
4. refrigerator
5. condominium
6. councilperson
7. efficiency
8. ceiling

CHAPTER 23
EXERCISE *Page 202.*

1. d
2. d
3. b
4. b
5. a
6. b
7. d
8. a
9. a
10. b
11. c
12. c
13. b
14. d
15. c

For Achievement Tests 1–7

ACHIEVEMENT TEST 1
CHAPTERS 1–4 *Pages 205–207.*

1. T
2. T
3. F
4. F
5. F
6. T
7. T
8. F
9. T
10. F
11. F
12. F
13. F
14. T
15. F
16. T
17. T
18. T
19. F
20. F
21. T
22. T
23. F
24. F

25. F
26. F
27. T
28. T
29. T
30. T
31. T
32. T
33. T
34. F
35. T
36. F
37. F
38. F
39. T
40. F

ACHIEVEMENT TEST 2
CHAPTER 6 *Pages 207–208.*

1. receipt
2. relief
3. shriek
4. yield
5. fiend
6. achievement
7. retrieve
8. friend
9. calories
10. chief
11. receiving
12. deceive
13. achieve
14. perceive
15. neighbors
16. mischievous
17. acronym
18. ceiling

ACHIEVEMENT TEST 3
CHAPTERS 7–8 *Pages 208–211.*

1. disadvantage
2. C
3. misstatement
4. recollect
5. C
6. innovation
7. renovate
8. unnatural
9. C
10. override
11. demoted
12. dissolve
13. pre-eminent
14. antiseptic
15. C
16. interstate
17. interrupt
18. postscript
19. suburban
20. superintendent
21. transient
22. admissible
23. laughable
24. unthinkable
25. eligible
26. invincible
27. legible
28. comfortable
29. perishable
30. demonstrable
31. C
32. recollect
33. C
34. unnoticeable
35. overrated

36. antecedent
37. C
38. C
39. seceded
40. perforated
41. perspective
42. C
43. precocious
44. drinkable
45. inaccessible
46. C
47. eligible
48. C
49. C
50. acquaintance
51. defendant
52. significance
53. hangar
54. C
55. C
56. C
57. radiator
58. C
59. supervisor
60. C

ACHIEVEMENT TEST 4
CHAPTERS 9–11 *Pages 211–214.*

1. buffaloes, buffalos, buffalo
2. vetoes
3. tomatoes
4. pianos
5. lassos, lassoes
6. medium
7. leaves
8. beliefs
9. vegetarian
10. oxen
11. chimneys
12. pulleys
13. volleys
14. salaries
15. tragedies
16. angrily
17. merciful
18. medleys
19. Tuesday
20. dignifies
21. dining
22. imaginable
23. judging
24. surprising
25. writing
26. whining
27. desirous
28. density
29. sincerely
30. families
31. dining
32. donkeys
33. encouragement
34. unimaginable
35. casualties
36. busily
37. accompanied
38. worried
39. portrayed
40. sublimity
41. inadvisable
42. singeing
43. vagueness
44. arguing
45. lovely
46. courageous

47. tasteless
48. contrivance
49. anniversaries
50. toxin
51. proofs
52. brothers-in-law
53. besieged
54. likeness
55. gracefully
56. truly
57. mimicking
58. sheep
59. alumni
60. academies
61. curriculum
62. bacilli

ACHIEVEMENT TEST 5
CHAPTERS 12–15 *Pages 214–216.*

1. low-priced
2. best-known
3. thirty-first
4. far-fetched
5. newly born
6. highest priced
7. preelection
8. co-owner
9. ex-governor
10. Vice-Admiral
11. conferred
12. preference
13. transferred
14. wrappings
15. hopper
16. hitter
17. trimmings
18. controlling
19. excelled
20. regretted
21. low ceiling
22. one half
23. dinning
24. low-cut
25. references
26. hoping
27. occurred
28. hangdog
29. unparalleled
30. twenty-ninth
31. predawn
32. high scorer
33. preferred
34. ex-policeman
35. conferred
36. chinned
37. proactive
38. flapped
39. red-cheeked
40. eighty-eight
41. subliminal
42. regretful
43. lowest priced
44. spaghetti
45. well timed
46. hitting
47. running
48. patrolled
49. all ready
50. run-on
51. senator-elect
52. mid-Atlantic
53. extolled
54. business
55. regaled

56. runner-up
57. spinning
58. omitted
59. scraped
60. recurred
61. annulled
62. programmer
63. panicked
64. rebelled
65. deferred

ACHIEVEMENT TEST 6
CHAPTERS 16–17 *Pages 217–218.*

1. don't
2. men's
3. his
4. who's
5. i's, t's
6. you've
7. ladies'
8. brother-in-law's
9. children's
10. couldn't
11. East, West
12. Grandma Moses
13. Hindu
14. Elks
15. "Dance Me to the End of Love"
16. *A Tale of Two Cities*
17. north
18. Columbus Day
19. *My Fair Lady*
20. House of Representatives
21. boy's
22. They're
23. doctors'
24. teachers'

25. 7s
26. Penn and Teller's
27. women's
28. theirs
29. t's
30. lawyer's
31. East
32. French
33. mathematics
34. Governor
35. Internet
36. Hawaii
37. Orient
38. Senate
39. Arbor Day
40. *Of Mice and Men*
41. Admiral
42. Uncle Floyd
43. boys'
44. south

ACHIEVEMENT TEST 7
CHAPTER 19 *Pages 219–221.*

1. advice
2. allies
3. aisle
4. all ready
5. illusion
6. alter
7. altogether
8. borne
9. angels
10. berth
11. beside
12. break
13. breath
14. bridle

15. canvass
16. Capitol
17. censure
18. cords
19. clothes
20. course
21. compliment
22. advice
23. core
24. incredulous
25. diaries
26. dissent
27. dessert
28. device
29. duel
30. formerly
31. instance
32. ingenious
33. compliments
34. boarder
35. consul
36. formally

37. morale
38. personnel
39. principle
40. stationery
41. waste
42. supersede
43. exceedingly
44. succeeds
45. proceeded
46. illusion
47. accede
48. receded
49. corpse
50. its
51. later
52. led
53. whether
54. loose
55. minors
56. peace
57. plain
58. quite

10,000 Word Ready Reference Spelling List

Spelling Reminders

It is not easy to become a good speller; in fact, many people never master the art. Even a computer spell-checker cannot always come to your rescue. English is full of confusing rules, strange spellings (like pneumonia and aerial), and words that sound alike but have different spellings (and you want to write the right word). In this book, you have found rules to help, some words that defy the rules, and lists of common misspellings. Like any other skill, spelling can be improved with practice.

There is no magic formula for learning how to spell. The ability to spell correctly results from persistent study. Here are some useful suggestions for studying the list of words that follows.

1. Use a small notebook exclusively for recording your personal spelling problem words.

2. Each time you discover a problem word, enter it in your notebook. Check a dictionary for the correct syllabification and pronunciation.

3. Look at the word and say it in syllables.

4. Try to apply a rule that will help you to understand *why* the word is spelled as it is.

5. Close your eyes and picture the way the word looks.

6. Write the word. Check it. Rewrite it if necessary.

7. Review words you have already studied until you are absolutely sure that you know how to spell them.

From *Grammar In Plain English*, 4th edition by P. Dutwin and H. Diamond. With permission of Barron's Educational Series, Inc.

Using the 10,000 Words as Practice

The list of 10,000 words is designed to be an ongoing resource for your study of spelling. Go through it in sections. Find the words you're not sure of and use the study tools above to write them, use them, and live with them until you're comfortable about their spelling. You have seen many of them throughout this book. The additional practice will reinforce what you've already learned; you will also notice your progress by finding a word that once was troubling for you, which you can now remember how to spell.

If you have someone to help you by reading some words as you write, it will be easier to identify your trouble spots and those words that will require some practice. However, if you're ready to learn and you don't have a study partner nearby, don't wait. Study what you can; there will be plenty of words left to study when your partner is available.

Like all learning, you won't wake up one day and be a perfect speller; few people are. Even professional writers stumble with troublesome words and keep dictionaries by their sides. However, having gone through this book, you are well on your way to becoming a confident, competent speller. You may already notice the time you save not looking up the same old words and you may, by now, have caught some errors that your spell-checker misses. Continue your study with the 10,000 words to reinforce and strengthen your skills.

About the List

Spelling. The words in this reference list are spelled according to American usage.
   When two spellings are valid, both are listed:

dem•a•gogue, dem•a•gog

Dividing words at the end of a line. Centered dots indicate division points at which a hyphen may be put at the end of a line of typing or writing. For example, *baccalaureate (bac•ca•lau•re•ate)* may be ended on one line with

bac-

bacca-

baccalau-

baccalaure-

and continued on the next line, respectively, with

-calaureate

-laureate

-reate

-ate

Note, however, that a single initial letter or a single terminal letter is not cut off.

The following words, for example, are not hyphenated:

abound   icy   o'clock   seamy

Plurals. Most English nouns form their plural by adding *s*. These regular plurals are not shown in the reference list. Irregular plurals are shown:

la•bo•ra•to•ry (–ries)
knife (knives)
lar•nyx (la•ryn•ges *or* lar•ynx•es)

las•so (las•sos *or* las•soes)
la•tex (la•ti•ces *or* la•tex•es)
oc•to•pus (–pus•es *or* –pi)

Definitions. Brief definitions of confusing pairs of words are given:

arc (something arched or curved; see *ark*)
ark (a boat; a repository for Torah scrolls, see *arc*)

af•fect (to influence; see *effect*)
ef•fect (to accomplish; see *affect*)

Brief definitions of commonly used foreign words and phrases are also given:

a la carte (French: each item is priced separately)
cul-de-sac (French: street closed at one end)

10,000 Words

A

aback
aba·cus (–cus·es)
aban·don
aban·don·ment
abase
abase·ment
abash
abate·ment
ab·bey
ab·bot
ab·bre·vi·ate
ab·bre·vi·a·tion
ab·di·cate
ab·di·ca·tion
ab·do·men
ab·dom·i·nal
ab·duct
ab·duc·tion
ab·er·ra·tion
abet
abet·ted
ab·hor
ab·hor·rence
abide
abil·i·ty (–ties)

ab·ject
ab·jur·ing
able-bod·ied
ab·lu·tion
a·bly
ab·nor·mal·i·ty (–ties)
ab·nor·mal·ly
aboard
abol·ish
ab·o·li·tion
abom·i·na·ble
abort
abor·tion
abound
about-face
abra·sive
abreast
abridge
abridg·ment, abridge·ment
abroad
ab·ro·gate
abrupt
ab·scess
ab·scond
ab·sence
ab·so·lute
ab·so·lute·ly

ab·solve
ab·sorb
ab·sor·bent
ab·stain
ab·strac·tion
abun·dant
abut·ment
abys·mal
abyss
ac·a·dem·i·cal·ly
ac·cede
ac·cel·er·ate
ac·cent
ac·cept (to receive; see *except*)
ac·ces·so·ry, ac·ces·sa·ry (–ries)
ac·ces·si·ble
ac·ci·dent
ac·ci·den·tal
ac·claim
ac·cli·mate
ac·cli·ma·tize
ac·co·lade
ac·com·mo·date
ac·com·mo·da·tion
ac·com·pa·nist
ac·com·pa·ny
ac·com·plice

ac·com·plish
ac·cord
ac·cost
ac·count
ac·coun·tant
ac·cru·al
ac·cu·mu·late
ac·cu·ra·cy
ac·cu·sa·tion
ac·cuse
ac·e·tate
acet·y·lene
achieve
achieve·ment
ac·knowl·edge
acous·tics
ac·quain·tance
ac·qui·esce
ac·quire
ac·qui·si·tion
ac·quit·tal
acre
acre·age
ac·ri·mo·ni·ous
across
ac·tiv·i·ty (–ties)
ac·tu·al
ac·tu·ar·i·al
ac·tu·ary
acu·punc·ture
acu·punc·tur·ist
ad·ap·ta·tion
ad·dict
ad·dic·tive
ad·di·tion·al
ad·dress·ee
ad·duce
ad·e·noid
ad·e·quate
ad·here
ad·he·sive
ad hoc (Latin: pertaining to the case
    at hand)
ad ho·mi·nem (Latin: argument based
    on personality)
adieu (adieus or adieux) (French:
    farewell)
ad in·fi·ni·tum (Latin: without end)
ad·ja·cent
ad·jec·tive
ad·join·ing
ad·journ
ad·journ·ment
ad·ju·di·cate
ad·junct
ad·just·able
ad-lib (Latin: without preparation)
ad·min·is·ter
ad·min·is·trate
ad·min·is·tra·tion

ad·min·is·tra·tor
ad·mi·ra·ble
ad·mi·ra·tion
ad·mis·si·ble
ad nau·se·am (Latin: to a sickening
    degree)
ad·o·les·cent
adopt
adop·tion
ad·re·nal
adren·a·line
adroit
ad·u·la·tion
ad·van·ta·geous
ad·ven·tur·ous
ad·ver·sary (–sar·ies)
ad·ver·si·ty (–ties)
ad·ver·tise·ment
ad·vice (recommendation; see advise)
ad·vis·able
ad·vise (to give advice; see advice)
ad·vis·er, ad·vi·sor
ad·vo·cate
aer·ate
ae·ri·al (relating to the air)
aer·i·al (antenna)
aer·o·bics
aero·dy·nam·ics
aero·nau·tics
aero·sol
aes·thet·ics
af·fa·ble
af·fect (to influence; see effect)
af·fec·tion·ate
af·fi·da·vit
af·fil·i·ate
af·fin·i·ty (–ties)
af·fir·ma·tive
af·flic·tion
af·flu·ent
af·ford
af·fray
af·front
Af·ghan
afore·men·tioned
afraid
af·ter·ward, af·ter·wards
again
agen·cy (–cies)
agen·da
agent
ag·glom·er·ate
ag·gran·dize·ment
ag·gra·vate
ag·gres·sion
ag·gres·sive
ag·grieved
aghast
ag·ile
agil·i·ty (–ties)

ag·i·tate
ag·i·ta·tor
ag·nos·tic
ag·o·nize
agrar·i·an
agree·able
ag·ri·cul·ture
agron·o·my
aid (to give assistance, a subsidy;
    see aide)
aide (military assistant; see aid)
air-con·di·tion
air con·di·tion·er
air force
air·line
air·port
aisle
ajar
a la carte (French: each item is priced
    separately)
alac·ri·ty
al·ba·tross
al·bu·men
al·che·my
al·co·hol
al·ge·bra
al·ga (al·gae)
ali·as
al·i·bi
alien·ate
align·ment, aline·ment
al·i·men·ta·ry
al·i·mo·ny (–nies)
alive
al·ka·li (–lies or –lis)
al·lay (relieve; see alley, ally)
al·le·ga·tion
al·lege
al·le·giance
al·le·go·ry (–ries)
al·ler·gy (–gies)
al·le·vi·ate
al·ley (narrow passage; see allay, ally)
al·li·ance
al·li·ga·tor
al·lit·er·ate
al·lit·er·a·tion
al·lo·cate
al·lo·path·ic
al·lot
al·lot·ment
al·low
al·low·able
al·low·ance
al·loy
all right
al·lude (to refer; see elude)
al·lure
al·lu·sion
al·ly (an associate; see allay, alley)

al·ma·nac
al·mond
al·most
alo·ha
alone
aloud
al·pha·bet
al·pha·bet·ize
al·ready
al·tar (structure used in religious
    ceremonies; see *alter*)
al·ter (to change; see *altar*)
al·ter·ation
al·ter·ca·tion
al·ter·nate
al·ter·na·tive
al·though
al·tim·e·ter
al·ti·tude
al·to·geth·er
al·tru·ism
al·um
alu·mi·num
alum·na (–nae)
alum·nus (–ni)
al·ways
amal·gam
amal·gam·ate
am·a·teur
am·a·to·ry
amaze
am·bas·sa·dor
am·bi·dex·trous
am·bi·ence, am·bi·ance
am·bi·gu·i·ty (–ties)
am·big·u·ous
am·bi·tious
am·biv·a·lence
am·bu·lance
am·bu·la·to·ry
ame·lio·rate
ame·na·ble
amend·ment
ame·ni·ty (–ties)
am·e·thyst
ami·a·ble
am·i·ca·ble
am·mo·nia
am·mu·ni·tion
am·ne·sia
am·nes·ty (–ties)
am·nio·cen·te·sis
amoe·ba (–bas *or* –bae)
among
amor·al
am·o·rous
amor·phous
am·or·ti·za·tion
am·or·tize
amount

am·phet·amine
am·phib·i·an
am·phi·the·ater
am·pli·fy
am·pu·tate
amuse·ment
anach·ro·nism
an·al·ge·sic
an·a·log
anal·o·gous
anal·o·gy
anal·y·sis
an·a·lyst
an·a·lyze
an·ar·chy
anat·o·my
an·ces·tor
an·ces·try
an·chor
an·cho·vy (–vies)
an·cient
an·cil·lary
an·ec·dote
an·es·the·sia
an·eu·rysm, an·eu·rism
an·gel (heavenly messenger; see *angle*)
an·gle (geometric figure; see *angel*)
angst
an·gu·lar
an·guish
an·i·mate
an·i·ma·tion
an·i·ma·tor
an·i·mos·i·ty (–ties)
an·nals
an·nex (noun), an·nex (verb)
an·ni·hi·late
an·ni·ver·sa·ry (–ries)
an·no·tate
an·nounce·ment
an·nounc·er
an·noy
an·nu·al
an·nu·ity (–ities)
an·nul
an·nun·ci·ate
anoint
anom·a·ly (–lies)
anon·y·mous
an·swer
ant (insect; see *aunt*)
an·tag·o·nize
an·te·ced·ent
an·te·date
an·te·lope
an·ten·na
an·te·ri·or
an·te·room
an·them
an·thol·o·gy (–gies)

an·thra·cite
an·thro·pol·o·gy
an·ti·bi·ot·ic
an·tic
an·tic·i·pate
an·ti·cli·max
an·ti·de·pres·sant
an·ti·dote
an·ti·his·ta·mine
an·ti·ox·i·dant
an·ti·pas·to
an·tip·a·thy (–thies)
an·ti·pol·lu·tion
an·ti·quar·i·an
an·tique
an·tiq·ui·ty (–ties)
an·ti·sep·tic
an·ti·so·cial
an·tith·e·sis (–e·ses)
an·to·nym
anx·i·ety (–eties)
anx·ious
aor·ta (–tas *or* –tae)
apart·heid
apart·ment
ap·a·thy
aper·i·tif
ap·er·ture
apex
aph·o·rism
aph·ro·di·si·ac
aplomb
apoc·a·lypse
apoc·ry·phal
apo·gee
apol·o·gize
apol·o·gy (–gies)
ap·o·plec·tic
ap·o·plexy
apos·tro·phe
apo·the·o·sis (–o·ses)
ap·pall, ap·pal
ap·pa·ra·tus (–tus·es *or* –tus)
ap·par·el
ap·par·ent
ap·pa·ri·tion
ap·peal
ap·pear·ance
ap·pease
ap·pel·lant
ap·pe·late
ap·pend·age
ap·pen·dec·to·my (–mies)
ap·pen·di·ci·tis
ap·pen·dix (–dix·es *or* –di·ces)
ap·per·tain
ap·pe·tite
ap·pe·tiz·er
ap·plaud
ap·plause

ap·pli·ance
ap·pli·ca·ble
ap·pli·ca·tion
ap·pli·ca·tor
ap·plied
ap·ply
ap·point·ment
ap·por·tion
ap·pose
ap·praise
ap·pre·ci·ate
ap·pre·hend
ap·pren·tice
ap·prise
ap·proach
ap·pro·ba·tion
ap·pro·pri·ate
ap·pro·pri·a·tion
ap·prov·al
ap·prox·i·mate
apri·cot
ap·ti·tude
apt·ly
aquar·i·um
aquat·ic
aq·ue·duct
ar·bi·ter
ar·bi·trary
ar·bi·trate
ar·bi·tra·tor
ar·bor
arc (curved line; see *ark*)
ar·cade
arch
ar·chae·ol·o·gy
ar·cha·ic
ar·chery
ar·che·type
ar·chi·tect
ar·chi·tec·tur·al
ar·chi·tec·ture
ar·chive
arc·tic
ar·dent
ar·dor
ar·du·ous
ar·ea
are·na
ar·gue
ar·id
ar·is·toc·ra·cy (–cies)
aris·to·crat
arith·me·tic
ark (boat; see *arc*)
ar·ma·ment
ar·ma·ture
ar·mi·stice
ar·moire
ar·mor
ar·my (–mies)

aro·ma
aro·ma·ther·a·py
ar·o·mat·ic
arouse
ar·raign
ar·range
ar·ray
ar·rear
ar·rest
ar·riv·al
ar·rive
ar·ro·gance
ar·se·nic
ar·son
ar·te·ri·al
ar·te·rio·scle·ro·sis
ar·tery (–ter·ies)
art·ful
ar·thri·tis
ar·ti·choke
ar·ti·cle
ar·tic·u·late
ar·ti·fact
ar·ti·fice
ar·ti·fi·cial
ar·ti·san
ar·tis·tic
ar·tis·ti·cal·ly
as·bes·tos
as·cend
as·cen·sion
as·cent (climb; see *assent*)
as·cer·tain
as·cet·ic
as·cribe
asep·tic
askew
as·par·a·gus (–gus·es)
as·pect
as·per·i·ty (–ties)
as·per·sion
as·phalt
as·phyx·i·ate
as·pire
as·pi·rin
as·sail
as·sas·sin
as·sas·si·na·tion
as·sault
as·sem·ble
as·sem·bly (–blies)
as·sent (to agree; see *ascent*)
as·sert
as·sess·ment
as·set
as·sid·u·ous
as·sign·ment
as·sim·i·late
as·sis·tant
as·so·ci·a·tion

as·so·nance
as·sort·ment
as·suage
as·sump·tion
as·sur·ance
as·ter·isk
as·ter·oid
asth·ma
as·trin·gent
as·trol·o·gy
as·tro·naut
as·tron·o·mer
as·tro·nom·i·cal, as·tro·nom·ic
as·tron·o·my (–mies)
as·tute
asun·der
asy·lum
asym·met·ric, asym·met·ri·cal
athe·ist
ath·lete
ath·let·ic
at·mo·sphere
atom·ic
atone·ment
atro·cious
at·ro·phy (–phies)
at·tach
at·ta·ché
at·tach·ment
at·tack
at·tain
at·tempt
at·ten·dance
at·ten·tive
at·ten·u·ate
at·test
at·tic
at·tire
at·ti·tude
at·tor·ney
at·trac·tive
at·tri·bute
at·tri·tion
at·tune
atyp·i·cal
au·burn
auc·tion·eer
au·da·cious
au·dac·i·ty (–ties)
au·di·ble
au·di·ence
au·dio·vi·su·al
au·dit
au·di·tion
au·di·to·ri·um
aug·ment
auld lang syne (Scottish: the good old
  times)
aunt (relative; see *ant*)
au·ral (relating to the ear; see *oral*)

au re·voir (French: good·bye)
au·ri·cle
aus·pic·es
aus·pi·cious
aus·tere
aus·ter·i·ty (–ties)
au·then·tic
au·then·ti·cate
au·then·tic·i·ty
au·thor
au·thor·i·ta·tive
au·thor·i·ty (–ties)
au·tho·ri·za·tion
au·tho·rize
au·tism
au·to·bio·graph·i·cal, au·to·bio·graph·ic
au·to·bi·og·ra·phy (–phies)
au·toc·ra·cy (–cies)
au·to·crat
au·to·graph
au·to·mat·ed
au·to·mat·ic
au·to·mat·i·cal·ly
au·to·ma·tion
au·tom·a·ton
au·to·mo·bile
au·to·mo·tive
au·ton·o·mous
au·ton·o·my (–mies)
au·top·sy (–sies)
au·to·sug·ges·tion
au·tumn
aux·il·ia·ry (–ries)
avail·abil·i·ty (–ties)
avail·able
av·a·lanche
av·a·rice
av·a·ri·cious
avenge
av·e·nue
av·er·age
averse
aver·sion
avert
avi·ary (–ar·ies)
avi·a·tion
avi·a·tor
av·id
av·o·ca·do (–dos or –does)
av·o·ca·tion
avoid·able
avoid·ance
av·oir·du·pois (French: weight)
await
awake
awak·en·ing
award
aware
away
awe·some

aw·ful
awhile
awk·ward
aw·ning
awoke
ax·i·al
ax·i·om
ax·is (ax·es)
ax·le
ay·ur·ve·dic
aza·lea
azure

B

bab·ble
bab·bling
ba·boon
ba·by (ba·bies)
bac·ca·lau·re·ate
bach·e·lor
ba·cil·lus (–li)
back·bone
back·fire
back·ground
back·log
back·stop
back·ward
ba·con
bac·te·ri·al
bac·te·ri·ol·o·gy
bac·te·ri·um (–ria)
bad·ger
bad·min·ton
baf·fle
bag·gage
bail (security for due appearance;
    see *bale*)
bai·liff
bai·li·wick
bak·ery (–er·ies)
bak·ing
bal·ance
bal·co·ny (–nies)
bale (large bundle; see *bail*)
balk
bal·lad
bal·last
bal·le·ri·na
bal·let
bal·lis·tics
bal·loon
bal·lot
balm
ba·lo·ney, bo·lo·ney
bal·sa
bam·boo
ba·nal
ba·nana

ban·dage
ban·dan·na
ban·dit·ry
band·width
bane·ful
ban·ish
ban·is·ter
bank·rupt
bank·rupt·cy (–cies)
ban·ner
ban·quet
ban·ter
bar·be·cue
bare (exposed; see *bear*)
bar·gain
ba·rom·e·ter
ba·ron (a lord of the realm;
    see *barren*)
bar·rack
bar·rel
bar·ren (not reproducing; see *baron*)
bar·rette (hair pin; see *beret*)
bar·ri·cade
bar·ri·er
bar·room
base (bottom; see *bass*)
bash·ful
ba·sic
ba·si·cal·ly
ba·sil·i·ca
ba·sis (ba·ses)
bas·ket·ry (–ries)
bass (a deep tone; see *base*)
bas·si·net
bas·soon
baste
bas·tion
bathe
bat·tal·ion
bat·tle
bau·ble
bay·o·net
bay·ou
ba·zaar (market; see *bizarre*)
beach (shore; see *beech*)
bea·con
beady
bear (an animal, to endure, to give
    birth; see *bare*)
beard
beast
beau
beau·ti·ful
beau·ti·fy
beau·ty (–ties)
be·cause
beech (tree; see *beach*)
beer (alcoholic beverage; see *bier*)
be·fore
be·fud·dle

beg·gar
be·gin·ning
be·go·nia
be·grudge
be·guile
be·hav·ior
be·he·moth
be·hest
be·hold·en
be·hoove
beige
be·ing
be·ir (a stand for a coffin; see *beer*)
be·la·bor
be·lat·ed
bel·fry (–fries)
be·lie
be·lief
be·lieve
bell (chime; see *belle*)
belle (beauty; see *bell*)
bel·lig·er·ent
bel·lows
be·neath
ben·e·fac·tor
be·nef·i·cence
ben·e·fi·cial
ben·e·fi·cia·ry (–ries)
be·nev·o·lence
be·nev·o·lent
be·nign
ben·zene, ben·zine
be·queath
be·quest
be·reave
be·ret (woolen cap; see *barrette*)
ber·serk
berth (place; see *birth*)
be·siege
bes·tial
be·stow
be·tray
be·tween
bev·el
bev·er·age
bevy (bev·ies)
be·wail
bi·an·nu·al
bi·as
bi·ble
bib·li·cal
bib·li·og·ra·phy (–phies)
bi·car·bon·ate
bi·cen·ten·ni·al
bi·ceps
bi·cy·cle
bi·en·ni·al
bi·fo·cal
big·a·my
big·ot

big·ot·ry (–ries)
bi·ki·ni
bi·lat·er·al
bi·lin·ear
bi·lin·gual
bill·board
bil·liards
bil·lion
bil·lion·aire
bi·na·ry (–ries)
bin·au·ral
bind·ery (–er·ies)
bin·oc·u·lar
bio·chem·is·try
bio·de·grad·able
bio·feed·back
bio·graph·i·cal
bi·og·ra·phy (–phies)
bi·o·log·i·cal
bi·ol·o·gy
bi·on·ic
bi·op·sy
bi·par·ti·san
bi·ra·cial
birth (originate; see *berth*)
bis·cuit
bi·son
bisque
bit·ter
bit·ter·ness
bi·zarre (out of the ordinary;
    see *bazaar*)
black·mail
blar·ney
bla·sé
blas·phe·my (–mies)
bla·tant
bla·zon
blem·ish
blight
blind·ly
bliz·zard
bloc (group; see *block*)
block (hinder; see *bloc*)
block·ade
blog
blog·ger
blos·som
blotch
blown
blud·geon
blue
blurb
boar (wild pig; see *bore*)
board (a piece of wood; see *bored*)
bodi·ly
bo·gey
bog·gle
bo·lo·gna, ba·lo·ney
bol·ster

bom·bard
bo·na fide (Latin: in good faith)
bo·nan·za
bond·age
bon·fire
bo·nus
bon voy·age (French: farewell)
book·keep·ing
boo·mer·ang
boor·ish
bo·rax
bor·der
bore (to drill; past of bear; dull person;
    see *boar*)
bored (past of bore; see *board*)
born (from birth; see *borne*)
borne (past participle of bear; see *born*)
bor·ough (town; see *borrow*)
bor·row (to receive with intention of
    returning; see *borough*)
borscht (Russian: soup of beets and
    sour cream)
bo·som
bossy
bot·a·ny (–nies)
bot·tle
bot·tom
bou·doir (French: bedroom, private
    sitting room)
bough (tree limb; see *bow*)
bouil·la·baisse (French: fish stew)
bouil·lon
boul·der
bou·le·vard
bound·ary (–aries)
boun·te·ous
bou·quet
bour·bon
bou·ton·niere (French: flower worn in
    buttonhole)
bo·vine
bow (to bend; see *bough*)
bow·el
boy·cott
brace·let
braid
braille
braise
brake (to stop; see *break*)
bram·ble
bras·siere
bra·va·do
brav·ery
bra·vo (bra·vos)
brawny
bra·zen
breach
breadth
break (to tear; see *brake*)
break·fast

breath
breathe
breath·less
breech·es
breeze
breth·ren
brev·i·ty
brib·ery
bric-a-brac
brid·al (relating to a bride; see *bridle*)
bridge
bri·dle (horse's headgear; see *bridal*)
brief
bri·gade
brig·a·dier
bright
bril·liant
brine
bri·quette, bri·quet
bris·tle
brit·tle
broach (to open up a subject for discussion; see *brooch*)
broad·band
broad·cast
bro·cade
broc·co·li
bro·chure
bro·ker·age
bro·mide
bron·chi·al
brooch (ornament; see *broach*)
broth·er·ly
brow·beat
browse
bruise
brun·et, brun·ette
brusque
bru·tal
bub·ble
buc·ca·neer
buck·et
bu·col·ic
bud·get
buf·fa·lo
buf·fet
buf·foon
bug·a·boo
bu·gle
build
bul·le·tin
bul·lion
bump·kin
bump·tious
bun·ga·low
bun·gle
buoy·an·cy
bur·den
bu·reau
bu·reau·cra·cy (–cies)

bu·reau·crat
bur·geon
bur·glar
buri·al
bur·lesque
bur·ly
burnt
bur·ro (donkey; see *burrow*)
bur·row (a hole made in the ground by an animal; see *burro*)
bush·el
busi·ness
bus·tle
busy
butch·er
but·ter·fly
but·tock
but·ton
but·tress
bux·om
buy (purchase; see *by, bye*)
buzz
buz·zard
by (near; see *buy, bye*)
bye (goodbye; see *buy, by*)
by·pass
by·pro·duct
by·stand·er
byte (computer term)
by·way

C

ca·bana
cab·a·ret
cab·bage
cab·i·net
ca·ble
ca·boose
cache
ca·chet
ca·coph·o·ny (–nies)
cac·tus
ca·dav·er
ca·dence
caf·e·te·ria
caf·feine
ca·gey
ca·jole
ca·lam·i·ty (–ties)
cal·ci·fy
cal·ci·um
cal·cu·late
cal·cu·la·tor
cal·cu·lus (–lus·es)
cal·en·dar
cal·i·ber, cal·i·bre
cal·i·brate
cal·i·co
cal·is·then·ics

cal·lig·ra·pher
cal·lig·ra·phy
cal·lous (feeling no emotion; see *callus*)
cal·lus (hard, thickened area of skin; see *callous*)
ca·lo·ric
cal·o·rie, cal·o·ry (–ries)
ca·lyp·so (–sos *or* –soes)
ca·ma·ra·de·rie
ca·mel·lia
cam·eo (cam·eos)
cam·i·sole
cam·ou·flage
cam·paign
cam·phor
ca·nal
ca·nard
ca·nas·ta
can·cel
can·cel·la·tion, can·cel·ation
can·cer
can·des·cence
can·di·da·cy (–cies)
can·di·date
can·dle
can·dor
ca·nine
can·is·ter, can·nis·ter
can·ker
can·ni·bal
can·non (gun; see *canon*)
can·not
ca·noe
canon (dogma; see *cannon*)
can·o·py (–pies)
can·ta·loupe, can·ta·loup
can·tan·ker·ous
can·ta·ta
can·teen
can·ti·cle
can·vas (closely woven cloth; see *canvass*)
can·vass (examine votes; see *canvas*)
can·yon
ca·pa·bil·i·ty (–ties)
ca·pa·ble
ca·pa·cious
ca·pac·i·ty (–ties)
ca·per
cap·il·lary (–lar·ies)
cap·i·tal (seat of government; see *capitol*)
cap·i·tal·ism
cap·i·tol (building in which legislature meets; see *capital*)
ca·pit·u·late
ca·pon
ca·price
ca·pri·cious
cap·sule

cap·tain
cap·tion
cap·ti·vate
car·a·mel
car·at, kar·at (unit of weight;
    see *caret, carrot*)
car·a·van
car·bine
car·bo·hy·drate
car·bon
car·bun·cle
car·bu·re·tor
car·cass
car·cin·o·gen
car·ci·no·gen·ic
car·di·ac
car·di·gan
car·di·nal
car·dio·gram
car·di·ol·o·gist
ca·reen
ca·reer
care·ful
ca·ress
car·et (printing symbol; see *carat,
    carrot*)
car·go
car·i·ca·ture
car·ies
car·il·lon
car·nage
car·nal
car·ni·val
car·niv·o·rous
car·ol
car·pen·ter
carp·ing
car·riage
car·ri·er
car·ri·on
car·rot (vegetable; see *carat, caret*)
carte blanche (French: full
    discretionary power)
car·tog·ra·pher
car·ton
car·toon
car·tridge
cas·cade
case·work
cash·ier
cash·mere
ca·si·no (–nos)
cas·ket
cas·se·role
cas·sette, ca·sette
cas·sock
cast (direct; see *caste*)
cas·ta·net
caste (class; see *cast*)
cas·ti·gate

cas·tle
cas·tor
ca·su·al·ty (–ties)
cat·a·clysm
cat·a·comb
cat·a·lep·sy (–sies)
cat·a·log, cat·a·logue
cat·a·lyst
cat·a·pult
cat·a·ract
ca·tas·tro·phe
cat·a·ton·ic
cat·e·chism
cat·e·go·rize
cat·e·go·ry (–ries)
ca·ter
cat·er·cor·ner, kit·ty-cor·ner
cat·er·pil·lar
ca·thar·sis
ca·the·dral
cath·e·ter
cat·sup, ketch·up
cau·cus
caught
caul·dron
cau·li·flow·er
caulk
caus·al
caus·tic
cau·tion
cau·tious
cav·a·lier
cav·al·ry (–ries)
cav·i·ar
cav·il
cav·i·ty (–ties)
ca·vort
cease
ce·dar
cede
ceil·ing
cel·e·brate
ce·leb·ri·ty (–ties)
cel·ery (–er·ies)
ce·les·tial
cel·i·ba·cy
cell (microscopic mass; see *sell*)
cel·lar (basement; see *seller*)
cel·lo
cel·lo·phane
cel·lu·lar
cel·lu·loid
ce·ment
cem·e·tery (–ter·ies)
cen·ser (incense burner; see *censor*)
cen·sor (supervisor of conduct and
    morals; see *censer*)
cen·sure
cen·sus
cent (monetary unit; see *sent*)

cen·te·na·ry (–ries)
cen·ten·ni·al
cen·ter·piece
cen·ti·grade
cen·ti·me·ter
cen·trif·u·gal
cen·trip·e·tal
cen·tu·ry (–ries)
ce·phal·ic
ce·ram·ic
ce·re·al (prepared grain; see *serial*)
cer·e·bel·lum
cer·e·bral
cer·e·mo·ny (–nies)
ce·rise
cer·tain
cer·tif·i·cate
cer·ti·fy
cer·ti·tude
ces·sa·tion
ces·sion
cess·pool
chafe
chaff
cha·grin
chair·man
cha·let
chal·ice
chalk
chal·lenge
chal·lis (chal·lises)
cham·ber·lain
cham·bray
cha·me·leon
cham·ois
cham·pagne
cham·pi·on
chan·cel·lor
chan·cery (–cer·ies)
chan·de·lier
change
chan·nel
chan·tey, chan·ty (chan·teys, chan·ties)
cha·os
cha·pel
chap·er·one, chap·er·on
chap·lain
chap·ter
char·ac·ter
cha·rade
char·coal
charge
char·i·ot
cha·ris·ma
char·i·ty (–ties)
char·la·tan
char·treuse
chary
chasm
chas·sis

chaste
chas·tise
chas·ti·ty
châ·teau (French: mansion)
chat·tel
chat·ty
chauf·feur
chau·vin·ism
check
chee·tah
chef
chem·i·cal
che·mise
chem·is·try (–tries)
che·mo·ther·a·py
che·nille
cher·ish
cher·ub
chess
che·va·lier
chev·ron
chic
chic·o·ry (–ries)
chief
chif·fon
child (chil·dren)
chime
chim·ney
chim·pan·zee
chin·chil·la
chintz
chi·ro·prac·tic
chi·ro·prac·tor
chis·el
chiv·al·ry (–ries)
chlo·rine
chlo·ro·form
chlo·ro·phyll
choc·o·late
choir
chol·era
cho·les·ter·ol
cho·ral
chord
cho·re·og·ra·phy (–phies)
chor·tle
cho·rus
chris·ten
chro·mat·ic
chrome
chro·mo·some
chron·ic
chron·i·cle
chro·no·log·i·cal
chro·nol·o·gy (–gies)
chry·san·the·mum
church
chute
ci·gar
cig·a·rette, cig·a·ret

cin·der
cin·e·ma
cin·na·mon
ci·pher
cir·cle
cir·cuit
cir·cu·lar
cir·cu·la·tion
cir·cum·cise
cir·cum·fer·ence
cir·cum·lo·cu·tion
cir·cum·scribe
cir·cum·spect
cir·cum·stance
cir·cum·stan·tial
cir·cum·vent
cir·rho·sis
cis·tern
ci·ta·tion
cite (to quote; see *site*)
cit·i·zen
city
civ·ic
civ·il
civ·il·ian
ci·vil·i·ty (–ties)
civ·i·li·za·tion
claim
claim·ant
clair·voy·ance
clam·my
clam·or
clan·des·tine
clan·gor
claque
clar·et
clar·i·fy
clar·i·net
clar·i·on
clar·i·ty
clas·sic
clas·si·cal
clas·si·cist
clas·si·fied
class·less
clause
claus·tro·pho·bia
clav·i·chord
clav·i·cle
cleanse
clear·ance
cleave
clef
cleft
clem·en·cy (–cies)
cler·i·cal
cli·ché (French: trite expression)
click (slight sharp noise; see *clique*)
cli·en·tele
cliff

cli·mate
climb
clin·ic
clique (exclusive group; see *click*)
clob·ber
clois·ter
clos·et
cloth
clothe
cloud
clout
clus·ter
clutch
co·ag·u·late
co·a·lesce
co·a·li·tion
coarse (rough; see *course*)
coax
co·bra
co·caine
cock·ney
co·coa
co·co·nut
co·coon
cod·dle
co·de·fend·ant
co·deine
cod·ger
cod·i·cil
cod·i·fy
co·ed·u·ca·tion
co·ef·fi·cient
co·erce
cof·fers
cof·fin
co·gent
cog·i·tate
co·gnac
cog·ni·tion
cog·ni·zant
co·here
co·he·sive·ness
coif·fure
co·in·cide
col·an·der
col·ic
col·i·se·um
col·lab·o·rate
col·lapse
col·laps·ible
col·late
col·lat·er·al
col·league
col·lec·tive
col·lege
col·lide
col·lie
col·li·sion
col·lo·qui·al
col·lo·quy (–quies)

col·lu·sion
co·logne
co·lon
col·o·nel (army officer; see *kernel*)
co·lo·nial
col·on·nade
col·o·ny (–nies)
col·or
co·los·sal
col·umn
col·um·nist
co·ma
comb
com·bat n., com·bat vb.
com·bi·na·tion
co·me·di·an
com·e·dy (–dies)
com·et
come·up·pance
com·fort·able
com·ma
com·man·deer
com·mand·ment
com·man·do (–dos *or* –does)
com·mem·o·rate
com·mem·o·ra·tive
com·mence
com·mend
com·men·da·tion
com·men·su·rate
com·men·tary (–tar·ies)
com·men·ta·tor
com·merce
com·mer·cial
com·min·gle
com·mis·er·ate
com·mis·sar
com·mis·sary (–sar·ies)
com·mis·sion
com·mit
com·mit·tee
com·mode
com·mo·di·ous
com·mod·i·ty (–ties)
com·mo·dore
com·mon
com·mo·tion
com·mu·nal
com·mune
com·mu·ni·ca·ble
com·mu·ni·cate
com·mun·ing
com·mu·nion
com·mu·ni·qué
com·mu·nism
com·mu·nist
com·mu·ni·ty (–ties)
com·mute
com·mut·ing
com·pa·ny (–nies)

com·pan·ion
com·pa·ra·ble
com·par·a·tive
com·pas·sion·ate
com·pat·i·bil·i·ty
com·pat·i·ble
com·pel
com·pen·sate
com·pete
com·pe·tence
com·pe·ti·tion
com·pet·i·tor
com·pi·la·tion
com·pla·cent (self-satisfied; see
     complaisant)
com·plain
com·plais·ant (obliging; see *complacent*)
com·ple·ment (something that
     completes; see *compliment*)
com·ple·men·ta·ry
com·plete
com·plex·ion
com·plex·i·ty (–ties)
com·pli·ant
com·pli·cate
com·plic·i·ty (–ties)
com·pli·ment (expression of praise;
     see *complement*)
com·pli·men·ta·ry
com·ply
com·po·nent
com·pos·ite
com·po·si·tion
com·pos·i·tor
com·pound
com·pre·hend
com·pre·hen·sive
com·press
com·prise
com·pro·mise
comp·trol·ler, con·trol·ler
com·pul·sion
com·punc·tion
com·put·er
com·put·er·ize
com·rade
con·ceal
con·cede
con·ceit
con·ceive
con·cen·trate
con·cen·tric
con·cept
con·cep·tu·al
con·cern
con·cert
con·cer·to
con·ces·sion
con·cil·i·ate
con·cise

con·clude
con·coct
con·cord
con·course
con·crete
con·cu·bine
con·cu·pis·cent
con·cur
con·cur·rent
con·cus·sion
con·dem·na·tion
con·dense
con·de·scend
con·di·ment
con·di·tion·al
con·do·lence
con·do·min·i·um
con·done
con·du·cive
con·duct
con·duit
con·fer
con·fer·ence
con·ferred
con·fes·sion
con·fet·ti
con·fi·dant (one to whom secrets are
     entrusted; see *confident*)
con·fi·dante (a female confidant)
con·fi·dence
con·fi·dent (assured; see *confidant*)
con·fig·u·ra·tion
con·fine
con·firm
con·fis·cate
con·fla·gra·tion
con·flict
con·form
con·frere
con·fron·ta·tion
con·fu·sion
con·geal
con·ge·nial
con·gest
con·glom·er·ate
con·grat·u·late
con·gre·gate
con·gres·sio·nal
con·gru·ent
con·ic
co·ni·fer
con·jec·ture
con·ju·gal
con·ju·gate
con·junc·tion
con·jure
con·nect
con·nec·tion
con·nive
con·nois·seur

con·no·ta·tion
con·nu·bi·al
con·quer
con·quis·ta·dor (Spanish: one that
    conquers)
con·science
con·sci·en·tious
con·scious
con·script
con·se·crate
con·sec·u·tive
con·sen·sus
con·sent
con·se·quence
con·ser·va·tion
con·ser·va·tive
con·ser·va·to·ry (–ries)
con·sid·er
con·sign
con·sis·tent
con·sole
con·sol·i·date
con·som·mé
con·so·nance
con·spic·u·ous
con·spir·a·cy (–cies)
con·spir·a·tor
con·spire
con·sta·ble
con·stab·u·lary (–lar·ies)
con·stant
con·stel·la·tion
con·ster·na·tion
con·sti·pa·tion
con·stit·u·ent
con·sti·tute
con·sti·tu·tion
con·sti·tu·tion·al·i·ty
con·strain
con·strict
con·struc·tive
con·strue
con·sul
con·sul·ta·tion
con·sume
con·sum·er
con·sum·mate
con·sump·tion
con·tact
con·ta·gious
con·tain·er
con·tam·i·na·tion
con·tem·plate
con·tem·po·ra·ne·ous
con·tem·po·rary
con·tempt·ible
con·temp·tu·ous
con·tend
con·tent (noun), con·tent (verb,
    adjective)

con·tes·tant
con·text
con·tig·u·ous
con·ti·nence
con·ti·nent
con·tin·gen·cy (–cies)
con·tin·u·al
con·tin·u·ous
con·tin·u·um
con·tort
con·tour
con·tra·band
con·tra·cep·tion
con·trac·tion
con·trac·tu·al
con·tra·dict
con·tral·to
con·trary (–trar·ies)
con·trast (noun), con·trast (verb)
con·trib·ute
con·trite
con·trive
con·trolled
con·trol·ler, comp·trol·ler
con·tro·ver·sial
con·tro·ver·sy (–sies)
con·tro·vert
con·tu·sion
co·nun·drum
con·va·lesce
con·vene
con·ve·nience
con·ven·tion
con·verge
con·ver·sa·tion
con·ver·sion
con·vert·er
con·vey
con·vic·tion
con·vince
con·viv·ial
con·vo·ca·tion
con·vo·lu·tion
con·vulse
co·op·er·ate
co·or·di·nate
co·pi·ous
cop·u·late
cor·dial
cor·don
cor·do·van
cor·du·roy
cor·nea
cor·ner
cor·net
cor·nu·co·pia
cor·ol·lary (–lar·ies)
cor·o·nary
cor·o·na·tion
cor·o·ner

cor·po·ral
cor·po·rate
cor·po·ra·tion
cor·po·re·al
corps (group; see *corpse*)
corpse (dead body; see *corps*)
cor·pu·lent
cor·pus·cle
cor·pus de·lic·ti (New Latin: fact
    necessary to prove a crime)
cor·ral
cor·rect
cor·rec·tion
cor·re·late
cor·re·la·tion
cor·re·spon·dence
cor·ri·dor
cor·rob·o·rate
cor·rode
cor·ro·sion
cor·rupt
cor·sage
cor·set
cor·ti·sone
co·sign·er
cos·met·ic
cos·mo·pol·i·tan
cos·mos
cost·ly
cos·tume
cot·tage
cou·gar
could
coun·cil (advisory group; see *counsel*)
coun·sel (advice; see *council*)
coun·sel·or, coun·sel·lor
coun·te·nance
coun·ter·feit
coun·ter·part
coun·ter·point
coun·ter·pro·duc·tive
coun·try
coup
coupe
cou·ple
cou·pon
cou·ra·geous
cou·ri·er
course (direction, customary
    procedure; see *coarse*)
cour·te·ous
cous·in
cou·tu·ri·er
cov·er·age
co·vert
co·work·er
coy·ote
crab·by
cra·dle
cra·ni·al

cra·vat
cray·on
crease
cre·a·tion
cre·a·tiv·i·ty
crea·ture
cre·dence
cre·den·tial
cred·i·bil·i·ty
cred·i·ble
cred·it
cre·do
cre·du·li·ty
cre·du·lous
cre·mate
cre·ole
crepe, crêpe
cre·scen·do
cres·cent
cre·tin
cre·vasse
crev·ice
cri·er
crim·i·nal
crim·i·nol·o·gy
cringe
crin·kle
crip·ple
cri·sis (–ses)
crisp·y
cri·te·ri·on (–ria or –ri·ons)
crit·i·cal
crit·i·cism
crit·i·cize
cri·tique
cro·chet
crock·ery
croc·o·dile
cro·cus
crois·sant
cro·ny (–nies)
cro·quet
cross·road
crotch·ety
crouch
crou·ton
crowd
cru·cial
cru·ci·fix (–fix·es)
cru·el
cruise
cru·sade
crus·ta·cean
crutch
crux
cry
cryp·tic
crys·tal
crys·tal·lize
cu·bi·cal (shaped like a cube;

see *cubicle*)
cu·bi·cle (sleeping compartment;
    see *cubical*)
cud·dle
cue (anything that excites to action;
    see *queue*)
cui·sine
cul-de-sac (culs-de-sac) (French: street
    closed at one end)
cu·li·nary
cul·mi·nate
cul·pa·ble
cul·ti·vate
cul·tur·al
cum·ber·some
cu·mu·la·tive
cun·ning
cup·board
cu·po·la
cu·rate
cu·ra·tor
cur·few
cu·ri·ous
cur·rant (berry; see *current*)
cur·ren·cy (–cies)
cur·rent (present; see *currant*)
cur·ric·u·lum
cur·so·ry
cur·tail·ment
cur·tain
cur·te·sy (–sies)
curt·sy, curt·sey (curt·sies or curt·seys)
cur·va·ture
curve
cush·ion
cus·tard
cus·to·di·an
cus·to·dy (–dies)
cus·tom
cus·tom·ary
cus·tom·er
cu·ti·cle
cut·lery
cy·ber·space
cy·cle
cy·clic, cy·cli·cal
cy·clone
cyl·in·der
cym·bal
cyn·ic
cy·press
cyst

D

dab·ble
dad·dy (daddies)
daf·fo·dil
dag·ger
dai·ly

dair·y (dair·ies)
dai·sy (daisies)
dam·age
dam·ask
dam·sel
dance
dan·de·li·on
dan·druff
dan·ger·ous
dan·gle
dash·board
da·ta
da·ta·base
date
daugh·ter
daunt·less
daw·dle
day care
daz·zle
dear (expensive; expression of
    endearment; see *deer*)
de·ba·cle
de·base·ment
de·bat·able
de·bil·i·tate
deb·it
deb·o·nair
de·brief
de·bris (plural also debris)
debt
debt·or
de·bug
de·but
de·cade
dec·a·dence
de·caf·fein·ate
de·cal
de·cap·i·tate
de·cath·lon
de·cay
de·ceased
de·ceit
de·ceive
de·cen·cy
de·cent
de·cen·tral·iza·tion
de·cep·tion
deci·bel
de·cide
de·cid·u·ous
dec·i·mal
dec·i·mate
de·ci·pher
de·ci·sion
dec·la·ma·tion
dec·la·ra·tion
de·clas·si·fy
de·cliv·i·ty (–ties)
de·code
de·com·pose

de·con·tam·i·nate
de·cor, dé·cor (French: decoration)
dec·o·rate
dec·o·rous
de·co·rum
de·coy (noun), de·coy (verb)
de·crease
de·cree
de·crep·it
de·cry
ded·i·cate
de·duct·ible
de·duc·tion
deer (an animal; see *dear*)
de fac·to (New Latin: in reality)
def·a·ma·tion
de·fault
de·fec·tive
de·fen·dant
de·fense
de·fen·sive
def·er·ence
de·fi·ance
de·fi·cien·cy (–cies)
def·i·cit
de·fine
def·i·nite
def·i·ni·tion
de·fo·li·ant
de·for·mi·ty (–ties)
de·fraud
de·fray
deft
de·fy
de·gen·er·ate
de·gree
de·hy·drate
de·i·fy
deign
de·i·ty (–ties)
de·lay
de·lec·ta·ble
del·e·gate
del·e·ga·tion
de·lete
del·e·te·ri·ous
de·lib·er·ate
del·i·cate
de·li·cious
de·light
de·lin·eate
de·lin·quent
de·lir·i·ous
de·liv·ery (–er·ies)
de·lude
del·uge
de·lu·sion
de·luxe
dem·a·gogue, dem·a·gog
de·mand

de·mean·or
de·mil·i·ta·rize
de·mise
demi·tasse
de·moc·ra·cy (–cies)
de·mol·ish
dem·on·strate
de·mor·al·ize
de·mur
de·mure
de·ni·al
den·i·grate
den·im
de·nom·i·na·tion
de·nom·i·na·tor
de·nounce
dense
den·tal
den·tist·ry
de·odor·ant
de·part·ment
de·par·ture
de·pen·dent
de·pict
de·plete
de·plor·able
de·ploy
de·por·ta·tion
de·pos·it
de·pos·i·to·ry (–ries)
de·pot
dep·re·cate
de·pre·ci·ate
dep·re·da·tion
de·pres·sion
de·pri·va·tion
depth
dep·u·ty (–ties)
de·reg·u·la·tion
der·e·lict
der·i·va·tion
de·riv·a·tive
der·ma·tol·o·gy
de·rog·a·to·ry
de·scend·ant, de·scend·ent
de·scen·sion
de·scent
de·scribe
de·scrip·tion
des·e·crate
de·seg·re·ga·tion
de·sert (arid barren tract; see *dessert*)
des·ic·cate
de·sign
des·ig·nate
de·sir·able
de·sist
des·o·la·tion
des·per·ate
de·spi·ca·ble

de·spise
de·spite
de·spon·dent
des·pot
des·sert (course served at end of meal;
     see *desert*)
des·ti·ny (–nies)
des·ti·tute
de·stroy
de·struc·tion
de·sue·tude
des·ul·to·ry
de·tach
de·tail
de·tect
de·ter·gent
de·te·ri·o·rate
de·ter·mi·na·tion
de·ter·rent
det·o·na·tion
de·tour
de·tox
de·tox·i·fy
de·tract
det·ri·ment
deuce
de·val·u·a·tion
dev·as·tate
de·vel·op
de·vel·op·ment
de·vi·ate
de·vice (mechanism; see *devise*)
de·vi·ous
de·vise (to invent; see *device*)
de·void
de·vour
de·vout
dew (moisture; see *due*)
dex·ter·i·ty (–ties)
di·a·be·tes
di·a·bol·ic
di·ag·no·sis (–no·ses)
di·ag·o·nal
di·a·gram·ing, di·a·gram·ming
di·a·lect
di·a·logue
di·am·e·ter
di·a·mond
di·a·per
di·a·phragm
di·ar·rhea
di·a·ry (–ries)
di·a·tribe
di·chot·o·my (–mies)
dic·tate
dic·ta·tion
dic·ta·tor
dic·tio·nary (–nar·ies)
dic·tum (dic·ta, dic·tums)
di·dac·tic

die (to expire; see *dye*)
die·sel
di·e·tary
dif·fer·ence
dif·fer·en·tial
dif·fi·cult
dif·fi·dence
dif·fuse
di·gest·ible
dig·it
dig·i·tal
dig·i·tal·is
dig·ni·fy
dig·ni·tary (–tar·ies)
di·gress
di·lap·i·dat·ed
di·late
dil·a·to·ry
di·lem·ma
dil·et·tante
dil·i·gence
dil·ly·dal·ly
di·lute
di·men·sion
di·min·ish
di·min·u·tive
din·er (restaurant; see *dinner*)
di·nette
din·ghy (dinghies)
din·gy
din·ner (meal; see *diner*)
di·no·saur
di·ora·ma
diph·the·ria
diph·thong
di·plo·ma
di·plo·ma·cy
di·rec·tion
di·rec·tor·ate
dirge
dis·abil·i·ty
dis·ad·van·tage
dis·agree
dis·al·low
dis·ap·pear
dis·ap·pear·ance
dis·ap·point
dis·ap·prove
dis·ar·ma·ment
dis·arm·ing
dis·ar·range
dis·ar·ray
dis·as·so·ci·ate
di·sas·ter
di·sas·trous
dis·avow
dis·burse
disc, disk
dis·cern
dis·cern·ible, dis·cern·able

dis·ci·ple
dis·ci·pline
dis·claim·er
dis·clo·sure
dis·com·fort
dis·con·cert·ing
dis·con·nect
dis·con·so·late
dis·con·tin·ue
dis·cor·dant
dis·count
dis·cour·age
dis·cour·te·ous
dis·cov·ery (–er·ies)
dis·creet (showing discernment in
    speech; see *discrete*)
dis·crep·an·cy (–cies)
dis·crete (individually distinct;
    see *discreet*)
dis·cre·tion
dis·crim·i·nate
dis·cus (disk; see *discuss*)
dis·cuss (to talk about; see *discus*)
dis·cus·sion
dis·dain
dis·ease
dis·em·bark
dis·en·chant
dis·en·fran·chise
dis·en·gage
dis·en·tan·gle
dis·grace
dis·guise
dis·gust·ing
dis·har·mo·ny
dis·heart·en
di·shev·el
dis·hon·es·ty
dis·il·lu·sion
dis·in·cline
dis·in·fec·tant
dis·in·her·it
dis·in·te·grate
disk, disc
dis·lodge
dis·mal
dis·miss
dis·obe·di·ent
dis·obey
dis·or·ga·nized
dis·par·age
dis·pa·rate
dis·pas·sion·ate
dis·patch
dis·pel
dis·pens·able
dis·pen·sa·ry (–ries)
dis·pen·sa·tion
dis·perse
dis·plea·sure

dis·pose
dis·pos·sess
dis·pro·por·tion
dis·pute
dis·re·gard
dis·re·pair
dis·re·pute
dis·rupt
dis·sat·is·fy
dis·sect
dis·sem·ble
dis·sem·i·nate
dis·sen·sion, dis·sen·tion
dis·sent
dis·ser·ta·tion
dis·ser·vice
dis·si·dent
dis·sim·i·lar
dis·sim·u·late
dis·si·pate
dis·so·ci·ate
dis·so·lute
dis·solve
dis·so·nance
dis·suade
dis·tain
dis·tance
dis·taste·ful
dis·tem·per
dis·tinct
dis·tin·guish
dis·tor·tion
dis·tract
dis·traught
dis·tress
dis·tri·bu·tion
dis·tur·bance
dis·uni·ty
di·verge
di·verse
di·ver·si·fy
di·ver·si·ty
div·i·dend
di·vine
di·vis·i·ble
di·vi·sion
di·vi·sive
di·vorce
div·ot
di·vulge
doc·ile
dock·et
doc·tor
doc·trine
doc·u·ment
dod·der·ing
dodge
doe (female deer; see *dough*)
dog·ger·el
dog·ma

doi·ly
dole·ful
dol·lar
do·lor·ous
dol·phin
do·main
do·mes·tic
dom·i·nance
dom·i·neer
do·min·ion
dom·i·no
do·nate
don·key
do·nor
doo·dle
dor·mant
dor·mi·to·ry (–ries)
dor·sal
dos·age
dos·sier
dou·ble
doubt
doubt·ful
dough (flour mixture; money; see *doe*)
dough·nut, do·nut
dour
douse, dowse
dow·a·ger
down·load
down·load·able
down·ward
dow·ry (dowries)
dox·ol·o·gy (–gies)
doz·en
draft
drag·net
drag·on
drain
dra·ma
dra·mat·ic
dra·mat·i·cal·ly
drap·ery (–er·ies)
drawl
drea·ry
dredge
driv·el
driz·zle
droll
droop·ing
drop·ping
drought
drow·sy
drudge
drug·gist
drunk·ard
dry
du·al (two parts; see *duel*)
du·bi·ous
duc·tile
dud·geon

due (owing; see *dew*)
du·el (combat; see *dual*)
du·et
duf·fel, duf·fle
dul·cet
dul·ci·mer
dumb·bell
dumb·found, dum·found
dun·ga·ree
dun·geon
du·plex
du·pli·cate
du·plic·i·ty (–ties)
du·ra·ble
du·ra·tion
du·ress
du·ti·ful
dwarf
dwin·dle
dye (color; see *die*)
dy·nam·ic
dy·na·mite
dy·nas·ty (–ties)
dys·en·tery (–ter·ies)
dys·lex·ia

E

ea·ger
ea·gle
ear·ache
ear·li·er
ear·ly
ear·nest
earn·ings
ear·piece
ear·ring
earth
earth·quake
ea·sel
ease·ment
eas·i·ly
east·ern
easy
eau de co·logne (French: cologne)
eaves·drop
eb·o·ny (–nies)
ebul·lient
ec·cen·tric
ec·cen·tric·i·ty
ech·e·lon
echo (ech·oes)
éclair
eclec·tic
eclipse
ecol·o·gy
eco·nom·ic
eco·nom·i·cal
eco·sys·tem

ec·sta·sy (–sies)
ec·stat·ic
ec·ze·ma
edge
edgy
ed·i·ble
edict
ed·i·fi·ca·tion
ed·i·fice
edi·tion
ed·i·tor
ed·i·to·ri·al·ize
ed·u·ca·tion
ee·rie, eery
ef·face
ef·fect (to accomplish; see *affect*)
ef·fem·i·nate
ef·fer·ves·cence
ef·fi·ca·cious
ef·fi·ca·cy (–cies)
ef·fi·cien·cy (–cies)
ef·fi·gy (–gies)
ef·fort·less
ef·fron·tery
ef·fu·sion
egal·i·tar·i·an
ego·cen·tric
ego·tist
egre·gious
eighth
ei·ther
ejac·u·late
elab·o·rate
elapse
elas·tic
ela·tion
el·bow
el·der·ly
elec·tion
elec·tor·al
elec·tric
elec·tro·car·dio·gram
elec·tro·cute
elec·trode
elec·trol·y·sis
elec·tro·mag·net·ic
elec·tron
elec·tron·ic
el·e·gance
el·e·gy (–gies)
el·e·men·ta·ry
el·e·phant
el·e·va·tion
elev·en
elic·it (draw out; see *illicit*)
el·i·gi·ble
elim·i·nate
elite
elix·ir
el·lipse

el·o·cu·tion
elon·gate
elope
el·o·quence
elu·ci·date
elude (avoid; see *allude*)
elu·sive
ema·ci·at·ed
e-mail
em·a·nate
eman·ci·pate
emas·cu·late
em·bar·go
em·bar·ka·tion
em·bar·rass
em·bas·sy (–sies)
em·bel·lish
em·ber
em·bez·zle
em·bit·ter
em·bla·zon
em·blem
em·body
em·brace
em·broi·der
em·broi·dery (–der·ies)
em·broil
em·bryo
em·bry·ol·o·gy
em·bry·on·ic
em·cee (also M.C.)
em·er·ald
emerge
emer·gen·cy (–cies)
emer·i·tus (–i·ti)
em·ery (–er·ies)
em·i·grate (to leave one's country;
    see *immigrate*)
émi·gré, emi·gré
em·i·nence
em·is·sary
emis·sion
emol·lient
emol·u·ment
emo·ti·con
emo·tion
em·pa·thet·ic
em·pa·thy
em·per·or
em·pha·sis
em·pha·size
em·phat·ic
em·pire
em·pir·i·cal
em·ploy·able
em·ploy·ee
em·ploy·ment
em·po·ri·um
emp·ty
em·u·late

emul·si·fy
en·able
en·act·ment
enam·el
en·camp·ment
en·ceph·a·li·tis (en·ceph·a·lit·i·des)
en·chant
en·cir·cle
en·close, in·close
en·clo·sure
en·code
en·com·pass
en·core
en·coun·ter
en·cour·age
en·croach
en·cum·ber
en·cum·brance
en·cyc·li·cal
en·cy·clo·pe·dia
en·dan·ger
en·dear·ment
en·deav·or
en·dem·ic
en·dive
end·less
en·do·crine
en·do·cri·nol·o·gy
en·dorse
en·dow·ment
en·dur·ance
en·dure
en·e·ma
en·e·my (–mies)
en·er·get·ic
en·er·gize
en·er·gy
en·er·vate
en·fran·chise
en·gage
en·gage·ment
en·gen·der
en·gi·neer
en·grave
en·gross
en·gulf
en·hance
enig·ma
en·join
en·joy·ment
en·large·ment
en·light·en·ment
en·list
en·liv·en
en masse
en·mesh
en·mi·ty (–ties)
en·no·ble
enor·mous
enough

en·plane
en·rage
en·rap·ture
en·rich
en·roll·ment
en route
en·sem·ble
en·shrine
en·sign
en·slave
en·sue
en·tail
en·tan·gle
en·ter·prise
en·ter·tain
en·thrall, en·thral
en·throne
en·thu·si·asm
en·tice
en·tire·ly
en·tire·ty (–ties)
en·ti·tle
en·ti·ty (–ties)
en·tomb
en·to·mol·o·gy
en·tou·rage
en·trails
en·trance
en·trant
en·treat
en·trée, en·tree
en·trench
en·tre·pre·neur
en·tre·pre·neur·ial
en·trust
en·try
en·twine
enu·mer·ate
enun·ci·ate
enun·ci·a·tion
en·vel·op (enclose completely;
    see *envelope*)
en·ve·lope (container for letter;
    see *envelop*)
en·vi·able
en·vi·ous
en·vi·ron·ment
en·vi·ron·men·tal
en·vi·ron·men·tal·ism
en·vi·rons
en·vi·sion
en·voy
en·vy
en·zyme
eon
ephem·er·al
ep·ic
ep·i·cure
ep·i·dem·ic
epi·der·mis

ep·i·gram
ep·i·gram·mat·ic
ep·i·lep·sy
ep·i·logue
ep·i·sode
ep·i·taph
ep·i·thet
epit·o·me
equa·ble
equal
equal·ize
equa·nim·i·ty (–ties)
equate
equa·tion
equa·tor
eques·tri·an
equi·dis·tant
equi·lat·er·al
equi·lib·ri·um
equine
equi·noc·tial
equi·nox
equip
equip·ment
eq·ui·ta·ble
eq·ui·ty (–ties)
equiv·a·lent
equiv·o·cate
era
erad·i·cate
eras·er (a device to remove marks;
    see *erasure*)
era·sure (act of erasing; see *eraser*)
er·go (Latin: therefore, hence)
er·mine
erode
erog·e·nous
ero·sion
erot·ic
err
er·rand
er·rant
er·rat·ic
er·ro·ne·ous
er·ror
er·u·dite
erup·tion
es·ca·late
es·ca·la·tor
es·ca·pade
es·cape
es·ca·role
es·chew
es·cort
es·crow
esoph·a·gus
es·o·ter·ic
es·pe·cial·ly
es·pi·o·nage
es·pla·nade

es·pouse
espres·so
es·quire
es·say (noun), es·say (verb)
es·sence
es·sen·tial
es·tab·lish
es·tate
es·teem
es·thet·ic
es·ti·ma·ble
es·ti·mate
es·trange
es·tu·ary (–ar·ies)
et cet·era (Latin: and so forth)
etch·ing
eter·nal
eter·ni·ty (–ties)
ether
ethe·re·al
Ether·net
eth·i·cal
eth·ics
eth·nic
ethos
eth·yl
eti·ol·o·gy
et·i·quette
étude
et·y·mol·o·gy (–gies)
eu·ca·lyp·tus (–ti)
eu·chre
eu·gen·ic
eu·lo·gy (–gies)
eu·nuch
eu·phe·mism
eu·phon·ic
eu·pho·ria
eu·re·ka
eu·tha·na·sia
evac·u·ate
evade
eval·u·ate
ev·a·nes·cence
evan·ge·list
evap·o·rate
eva·sion
even·tu·al·i·ty (–ties)
ev·ery·where
evict
ev·i·dent
evil
evis·cer·ate
evoc·a·tive
evoke
evo·lu·tion
evo·lu·tion·ary
evolve
ex·ac·er·bate
ex·act

ex·act·ly
ex·ag·ger·ate
ex·alt
ex·am·i·na·tion
ex·am·ple
ex·as·per·ate
ex·ca·va·tion
ex·ceed
ex·cel
ex·cel·lent
ex·cel·si·or
ex·cept (leave out; see *accept*)
ex·cep·tion·al
ex·cerpt
ex·cess
ex·ces·sive
ex·change
ex·che·quer
ex·cise
ex·cite·ment
ex·claim
ex·cla·ma·tion
ex·clude
ex·clu·sive
ex·com·mu·ni·cate
ex·cre·ment
ex·cru·ci·at·ing
ex·cur·sion
ex·cus·ably
ex·e·cute
ex·e·cut·able
ex·ec·u·tive
ex·ec·u·tor
ex·em·pla·ry
ex·em·pli·fy
ex·empt
ex·emp·tion
ex·er·cise
ex·ert
ex·ha·la·tion
ex·haust
ex·haus·tion
ex·hib·it
ex·hil·a·rate
ex·hume
ex·i·gen·cy (–cies)
ex·ile
ex·is·tence
ex·is·ten·tial·ism
ex·it
ex·o·dus
ex·on·er·ate
ex·or·bi·tant
ex·or·cise
ex·o·ter·ic
ex·ot·ic
ex·pand
ex·pand·able
ex·panse
ex·pa·tri·ate

ex·pec·tan·cy (–cies)
ex·pec·to·rate
ex·pe·di·en·cy (–cies)
ex·pe·dite
ex·pe·di·tion
ex·pe·di·tious
ex·pel
ex·pend·able
ex·pen·di·ture
ex·pense
ex·pe·ri·ence
ex·per·i·ment
ex·per·i·men·tal
ex·pert
ex·per·tise
ex·pi·ate
ex·pi·ra·tion
ex·plain
ex·plan·a·tory
ex·ple·tive
ex·pli·ca·ble
ex·plic·it
ex·plode
ex·ploi·ta·tion
ex·plore
ex·plor·a·to·ry
ex·plo·sion
ex·po·nent
ex·port (noun), ex·port (verb)
ex·pose (to disclose; see *exposé*)
ex·po·sé (a statement; see *expose*)
ex·po·si·tion
ex·pos·tu·late
ex·po·sure
ex·pound
ex·press
ex·pres·sion
ex·press·way
ex·pro·pri·ate
ex·pul·sion
ex·punge
ex·pur·gate
ex·qui·site
ex·tant
ex·tem·po·ra·ne·ous
ex·tem·po·rize
ex·tend
ex·ten·sion
ex·ten·sive
ex·tent
ex·ten·u·ate
ex·te·ri·or
ex·ter·mi·nate
ex·ter·nal
ex·tinct
ex·tin·guish
ex·tir·pate
ex·tol
ex·tort
ex·tra

ex·tract
ex·tra·cur·ric·u·lar
ex·tra·dite
ex·tra·mar·i·tal
ex·tra·ne·ous
ex·traor·di·nary
ex·trap·o·late
ex·tra·sen·so·ry
ex·tra·ter·res·tri·al
ex·trav·a·gance
ex·treme
ex·trem·i·ty (–ties)
ex·tri·cate
ex·trin·sic
ex·tro·vert, ex·tra·vert
ex·u·ber·ance
ex·u·ber·ant
ex·ude

F

fa·ble
fab·ric
fab·ri·cate
fab·u·lous
fa·cade
face
fac·et
fa·ce·tious
fa·cial
fac·ile
fa·cil·i·tate
fa·cil·i·ta·tor
fa·cil·i·ty (–ties)
fac·sim·i·le
fac·tion
fac·to·ry (–ries)
fac·tu·al
fac·ul·ty (–ties)
Fahr·en·heit
fail·ure
faint (lose consciousness; see *feint*)
fairy
fait ac·com·pli (French: accomplished
    fact)
faith·ful
fak·er
fal·con
fall
fal·la·cious
fal·la·cy (–cies)
fal·li·ble
fal·low
false·ly
fal·set·to
fal·si·fy
fal·ter
fa·mil·iar
fa·mil·iar·i·ty

fa·mil·iar·ize
fam·i·ly (–lies)
fam·ine
fam·ish
fa·mous
fa·nat·ic
fa·nat·i·cism
fan·ci·ful
fan·fare
fan·tasm, phan·tasm
fan·tas·tic
fan·ta·sy (–sies)
farce
far·ci·cal
fare·well
farm·er
far·ther
fas·ci·nate
fas·cism
fash·ion·able
fas·ten
fas·tid·i·ous
fa·tal
fate
fa·ther
fath·om
fa·tigue
fat·ten
fau·cet
fault·less
faun (mythological being; see *fawn*)
fau·na
faux (French: fake)
faux pas (French: a social blunder)
fa·vor·able
fawn (young deer; see *faun*)
fear·ful
fea·si·ble
feast
feat (deed; see *feet*)
feath·er
fea·ture
fed·er·al
fee·ble
feet (plural of foot; see *feat*)
feign
feint (something feigned; see *faint*)
fe·line
fel·low·ship
fel·o·ny (–nies)
fe·male
fem·i·nine
fence
fe·ral
fer·ment
fe·ro·cious
fer·ret
fer·ry (–ries)
fer·tile
fer·til·ize

fer·vent

fer·vid

fer·vor

fes·ti·val

fes·toon

fe·tal

fet·id

fe·tus

feud

feu·dal

fe·ver

few

fi·an·cé (French: engaged man)

fi·an·cée (French: engaged woman)

fi·as·co

fi·ber·glass

fi·bro·my·al·gia

fick·le

fic·tion

fic·ti·tious

fid·dle

fi·del·i·ty (–ties)

fid·get

fi·du·cia·ry (–ries)

field

fiend

fierce

fi·ery

fi·es·ta

fifth

fif·ti·eth

fight

fig·ment

fig·ure

fig·u·rine

fil·a·ment

fil·ial

fil·i·bus·ter

fil·i·gree

fil·let, fi·let

fil·ly (fillies)

film

fil·ter

fi·nal

fi·na·le

fi·nance

fi·nan·cier

fi·nesse

fin·ger·print

fi·nis (French: end)

fin·ish

fi·nite

fir·ma·ment

first

fis·cal

fis·sure

fix·ture

flac·cid

flag·pole

fla·grant

flair (natural aptitude; see *flare*)

flam·boy·ant

fla·min·go

flam·ma·ble

flan·nel

flap·per

flare (unsteady glaring light; see *flair*)

flat·tery (–ter·ies)

flaunt

fla·vor

flaw·less

flax·en

flea (insect; see *flee*)

fledg·ling

flee (to run from; see *flea*)

fleece

flew (past tense of fly; see *flue, flu*)

flex·i·ble

fli·er

flight

flir·ta·tion

float·ing

floc·cu·lent

flock

flog

flood·light

floor·board

flor·al

flo·res·cence

flo·ri·cul·ture

flor·id

flo·rist

flo·ta·tion

flo·til·la

flot·sam

flounce

floun·der

flour (from grain; see *flower*)

flour·ish

flow·chart

flow·er (blossom; see *flour*)

fluc·tu·ate

flu

flue (air channel; see *flew*)

flu·ent

flu·id

fluo·res·cent

fluo·ri·date

fluo·ri·nate

fluo·ro·scope

flute

fly (flies)

fo·cal

fo·cus (–cus·es *or* –ci)

foe

foi·ble

fold·er

fo·liage

fo·lio

folk

fol·li·cle

fol·low

fol·ly (follies)

fo·ment

fon·dle

fon·due, fon·du

food

fool·ish

foot·age

foot·note

for·age

for·ay

for·bear·ance

for·bid·den

force

for·ceps

forc·ible

fore·bear, for·bear

fore·cast

fore·clo·sure

fore·ground

for·eign

fore·man

fore·most

fo·ren·sic

for·est·ry

fore·word (preface; see *forward*)

for·ev·er

for·feit

forg·ery (–ies)

for·get·ful

for·give·ness

for·giv·ing

for·go, fore·go

for·got·ten

fork

for·lorn

form·al·de·hyde

for·mal·i·ty (–ties)

for·mal·ly (following established custom; see *formerly*)

for·mat

for·ma·tion

for·ma·tive

for·mer·ly (at an earlier time; see *formally*)

for·mi·da·ble

for·mu·la (–las *or* –lae)

for·mu·late

for·syth·ia

fort (fortified place; see *forte*)

forte (one's strong point; see *fort*)

forth (forward; see *fourth*)

forth·right

for·ti·eth

for·ti·fi·ca·tion

for·tis·si·mo

for·ti·tude

fort·night

for·tress

for·tu·itous
for·tu·nate
fo·rum
for·ward (in front; see *foreword*)
fos·sil
fos·sil·ize
fos·ter
foul (offensive to the senses; see *fowl*)
foun·da·tion
found·ry (–ries)
foun·tain
four
fourth (numeric order; see *forth*)
fowl (bird; see *foul*)
foy·er
frac·tion
frac·ture
frag·ile
frag·ment
fra·grant
frail
fran·chise
frank·furt·er
frank·in·cense
fran·tic
frappe, frap·pé
fra·ter·ni·ty (–ties)
fraud
fraud·u·lent
fraught
free·dom
free·lance
freeze (turn into ice; see *frieze*)
freight
fre·net·ic, phre·net·ic
fren·zy (fren·zies)
fre·quent (adjective), fre·quent (verb)
fresh·man (–men)
Freud·ian
fri·ar (monk; see *fryer*)
fric·as·see, fric·as·sée
fric·tion
friend
frieze (architectural decoration;
    see *freeze*)
frig·ate
fright·en
fringe
frisky
frit·ter
friv·o·lous
frol·ic
front·age
fron·tier
fron·tis·piece
fro·zen
fru·gal
fru·i·tion
fruit·ful
frus·trate

fry·er (something intended for frying;
    see *friar*)
fuch·sia
fu·el
fu·gi·tive
fugue
ful·crum
ful·fill, ful·fil
ful·some
fu·mi·gate
func·tion·al
fun·da·men·tal
fu·ner·al
fu·ne·re·al
fun·nel
fu·ri·ous
furl
fur·lough
fur·nace
fur·ni·ture
fu·ror
fur·ri·er
fur·row
fur·ther
fur·tive
fuse
fu·se·lage
fus·ible
fu·sion
fu·tile
fu·til·i·ty (–ties)
fu·ture
fu·tur·is·tic

G

gab·er·dine
gad·get
gai·ety (–eties)
gain·ful·ly
gait (manner of walking; see *gate*)
ga·la
gal·axy (gal·ax·ies)
gal·lant
gal·lery (–ries)
gal·ley
gall·ing
gal·lon
gal·lop
ga·lore
ga·losh (–es)
gal·lows
gal·va·nize
gam·bit
gam·ble
game·keep·er
gam·ut
gan·der
gan·gli·on (gan·glia)

gan·grene
ga·rage
gar·bage
gar·ble
gar·den·er
gar·de·nia
gar·gan·tuan
gar·goyle
gar·ish
gar·land
gar·ment
gar·ner
gar·nish
gar·nish·ee
gar·ri·son
gas·eous
gas·ket
gas·o·line, gas·o·lene
gas·tric
gas·tron·o·my
gate (opening in wall *or* fence; see *gait*)
gath·er·ing
gauche
gau·dy
gauge
gaunt
gaunt·let
gauze
gav·el
ga·ze·bo
ga·zelle
ga·zette
gei·sha
gel·a·tin, gel·a·tine
gene
ge·ne·al·o·gy (–gies)
gen·er·al·i·ty (–ties)
gen·er·ate
gen·er·a·tion
gen·er·a·tor
ge·ner·ic
gen·er·ous
genes (the basic physical unit
    of heredity; see *jeans*)
gen·e·sis (–e·ses)
ge·net·ic
ge·net·i·cal·ly
ge·nial
gen·i·tal
ge·nius (–nius·es *or* –nii)
geno·cide
genre
gen·teel
gen·tile
gen·til·i·ty (–ties)
gen·tle·man (–men)
gen·try
gen·u·flect
gen·u·ine
ge·og·ra·phy (–phies)

ge·ol·o·gy (–gies)
ge·om·e·try (–tries)
ge·ra·ni·um
ge·ri·at·rics
ger·mane
ger·mi·cide
ger·mi·na·tion
ger·on·tol·o·gy
gest
ges·ta·tion
ges·tic·u·late
ges·ture
gey·ser
ghast·ly
ghet·to (ghettos or ghettoes)
ghoul·ish
gi·ant
gib·ber·ish
gibe
gib·lets
gift
gi·gan·tic
gig·o·lo
gild (to overlay with a thin covering of gold or something similar; see *gilt*)
gilt (covered with gold, or with something that resembles gold; see *gild*)
gim·mick
gin·ger
gi·raffe
gird·er
gir·dle
girth
gist
giz·zard
gla·cial
gla·cier
glad·i·a·tor
glad·i·o·la
glam·or·ous, glam·our·ous
glam·our, glam·or
glan·du·lar
glass·ware
glau·co·ma
gla·zier
glib
glim·mer
glimpse
glis·ten
glitch
glob·al
glob·al·i·za·tion
glob·u·lar
gloomy
glo·ri·ous
glos·sa·ry (–ries)
glossy (gloss·ies)
glove
glu·cose

glue
glut·ton
glyc·er·in, glyc·er·ine
gnarl
gnash
gnat
gnaw
gnome
gnu (African antelope; see *knew* and *new*)
goal
gob·let
gog·gles
goi·ter
gold·en
golf (a game; see *gulf*)
gon·do·la
good·will
go·pher
gor·geous
go·ril·la (an ape; see *guerrilla*)
gos·sa·mer
gos·sip
gouge
gou·lash
gourd
gour·met
gout
gov·ern·ment
gov·er·nor
gra·cious
gra·da·tion
gra·di·ent
grad·u·al
grad·u·ate
grad·u·a·tion
graph·ics
grain
gram·mar
gram·mat·i·cal·ly
gra·na·ry (–ries)
gran·deur
grand·fa·ther
gran·di·ose
grand·moth·er
gran·ite
grant
gran·u·late
graph·ic
graph·ite
grap·ple
grate (rasp noisily; see *great*)
grate·ful
grat·i·fy
grat·i·tude
gra·tu·itous
gra·tu·ity (–i·ties)
grav·i·tate
grav·i·ty (–ties)
great (large; see *grate*)

greedy
gre·gar·i·ous
grem·lin
gre·nade
gren·a·dine
grey·hound
grid·dle
grid·iron
griev·ance
griev·ous
gri·mace
grime
grippe
gris·ly (inspiring horror; see *grizzly*)
griz·zly (bear; see *grisly*)
groan
gro·cery (–cer·ies)
gro·tesque
grot·to (–toes)
group
grouse (grouse or grouses)
grov·el
grudge
gru·el
gru·el·ing, gru·el·ling
grue·some
grum·ble
grun·gy
guar·an·tee (assurance of quality; see *guaranty*)
guar·an·ty (something given as security; see *guarantee*)
guard
guard·ian
gu·ber·na·to·ri·al
guer·ril·la (one who engages in irregular warfare; see *gorilla*)
guess
guest
guid·ance
guild
guile
guil·lo·tine
guilt
guise
gui·tar
gulf (part of an ocean, a chasm; see *golf*)
gull·ible, gull·able
gul·ly (–lies)
gur·gle
gu·ru
gut·tur·al
guz·zle
gym·na·si·um
gym·nast
gy·ne·col·o·gy
gyp·sum
gyp·sy

gy·rate
gy·ro·scope

H

ha·be·as cor·pus (Latin: legal writ
    to bring a person before
    a court)
hab·er·dash·ery (–er·ies)
hab·it·able
hab·i·tat
ha·bit·u·al
hack·ney
had·dock
hag·gard
hag·gle
hail (greet; see *hale*)
hair (threadlike outgrowth on skin;
    see *hare*)
hal·cy·on
hale (free from disease; see *hail*)
half
hal·i·but
hal·i·to·sis
hal·low
Hal·low·een
hal·lu·ci·na·tion
hal·lu·ci·no·gen
halve
ham·burg·er
ham·mer
ham·mock
ham·per
hand·i·cap
hand·i·craft
hand·ker·chief (–chiefs, chieves)
han·dle
hand·some (pleasing appearance;
    see *hansom*)
handy
han·gar (place for housing aircraft;
    see *hanger*)
hang·er (device on which something is
    hung; see *hangar*)
han·som (cab; see *handsome*)
hap·haz·ard
hap·pen
hap·pi·ness
hap·py
ha·rangue
ha·rass
har·bin·ger
har·bor
hard·ly
hard·ship
har·dy
hard·ware
hare (animal resembling rabbit;
    see *hair*)
har·em

harm·less
har·mon·ic
har·mo·ni·ous
har·mo·ny (–nies)
har·ness
har·poon
harp·si·chord
har·row·ing
har·ry
har·vest
hash·ish
has·sock
hatch·et
hate·ful
ha·tred
haugh·ty
haul
haunch
haunt
ha·ven
hav·oc
haw·thorn
haz·ard·ous
haze
ha·zel
head·ache
head·quar·ters
head·set
heal (restore to health; see *heel*)
heal·er
health·ful
healthy
hear (listen; see *here*)
hear·ken
hearse
heart
heart·ache
hearth
heart·i·ly
heat
heath
heath·er
heav·en
heavy
heck·le
hec·tic
hedge
he·do·nism
heed·less
heel (part of foot; see *heal*)
hefty
heif·er
height
hei·nous
heir
heir·loom
heist
he·li·cop·ter
he·li·um
help·ful

hemi·sphere
hem·lock
he·mo·phil·ia
hem·or·rhage
hem·or·rhoid
hence·forth
hen·na
hep·a·ti·tis
her·ald
herb
herb·al
herb·al·ist
Her·cu·le·an
here (in this place; see *hear*)
he·red·i·tary
her·e·sy (–sies)
her·e·tic
her·i·tage
her·maph·ro·dite
her·met·ic
her·mit
her·nia
her·o·in (drug; see *heroine*)
her·o·ine (central figure in drama;
    see *heroin*)
her·on
her·ring·bone
hes·i·tate
het·ero·dox
het·ero·ge·neous
het·ero·sex·u·al
hew (to cut by blows; see *hue*)
hexa·gon
hex·am·e·ter
hi·a·tus
hi·ba·chi
hi·ber·nate
hi·bis·cus
hic·cough, hic·cup
hid·eous
hi·er·ar·chy (–chies)
hi·ero·glyph·ic
high·er (more elevated, taller; see *hire*)
hi·jack
hi·lar·i·ous
hin·drance
hinge
hip·po·drome
hip·po·pot·a·mus (–mus·es *or* –mi)
hire (employ, wage; see *higher*)
his·ta·mine
his·to·ri·an
his·tor·i·cal
his·to·ry (–ries)
his·tri·on·ic
hith·er·to
hives
hoard
hoarse
hoax

hob·ble
hock·ey
ho·cus-po·cus
hodge·podge
hoe
hoist
ho·li·ness
ho·lis·tic
hol·lan·daise
hol·low
ho·lo·caust
ho·lo·gram
ho·lo·graph
hol·ster
hom·age
home·ly
ho·meo·path
ho·me·op·a·thy
ho·mi·cide
hom·i·ly (–lies)
ho·mo·ge·neous
ho·mog·e·nize
hom·onym
ho·mo·sex·u·al
hon·es·ty (–ties)
hon·ey
hon·or
hon·o·rar·i·um
hon·or·ary (–ar·ies)
hood·lum
hoo·li·gan
hope
hop·ing (longing for; see *hopping*)
hop·ping (jumping; see *hoping*)
horde
ho·ri·zon
hor·i·zon·tal
hor·mone
horo·scope
hor·ren·dous
hor·ri·ble
hor·rid
hor·ror
hors d'oeuvre (French: appetizers)
horse
hor·ti·cul·ture
ho·siery
hos·pi·tal
hos·tage
hos·tel
host·ess
hos·tile
ho·tel
hour (time; see *our*)
house·hold
hov·el
hov·er
howl
huck·le·ber·ry (–ries)
huck·ster

hue (complexion, see *hew*)
huge
hu·mane
hu·man·i·tar·i·an
hu·man·i·ty
hu·man·ize
hum·ble
hu·mid
hu·mi·dor
hu·mil·i·ate
hu·mil·i·ty
hu·mor
hu·mor·ous
hu·mus
hun·dredth
hun·ger
hur·dle
hurl
hur·ri·cane
hur·ried
hur·tle
hus·band
hus·ky (–kies)
hus·tle
hy·a·cinth
hy·brid
hy·dran·gea
hy·drant
hy·drate
hy·drau·lic
hy·dro·chlo·ric
hy·dro·elec·tric
hy·dro·gen
hy·drom·e·ter
hy·dro·pho·bia
hy·drox·ide
hy·giene
hy·gien·ic
hy·men
hymn
hy·per·bo·le
hy·per·ten·sion
hy·per·ven·ti·la·tion
hy·phen
hy·phen·ate
hyp·no·sis (–ses)
hyp·no·tism
hy·po·chon·dria
hy·poc·ri·sy (–sies)
hy·po·crite
hy·po·der·mic
hy·pot·e·nuse, hy·poth·e·nuse
hy·poth·e·sis (–ses)
hy·poth·e·size
hy·po·thet·i·cal
hys·ter·ec·to·my (–mies)
hys·te·ria

I

ice·berg
ice floe
ici·cle
ic·ing
icy
icon
icon·o·clast
idea
ide·al
iden·ti·cal
iden·ti·fi·ca·tion
iden·ti·fy
ide·ol·o·gy, ide·al·o·gy (–gies)
id·i·o·cy (–cies)
id·i·om
id·i·o·mat·ic
id·i·o·syn·cra·sy (–sies)
id·i·ot
idle (not occupied; see *idol, idyll*)
idol (symbolic object of worship;
    see *idle, idyll*)
idol·a·try (–tries)
idol·ize
idyll, idyl (narrative poem; see *idle,
    idol*)
ig·loo
ig·ne·ous
ig·nite
ig·ni·tion
ig·no·ble
ig·no·min·i·ous
ig·no·rance
ig·nore
igua·na
il·le·gal
il·leg·i·ble
il·le·git·i·mate
ill-got·ten
il·lib·er·al
il·lic·it (not permitted; see *elicit*)
il·lit·er·ate
ill·ness
il·log·i·cal
il·lu·mi·na·tion
il·lu·sion (misleading
    image; see *allusion*)
il·lu·so·ry
il·lus·trate
il·lus·tra·tion
il·lus·tri·ous
im·age
imag·in·able
imag·i·na·tive
imag·ine
im·bal·ance
im·be·cile
im·bibe

im·bue
im·i·ta·tion
im·i·ta·tive
im·mac·u·late
im·ma·nent (inherent; see *imminent*)
im·ma·te·ri·al
im·ma·ture
im·mea·sur·able
im·me·di·ate
im·me·mo·ri·al
im·mense
im·merse
im·mer·sion
im·mi·grate (to come into a country;
    see *emigrate*)
im·mi·nent (ready to take place;
    see *immanent*)
im·mo·bile
im·mod·er·ate
im·mod·est
im·mo·late
im·mor·al
im·mor·tal
im·mov·able
im·mune
im·mu·ni·ty (–ties)
im·pact (noun), im·pact (verb)
im·pair
im·pale
im·pal·pa·ble
im·par·tial
im·pass·able, im·pas·si·ble
im·passe
im·pas·sioned
im·pas·sive
im·pa·tience
im·peach
im·pec·ca·ble
im·pede
im·ped·i·ment
im·pel
im·pend·ing
im·pen·e·tra·ble
im·per·a·tive
im·per·cep·ti·ble
im·per·fect
im·pe·ri·al
im·pe·ri·ous
im·per·ish·able
im·per·ma·nence
im·per·me·able
im·per·mis·si·ble
im·per·son·al
im·per·son·ate
im·per·ti·nent
im·per·vi·ous
im·pet·u·ous
im·pe·tus
im·pi·e·ty (–ties)
im·pinge

im·pi·ous
imp·ish
im·pla·ca·ble
im·plant
im·plau·si·ble
im·ple·ment
im·pli·cate
im·pli·ca·tion
im·plic·it
im·plore
im·ply
im·po·lite
im·pol·i·tic
im·pon·der·a·ble
im·port
im·por·tance
im·pose
im·po·si·tion
im·pos·si·bil·i·ty (–ties)
im·pos·si·ble
im·pos·tor, im·pos·ter
im·pos·ture
im·po·tent
im·pound
im·pov·er·ish
im·prac·ti·ca·ble
im·prac·ti·cal
im·pre·cate
im·pre·cise
im·preg·na·ble
im·pre·sa·rio
im·press
im·pres·sive
im·pri·ma·tur
im·print
im·pris·on·ment
im·prob·a·ble
im·promp·tu
im·prop·er
im·pro·pri·e·ty (–ties)
im·prove·ment
im·prov·i·dent
im·pro·vise
im·pru·dent
im·pu·dent
im·pugn
im·pulse
im·pu·ni·ty (–ties)
im·pu·ri·ty (–ties)
in·abil·i·ty (–ties)
in ab·sen·tia
in·ac·ces·si·ble
in·ac·cu·ra·cy (–cies)
in·ac·tive
in·ad·e·qua·cy (–cies)
in·ad·e·quate
in·ad·mis·si·ble
in·ad·ver·tent
in·ad·vis·able
in·alien·able

in·al·ter·able
inane
in·an·i·mate
in·ap·pli·ca·ble
in·ap·pro·pri·ate
in·ar·tic·u·late
in·ar·tis·tic
in·at·ten·tive
in·au·di·ble
in·au·gu·ral
in·au·gu·rate
in·aus·pi·cious
in·born
in·cal·cu·la·ble
in·can·des·cent
in·can·ta·tion
in·ca·pa·ble
in·ca·pac·i·tate
in·car·cer·ate
in·car·nate
in·cau·tious
in·cen·di·ary (–ar·ies)
in·cense
in·cen·tive
in·cep·tion
in·ces·sant
in·ci·den·tal·ly
in·cin·er·ate
in·cip·i·ent
in·cise
in·ci·sion
in·ci·sive
in·cite (to stir up; see *insight*)
in·clem·ent
in·cli·na·tion
in·cline
in·close, en·close
in·clude
in·cog·ni·to
in·co·her·ent
in·com·bus·ti·ble
in·come
in·com·men·su·ra·ble
in·com·pa·ra·ble
in·com·pat·i·ble
in·com·pe·tence
in·com·plete
in·com·pre·hen·si·ble
in·con·ceiv·able
in·con·clu·sive
in·con·gru·ous
in·con·se·quen·tial
in·con·sid·er·ate
in·con·sist·ent
in·con·sol·able
in·con·spic·u·ous
in·con·stant
in·con·test·able
in·con·tro·vert·ible
in·con·ve·nient

in·cor·po·rate
in·cor·rect
in·cor·ri·gi·ble
in·cor·rupt·ible
in·crease
in·creas·ing·ly
in·cred·i·ble
in·cred·i·bly
in·cre·du·li·ty
in·cred·u·lous
in·cre·ment
in·crim·i·nate
in·cu·bate
in·cu·ba·tor
in·cu·bus (–bus·es *or* –bi)
in·cul·cate
in·cum·bent
in·cur
in·cur·able
in·debt·ed
in·de·cent
in·de·ci·pher·able
in·de·ci·sion
in·de·fen·si·ble
in·de·fin·able
in·def·i·nite
in·del·i·ble
in·del·i·cate
in·dem·ni·fy
in·den·ta·tion
in·de·pen·dent
in·de·scrib·able
in·de·struc·ti·ble
in·de·ter·min·able
in·dex (in·dex·es *or* in·di·ces)
in·di·cate
in·dict (charge with offence; see *indite*)
in·dif·fer·ent
in·dig·e·nous
in·di·gent
in·di·gest·ible
in·di·ges·tion
in·dig·nant
in·dig·ni·ty (–ties)
in·di·go (–gos *or* –goes)
in·di·rect
in·dis·creet
in·dis·cre·tion
in·dis·crim·i·nate
in·dis·pens·able
in·dis·pose
in·dis·put·able
in·dis·sol·u·ble
in·dis·tinct
in·dis·tin·guish·able
in·dite (to put down in writing; see *indict*)
in·di·vid·u·al
in·di·vid·u·al·i·ty
in·di·vis·i·ble

in·doc·tri·nate
in·do·lence
in·dom·i·ta·ble
in·du·bi·ta·ble
in·duce
in·duct
in·dulge
in·dul·gence
in·dus·tri·al·ist
in·dus·try (–tries)
in·ebri·ate
in·ed·i·ble
in·ef·fa·ble
in·ef·fec·tive
in·ef·fec·tu·al
in·ef·fi·cien·cy (–cies)
in·elas·tic
in·el·i·gi·ble
in·ept
in·ep·ti·tude
in·equal·i·ty (–ties)
in·eq·ui·ta·ble
in·eq·ui·ty
in·ert
in·er·tia
in·es·cap·able
in·es·ti·ma·ble
in·ev·i·ta·ble
in·ex·cus·able
in·ex·haust·ible
in·ex·o·ra·ble
in·ex·pe·di·ent
in·ex·pen·sive
in·ex·pe·ri·enced
in·ex·pert
in·ex·pli·ca·ble
in·ex·press·ible
in·ex·tin·guish·able
in·ex·tri·ca·ble
in·fal·li·ble
in·fa·mous
in·fan·cy (–cies)
in·fan·tile
in·fan·try (–tries)
in·fat·u·a·tion
in·fec·tion
in·fec·tious
in·fer
in·fer·ence
in·fe·ri·or·i·ty (–ties)
in·fer·nal
in·fer·no (–nos)
in·ferred
in·fer·tile
in·fi·del·i·ty (–ties)
in·field
in·fil·trate
in·fi·nite
in·fin·i·tes·i·mal
in·fin·i·tive

in·fin·i·ty (–ties)
in·fir·ma·ry (–ries)
in·fir·mi·ty (–ties)
in·flame
in·flam·ma·ble
in·flam·ma·tion
in·flate
in·fla·tion
in·flec·tion
in·flex·i·ble
in·flict
in·flu·ence
in·flu·en·za
in·flux
in·for·mal
in·for·ma·tion
in·form·er
in·frac·tion
in·fra·red
in·fra·struc·ture
in·fre·quent
in·fringe
in·fu·ri·ate
in·fuse
in·fu·sion
in·ge·nious (clever; see *ingenuous*)
in·ge·nu·i·ty (–ities)
in·gen·u·ous (showing childlike simplicity; see *ingenious*)
in·gest
in·glo·ri·ous
in·got
in·grained
in·grate
in·gra·ti·ate
in·grat·i·tude
in·gre·di·ent
in·gress
in·hab·it
in·hab·i·tant
in·ha·la·tion
in·hale
in·her·ent
in·her·i·tance
in·hib·it
in·hi·bi·tion
in·hos·pi·ta·ble
in·hu·man
in·hu·mane
in·im·i·cal
in·im·i·ta·ble
in·iq·ui·ty (–ties)
ini·tial
ini·ti·ate
ini·tia·tive
in·jec·tion
in·ju·di·cious
in·junc·tion
in·jure
in·ju·ri·ous

in·ju·ry (–ries)
in·jus·tice
in·kling
in·land
in·let
in·mate
in me·mo·ri·am
in·nate
in·ning
in·no·cent
in·noc·u·ous
in·no·vate
in·no·va·tor
in·nu·en·do (–dos *or* –does)
in·nu·mer·a·ble
in·oc·u·late
in·of·fen·sive
in·op·er·a·ble
in·op·er·a·tive
in·op·por·tune
in·or·di·nate
in·or·gan·ic
in·quest
in·quire
in·qui·si·tion
in·quis·i·tive
in·road
in·sane
in·san·i·ty (–ties)
in·sa·tia·ble
in·scribe
in·scrip·tion
in·scru·ta·ble
in·sec·ti·cide
in·se·cure
in·sem·i·na·tion
in·sen·sate
in·sen·si·ble
in·sen·si·tive
in·sep·a·ra·ble
in·sert
in·side
in·sid·i·ous
in·sight (act of apprehending inner
    nature of things; see *incite*)
in·sig·nia, in·sig·ne (–nia *or* –ni·as)
in·sig·nif·i·cant
in·sin·cere
in·sin·u·ate
in·sip·id
in·sist
in·sis·tence
in·sole
in·so·lent
in·sol·u·ble
in·solv·able
in·sol·vent
in·som·nia
in·spec·tor
in·spi·ra·tion

in·sta·bil·i·ty
in·stall, in·stal
in·stant
in·stan·ta·neous
in·stead
in·step
in·sti·gate
in·stinct
in·sti·tute
in·struct
in·stru·ment
in·sub·or·di·nate
in·sub·stan·tial
in·suf·fer·able
in·suf·fi·cient
in·su·lar
in·su·late
in·su·lin
in·sult
in·su·per·a·ble
in·sup·port·able
in·sup·press·ible
in·sur·ance
in·sur·gent
in·sur·mount·able
in·sur·rec·tion
in·tact
in·tan·gi·ble
in·te·ger
in·te·gral
in·te·grate
in·teg·ri·ty
in·tel·lect
in·tel·li·gence
in·tel·li·gent·sia
in·tel·li·gi·ble
in·tem·per·ate
in·tend
in·tense
in·ten·tion·al
in·ter
in·ter·ac·tion
in·ter·cede
in·ter·cept
in·ter·ces·sion
in·ter·change·able
in·ter·com·mu·ni·ca·tion
in·ter·con·nect
in·ter·course
in·ter·de·part·men·tal
in·ter·dict
in·ter·est
in·ter·fere
in·ter·fer·ence
in·ter·im
in·te·ri·or
in·ter·ject
in·ter·line
in·ter·lin·ear
in·ter·lock

in·ter·lop·er
in·ter·lude
in·ter·mar·ry
in·ter·me·di·ary (–ar·ies)
in·ter·me·di·ate
in·ter·mez·zo (–zi *or* –zos)
in·ter·mi·na·ble
in·ter·mis·sion
in·ter·mit·tent
in·ter·mix
in·tern (noun), in·tern (verb)
in·ter·nal
in·ter·nal·ize
in·ter·na·tion·al
In·ter·net
in·tern·ment
in·ter·pose
in·ter·pret
in·ter·pre·tive
in·ter·ra·cial
in·ter·ro·gate
in·ter·rupt
in·ter·sect
in·ter·ses·sion
in·ter·sperse
in·ter·state
in·ter·stel·lar
in·ter·stice
in·ter·val
in·ter·vene
in·ter·view
in·tes·tine
in·ti·ma·cy (–cies)
in·ti·mate
in·tim·i·date
in·tol·er·a·ble
in·tol·er·ant
in·to·na·tion
in·tox·i·cate
in·trac·ta·ble
in·tra·mu·ral
in·tran·si·gent
in·tran·si·tive
in·tra·ve·nous
in·trep·id
in·tri·ca·cy (–cies)
in·tri·cate
in·trigue
in·trin·sic
in·tro·duce
in·tro·spec·tion
in·tro·ver·sion
in·tro·vert
in·tru·sion
in·tu·i·tion
in·tu·i·tive
in·un·date
in·val·id
in·valu·able
in·vari·able

in·va·sion
in·vec·tive
in·veigh
in·ven·tion
in·ven·to·ry (–ries)
in·verse
in·ver·te·brate
in·ves·ti·ga·tor
in·ves·ti·ture
in·ves·tor
in·vet·er·ate
in·vig·o·rate
in·vin·ci·ble
in·vi·o·la·ble
in·vis·i·ble
in·vi·ta·tion
in·vo·ca·tion
in·voice
in·voke
in·vol·un·tary
in·volve
in·vul·ner·a·ble
in·ward
io·dine
ion
io·ta
iras·ci·ble
irate
ire
ir·i·des·cence
iris (iris·es *or* iri·des)
irk·some
iron
ir·ra·di·a·tion
ir·ra·tio·nal
ir·rec·on·cil·able
ir·re·cov·er·able
ir·re·deem·able
ir·re·duc·ible
ir·re·fut·able
ir·reg·u·lar
ir·rel·e·van·cy (–cies)
ir·rel·e·vant
ir·rep·a·ra·ble
ir·re·place·able
ir·re·proach·able
ir·re·sist·ible
ir·res·o·lute
ir·re·spec·tive
ir·re·spon·si·ble
ir·re·triev·able
ir·rev·er·ent
ir·re·vers·ible
ir·rev·o·ca·ble
ir·ri·gate
ir·ri·ta·ble
ir·ri·tate
is·land
isle
iso·late

isos·ce·les
iso·tope
is·sue
ital·ic
item·ize
itin·er·ary (–ar·ies)
it's
its
ivo·ry (–ries)
ivy (ivies)

J

jab·ber
jack·et
jade
jag·ged
jag·uar
jail·er, jail·or
ja·lopy (ja·lop·ies)
jam·bo·ree
jan·gle
jan·i·tor
jar·gon
jas·mine, jes·sa·mine
jaun·dice
jaunt
jav·e·lin
jeal·ous
jeans (denim pants; see *genes*)
jeer
jel·ly (jellies)
jeop·ar·dize
jer·sey
jest
jet-pro·pelled
jet·ti·son
jet·ty (jetties)
jew·el·ry
jibe, gibe
jig·ger
jit·ney
jock·ey
joc·u·lar
jog·ging
join·ing
joint
jos·tle
jour·nal
jour·nal·ism
jour·ney
joust
jo·vial
joy·ful
joy·ous
ju·bi·lant
ju·bi·lee
judge
judg·ment, judge·ment
ju·di·ca·ture

ju·di·cial
ju·di·cia·ry
ju·di·cious
jug·gler
jug·u·lar
juicy
ju·jit·su, ju·jut·su, jiu·jit·su
juke·box
ju·lep
ju·li·enne
jum·ble
jum·bo
jump
junc·tion
junc·ture
jun·gle
ju·nior
ju·ni·per
jun·ket
jun·ta
ju·ris·dic·tion
ju·ris·pru·dence
ju·rist
ju·ror
jus·tice
jus·ti·fi·able
jus·ti·fi·ca·tion
ju·ve·nile
jux·ta·pose

K

ka·lei·do·scope
kan·ga·roo
kar·a·kul
kar·at, car·at
ka·ra·te
kay·ak
kayo
keel
keen
keen·ness
keep·sake
kelp
ken·nel
kept
ker·chief (–chieves)
ker·nel (inner part of a seed;
    see *colonel*)
ker·o·sene, ker·o·sine
ketch·up, cat·sup
ket·tle
kha·ki
ki·bosh
kid·nap
kid·nap·per
kid·ney
kiln
ki·lo·gram
kilo·li·ter

ki·lo·me·ter
kilo·watt
kil·ter
ki·mo·no
kin·der·gar·ten
kin·dle
kind·li·ness
kin·dling
kin·dred
ki·ne·scope
kin·es·thet·ic
ki·net·ic
ki·osk
kitch·en·ette
klep·to·ma·ni·ac
knack
knap·sack
knave (tricky fellow; see *nave*)
knead (press into a mass; see *need*)
knee
kneel
knell
knew (past tense of know; see *gnu, new*)
knife (knives)
knight (feudal nobleman; see *night*)
knob
knoll
knot
knowl·edge
knowl·edge·able
knuck·le
ko·ala
ko·sher
ku·dos
kum·quat

L

la·bel
la·bor
lab·o·ra·to·ry (–ries)
la·bo·ri·ous
lab·y·rinth
lac·er·ate
lack·ey
lack·lus·ter
la·con·ic
lac·quer
lad·der
la·den
lading
la·dle
la·ger
lag·gard
la·gniappe
la·goon
lair
lais·sez-faire (French: doctrine of individual freedom)

la·ity
lam·baste, lam·bast
lame (cripple; see *lamé*)
lamé (fabric; see *lame*)
la·men·ta·ble
lam·i·nate
lamp·light
lam·poon
lance
land·lord
lan·guage
lan·guid
lan·guish
lan·guor
lan·o·lin
lan·tern
lan·yard
la·pel
lap·i·dary (–dar·ies)
lapse
lar·ce·ny (–nies)
large
lar·gess, lar·gesse
lar·i·at
lar·va (–vae)
lar·yn·gi·tis
lar·ynx (lar·ynxes)
la·sa·gna
las·civ·i·ous
la·ser
las·si·tude
las·so (las·sos *or* las·soes)
la·tent
lat·er·al
la·tex (la·ti·ces *or* la·tex·es)
lath (thin strip of wood; see *lathe*)
lathe (shaping machine; see *lath*)
lat·i·tude
la·trine
lat·ter
laud
lau·da·to·ry
laugh
laugh·able
launch
laun·der
laun·dry (–dries)
lau·re·ate
lau·rel
lav·a·to·ry (–ries)
lav·en·der
lav·ish
law·ful
law·ful·ly
lawn
law·yer
lax·a·tive
lax·ity
lay·ette
lay·per·son

la·zy
leach (to dissolve out; see *leech*)
lead
lead·er
leaf·let
league
leak (to escape through an opening; see *leek*)
lean (to incline; see *lien*)
learn
lease
leash
least
leath·er
leave
leav·en
lech·er
lech·er·ous
lec·tern
lec·ture
led·ger
leech (bloodsucking worm; see *leach*)
leek (herb; see *leak*)
leer
leery
lee·ward
lee·way
left
leg·a·cy (–cies)
le·gal
le·gal·i·ty (–ties)
leg·ate
le·ga·to
leg·end
leg·end·ary
leg·gy
leg·horn
leg·i·ble
le·gion
le·gion·naire
leg·is·late
leg·is·la·tive
leg·is·la·ture
le·git·i·ma·cy
le·git·i·mate
le·gume
lei·sure
lem·ming
length
length·en
le·nient
len·til
leop·ard
le·o·tard
lep·er
lep·re·chaun
lep·ro·sy
les·bi·an
le·sion
les·see

les·son
les·sor
le·thal
le·thar·gic
let·ter
let·tuce
leu·ke·mia
lev·ee (embankment; see *levy*)
lev·el
lev·i·ty
levy (assessment; see *levee*)
lewd
lex·i·cog·ra·phy
lex·i·con
li·a·ble
li·ai·son
li·ar
li·ba·tion
li·bel
lib·er·al
lib·er·ate
lib·er·tar·i·an
lib·er·ty (–ties)
li·brar·i·an
li·brary (–brar·ies)
li·bret·to (–tos *or* –ti)
li·cense, li·cence
li·cen·tious
li·chen
lic·o·rice
lie (untruth; see *lye*)
lien (payment of debt; see *lean*)
lieu
lieu·ten·ant
life (lives)
lig·a·ment
lig·a·ture
light·ning
like·li·hood
li·lac
lily (lil·ies)
limb
lim·bo
lime·light
lim·er·ick
lim·i·ta·tion
lim·ou·sine
lim·pid
lin·e·al
lin·e·ar
lin·ge·rie
lin·go (lingoes)
lin·gual
lin·guis·tic
lin·i·ment
lin·ing
li·no·leum
lin·seed
lin·tel
liq·ue·fy

li·queur
liq·ui·date
li·quor
lis·ten
lit·a·ny (–nies)
li·ter
lit·er·a·cy
lit·er·al
lit·er·al·ly
lit·er·ary
lit·er·ate
lit·er·a·ture
lith·o·graph
lit·i·gant
lit·i·gate
lit·i·ga·tion
lit·mus
lit·tle
li·tur·gi·cal
lit·ur·gy (–gies)
liv·able, live·able
live·li·hood
live·li·ness
live·ly
liv·er
liv·er·wurst
live·stock
liv·id
liz·ard
lla·ma
loan
loath (unwilling, reluctant; see *loathe*)
loathe (dislike greatly; see *loath*)
lob·by (lobbies)
lob·ster
lo·cal (not general *or* widespread; see *locale*)
lo·cale (place related to a particular event; see *local*)
lo·cate
lock·et
lo·co·mo·tion
lo·cust
lodge
log·a·rithm
log·i·cal
lo·gis·tics
lo·gy, log·gy
loi·ter
lol·li·pop, lol·ly·pop
lone·li·ness
lone·ly
lone·some
lon·gev·i·ty
lon·gi·tude
lore
loose
loot (something taken by force; see *lute*)
lop·sid·ed

lo·qua·cious
lose
lo·tion
lot·tery (–ter·ies)
lo·tus, lo·tos
loud
lounge
lou·ver, lou·vre
lov·able, love·able
love·ly
loy·al
loz·enge
lu·bri·cate
lu·cid
lu·cid·i·ty
luck·i·ly
lu·cra·tive
lu·di·crous
lug·gage
lull
lum·ba·go
lum·ber
lu·mi·nary (–nar·ies)
lum·mox
lu·na·cy (–cies)
lu·nar
lu·na·tic
lun·cheon
lun·cheon·ette
lunge
lurch
lu·rid
lurk
lus·cious
lus·trous
lute (musical instrument; see *loot*)
lux·u·ri·ous
lux·u·ry (–ries)
ly·ce·um
lye (a highly concentrated aqueous solution; see *lie*)
lymph
lynch
lynx (lynx *or* lynx·es)
lyre
lyr·ic

M

ma·ca·bre
mac·ad·am
mac·a·ro·ni
mac·a·roon
mac·er·ate
ma·chete
mach·i·na·tion
ma·chine
ma·chin·ery
ma·chin·ist
mack·er·el

mack·i·naw
mac·ro·bi·ot·ic
mac·ro·cosm
mac·ro·scop·ic
mad·am, ma·dame
mad·den·ing
ma·de·moi·selle (ma·de·moi·selles *or* mes·de·moi·selles)
ma·dras
mad·ri·gal
mael·strom
mae·stro (mae·stros *or* mae·stri)
mag·a·zine
ma·gen·ta
mag·got
mag·i·cal
ma·gi·cian
mag·is·trate
mag·nan·i·mous
mag·nate (person of rank and power; see *magnet*)
mag·ne·sia
mag·ne·sium
mag·net (something that attracts; see *magnate*)
mag·net·ic
mag·nif·i·cent
mag·ni·fy
mag·ni·tude
mag·no·lia
mag·pie
ma·hog·a·ny (–nies)
maid·en
mail (letters; see *male*)
maim
main (chief; see *mane*)
main·tain
main·te·nance
mai·tre d' (maitre d's)
maize (Indian corn; see *maze*)
ma·jes·tic
ma·jor·i·ty (–ties)
mal·ad·just·ment
mal·a·dy (–dies)
mal·aise (French: indefinite feeling of ill health)
ma·lar·ia
mal·con·tent
male (masculine; see *mail*)
ma·lev·o·lent
mal·fea·sance
mal·formed
mal·func·tion
mal·ice
ma·li·cious
ma·lign
ma·lig·nan·cy (–cies)
ma·lin·ger
ma·lin·ger·er
mall

mal·lard
mal·lea·ble
mal·let
mal·nour·ished
mal·nu·tri·tion
mal·prac·tice
malt
mam·mal
mam·moth
man·age·able
man·age·ment
man·da·mus
man·da·rin
man·date
man·da·to·ry
man·di·ble
man·do·lin, man·do·line
mane (long, heavy hair on neck of horses; see *main*)
ma·neu·ver
man·gle
man·go (man·gos *or* man·goes)
mangy
ma·nia
ma·ni·ac
man·ic
ma·ni·cot·ti
man·i·cure
man·i·fest
man·i·fes·to (–tos *or* –toes)
man·i·fold
ma·nip·u·late
man·li·ness
man·ne·quin
man·ner
man·or
man·sion
man·tel (shelf; see *mantle*)
man·tle (cloak; see *mantel*)
man·u·al
man·u·fac·ture
man·u·mit
ma·nure
man·u·script
mar·a·schi·no
mar·a·thon
ma·raud·er
mar·ble
mare
mar·ga·rine
mar·gin
mar·gin·al
mari·gold
mar·i·jua·na, mar·i·hua·na
ma·rim·ba
mar·i·nate
ma·rine
mar·i·o·nette
mar·i·tal
mar·i·time

mar·jo·ram
mar·ket·able
mar·lin
mar·ma·lade
ma·roon
mar·quee
mar·quise
mar·qui·sette
mar·riage
mar·row
mar·shal, mar·shall (officer; see *martial*)
marsh·mal·low
mar·su·pi·al
mar·tial (relating to war; see *marshal*)
mar·ti·net
mar·tyr
mar·vel
mar·vel·ous, mar·vel·lous
mar·zi·pan
mas·cara
mas·cot
mas·cu·line
mas·och·ism
mas·och·ist
ma·son·ry (–ries)
mas·quer·ade
mas·sa·cre
mas·sage
mas·seur
mas·seuse
mas·sive
mas·ter·piece
mast·head
mas·ti·cate
mas·toid
mat·a·dor
ma·te·ri·al (substance; see *matériel*)
ma·te·ri·al·ism
ma·té·ri·el, ma·te·ri·el (equipment and supplies; see *material*)
ma·ter·nal
ma·ter·ni·ty (–ties)
math·e·mat·ics
mat·i·nee, mat·i·née
ma·tri·arch
ma·tric·u·late
mat·ri·mo·ny
ma·trix (ma·tri·ces *or* ma·trix·es)
ma·tron·ly
mat·ter
mat·tress
ma·ture
ma·tu·ri·ty
maud·lin
maul
mau·so·le·um (mau·so·le·ums *or* mau·so·lea)
mauve
mav·er·ick
max·i·mum (–ma *or* –mums)

may·hem
may·on·naise
may·or·al·ty
maze (network of passages; see *maize*)
mead·ow
mea·ger, mea·gre
me·an·der
mean·ing·ful
mean·while
mea·sles
mea·sure
meat (flesh of domestic animals;
    see *meet*, *mete*)
me·chan·ic
me·chan·i·cal
mech·a·nism
med·al (metal disk; see *meddle*, *metal*)
med·dle (interfere; see *medal*)
me·dia (–di·ae)
me·di·an
me·di·ate
me·di·a·tion
med·i·cal
med·i·ca·tion
me·dic·i·nal
med·i·cine
me·di·e·val, me·di·ae·val
me·di·o·cre
me·di·oc·ri·ty (–ties)
med·i·tate
med·i·ta·tion
me·di·um (me·di·ums *or* me·dia)
med·ley
meet (to become acquainted with; see
    meat, *mete*)
mega·cy·cle
mega·phone
mega·ton
mel·an·choly (–chol·ies)
me·lee (French: fight)
mel·lif·lu·ent
mel·lif·lu·ous
mel·low
me·lo·di·ous
melo·dra·ma
mel·o·dy (–dies)
mem·ber·ship
mem·brane
me·men·to
mem·oir
mem·o·ra·bil·ia
mem·o·ra·ble
mem·o·ran·dum
me·mo·ri·al
mem·o·ry (–ries)
men·ace
me·nag·er·ie
me·nial
men·o·pause
men·stru·ate

men·su·ra·tion
men·tal
men·thol
men·tion
men·tor
menu
mer·ce·nary (–nar·ies)
mer·chan·dise
mer·chant
mer·ci·ful
mer·cy (mer·cies)
mer·e·tri·cious
merge
merg·er
me·rid·i·an
me·ringue
mer·i·to·ri·ous
mer·maid
mesdames
mes·mer·ize
mes·sage
mes·sag·ing
mes·sen·ger
me·tab·o·lism
me·tal·ic
meta·mor·pho·sis (–ses)
met·a·phor
meta·phys·ics
mete (allot; see *meat*, *meet*)
me·te·or·ic
me·te·or
me·te·or·ite
me·ter
meth·a·done, meth·a·don
meth·od
meth·od·ol·o·gy (–gies)
me·tic·u·lous
met·ric
met·ro·nome
me·trop·o·lis
met·ro·pol·i·tan
met·tle
mez·za·nine
mez·zo-so·pra·no
mi·as·ma (–mas *or* –ma·ta)
mi·ca
mi·cro·anal·y·sis
mi·crobe
mi·cro·cosm
mi·crom·e·ter
mi·cro·phone
mi·cro·scope
mid·dle
mid·night
mid·riff
midst
mien
might (power; see *mite*)
mi·graine
mi·grate

mi·gra·to·ry
mil·dew
mile·age
mi·lieu (mi·lieus *or* mi·lieux)
mil·i·tan·cy
mil·i·ta·rist
mil·i·tary
mil·i·tate
mi·li·tia
mil·len·ni·um
mil·li·gram
mil·li·li·ter
mil·li·me·ter
mil·li·nery
mil·lion
mil·lion·aire
mim·eo·graph
mim·ic
minc·ing·ly
mind·less
min·er (mine worker; see *minor*)
min·er·al·o·gy
min·gle
min·i·a·ture
min·i·mize
min·i·mum
min·is·cule, mi·nus·cule
min·is·te·ri·al
mi·nor (comparatively unimportant;
    see *miner*)
mi·nor·i·ty (–ties)
min·strel
min·u·et
mi·nus·cule, min·is·cule
min·ute (space of time)
mi·nute (of small importance)
minx
mi·rac·u·lous
mi·rage
mire
mir·ror
mirth·ful
mis·al·li·ance
mis·an·thrope
mis·car·riage
mis·cel·la·neous
mis·cel·la·ny (–nies)
mis·chie·vous
mis·con·ceive
mis·con·strue
mis·de·mean·or
mis·er·a·ble
mi·ser·ly
mis·for·tune
mis·han·dle
mis·in·ter·pret
mis·judge
mis·man·age
mis·no·mer
mis·rep·re·sent

mis·shap·en
mis·sile
mis·sion·ary (–ar·ies)
mis·sive
mis·spell
mis·state
mis·take
mis·tle·toe
mis·tress
mis·tri·al
mite (small object *or* creature;
   see *might*)
mit·i·gate
mix·ture
mne·mon·ic
moat (trench; see *mote*)
mo·bile
mo·bi·li·za·tion
moc·ca·sin
mod·el
mod·er·ate
mod·er·a·tor
mod·ern·i·za·tion
mod·es·ty
mod·i·fi·er
mod·ish
mod·u·late
mo·gul
mo·hair
moist·en
mo·lar
mo·las·ses
mo·lec·u·lar
mol·e·cule
mol·li·fy
mol·ten
mo·men·tary
mo·men·tum
mon·arch
mon·as·tery (–ter·ies)
mon·e·tary
mon·ey (moneys *or* mon·ies)
Mon·gol·oid
mon·grel
mon·i·tor
mon·key
mono·chro·mat·ic
mon·o·cle
mo·nog·a·my
mono·gram
mono·logue, mono·log
mono·logu·ist, mo·no·lo·gist
mo·nop·o·ly (–lies)
mono·syl·lab·ic
mono·the·ism
mono·tone
mo·not·o·nous
mon·soon
mon·stros·i·ty (–ties)
mon·strous

mon·tage
month·ly
mon·u·men·tal
moon·light
mor·al
mo·rale
mo·rass
mor·a·to·ri·um (mor·a·to·ri·ums *or*
   mor·a·to·ria)
mor·bid
mor·dant
more·over
mo·res
morgue
mor·i·bund
morn·ing (time from sunrise to noon;
   see *mourning*)
mor·phine
mor·sel
mor·tal·i·ty
mort·gage
mor·ti·cian
mor·ti·fy
mor·tu·ary (–ar·ies)
mo·sa·ic
mosque
mos·qui·to (–tos *or* –toes)
mote (speck; see *moat*)
mo·tif
mo·tion
mo·ti·va·tion
mo·tor
mot·tled
mot·to (mot·tos *or* mot·toes)
moun·tain·ous
mourn
mourn·ing (act of sorrowing;
   see *morning*)
mouse
mousse
mouth·ful
mov·able, move·able
mov·ie
moz·za·rel·la
mu·ci·lage
mu·cous
mug·ger
mug·gy
mul·ber·ry (–ries)
mul·ti·cul·tur·al
mul·ti·eth·nic
mul·ti·fac·e·ted
mul·ti·far·i·ous
mul·ti·lat·er·al
mul·ti·me·dia
mul·ti·mil·lion·aire
mul·ti·na·tion·al
mul·ti·ple
mul·ti·tude
mum·ble

mum·bo jum·bo
mum·my (mummies)
mun·dane
mu·nic·i·pal
mu·ni·tion
mu·ral
mur·der·ous
mus·cle (body tissue; see *mussel*)
mus·cu·lar
muse
mu·se·um
mu·si·cal
mu·si·cian
mus·ke·teer
musk·rat
mus·lin
mus·sel (mollusk; see *muscle*)
mus·tache, mous·tache
mus·tard
mu·ta·ble
mu·ta·tion
mu·ti·late
mu·ti·neer
mut·ter
mut·ton
mu·tu·al
muz·zle
my·o·pic
myr·i·ad
myrrh
myr·tle
mys·te·ri·ous
mys·tery (–ter·ies)
mys·tic
mys·ti·cal
mys·ti·cism
mys·tique
myth
myth·i·cal
my·thol·o·gy (–gies)

N

na·ive
na·ive·té, na·ive·te
na·ked·ness
na·palm
nap·kin
nar·cis·sism
nar·cis·sus
nar·cot·ic
nar·rate
nar·ra·tor
nar·row
na·sal·i·ty (–ties)
na·scent
nas·ty
na·tion·al·i·ty (–ties)
na·tive
na·tiv·i·ty (–ties)

nat·u·ral·ize

na·tu·ro·path

naugh·ti·ness

nau·se·ate

nau·seous

nau·ti·cal

na·val (relating to ships; see *navel*)

nave (church aisle; see *knave*)

na·vel (depression in abdomen; see *naval*)

nav·i·gate

nav·i·ga·tor

near·by

neb·u·lous

nec·es·sary

ne·ces·si·tate

neck·lace

nec·tar·ine

need (a requirement, necessity; see *knead*)

nee·dle·work

ne'er-do-well

ne·far·i·ous

ne·gate

neg·a·tive

ne·glect

neg·li·gee, neg·li·gé

neg·li·gent

neg·li·gi·ble

ne·go·ti·a·tion

neigh

neigh·bor

neigh·bor·hood

nei·ther

nem·e·sis (–ses)

ne·on

neo·na·tal

neo·phyte

neph·ew

nep·o·tism

ner·vous

ner·vous·ness

nes·tle

net·ting

net·tle

net·work

neu·ral·gia

neu·ron

neu·ro·sis (–ses)

neu·rot·ic

neu·ro·tox·in

neu·ter

neu·tral·ize

neu·tron

new (recent; see *gnu* and *knew*)

news·group

news·stand

nib·ble

nice·ty (–ties)

niche

nick·el, nick·le

nick·nack, knick·knack

nic·o·tine

niece

night (time from dusk to dawn; see *knight*)

night·in·gale

night·mare

nim·ble

nine·teen

nine·ty (nineties)

ninth

nip·ple

ni·trate

ni·tro·gen

ni·tro·glyc·er·in, ni·tro·glyc·er·ine

no·bil·i·ty

no·ble

noc·tur·nal

noc·turne

nod·ule

noi·some

noisy

no·mad

nom de plume (French: pen name, pseudonym)

no·men·cla·ture

nom·i·nal

nom·i·nate

nom·i·na·tion

nom·i·nee

non·al·co·hol·ic

non·be·liev·er

non·bel·lig·er·ent

non·cha·lance

non·com·bat·ant

non·com·mis·sioned

non·com·mit·tal

non·com·pli·ance

non·con·duc·tor

non·con·form·ist

non·de·script

non·en·ti·ty (–ties)

non·es·sen·tial

non·fic·tion

non·in·ter·ven·tion

non·pa·reil (French: having no equal)

non·par·ti·san

non·poi·son·ous

non·pro·duc·tive

non·prof·it

non·re·new·able

non·sec·tar·i·an

non·sense

non se·qui·tur

non·tax·able

non·vi·o·lence

noo·dle

noose

nor·mal

north·ern

nose

nos·tal·gia

nos·tril

nos·trum

no·ta·bly

no·ta·rize

no·ta·ry public (no·ta·ries public *or* no·ta·ry publics)

no·ta·tion

notch

note·wor·thy

no·tice·able

no·ti·fy

no·tion

no·to·ri·e·ty (–eties)

no·to·ri·ous

nou·gat

nought

noun

nour·ish·ment

nov·el·lette

nov·el·ty (–ties)

nov·ice

nox·ious

noz·zle

nu·ance

nu·bile

nu·cle·ar

nu·cle·us (–clei *or* –cle·us·es)

nu·di·ty

nug·get

nui·sance

nul·li·fy

numb

num·ber

nu·mer·al

nu·mer·a·tor

nu·mer·ous

nu·mis·mat·ic

nup·tial

nurse

nurs·ery (–er·ies)

nur·ture

nu·tri·ent

nu·tri·tion

nu·tri·tious

nuz·zle

ny·lon

O

oa·sis (–ses)

oath

oat·meal

obe·di·ence

obe·lisk

obese

obe·si·ty

obey

ob·fus·cate
obit·u·ary (–ar·ries)
ob·jec·tion
ob·jec·tive
ob·jec·tor
ob·li·gate
ob·li·ga·tion
oblig·a·to·ry
oblige
oblique
oblit·er·ate
obliv·i·on
obliv·i·ous
ob·long
ob·lo·quy (–quies)
ob·nox·ious
oboe
obo·ist
ob·scene
ob·scen·i·ty (–ties)
ob·scure
ob·scu·ri·ty (–ties)
ob·se·qui·ous
ob·se·quy (–quies)
ob·ser·vant
ob·ser·va·to·ry (–ries)
ob·ses·sion
ob·so·les·cence
ob·so·lete
ob·sta·cle
ob·ste·tri·cian
ob·stet·rics
ob·sti·nate
ob·struc·tion
ob·tain
ob·tru·sive
ob·tuse
ob·vi·ate
ob·vi·ous
oc·ca·sion
oc·cip·i·tal
oc·clu·sion
oc·cult
oc·cu·pan·cy (–cies)
oc·cu·pant
oc·cu·pa·tion
oc·cu·py
oc·cur
oc·curred
oc·cur·rence
ocean
ocean·og·ra·phy
oc·ta·gon
oc·tag·o·nal
oc·tane
oc·tave
oc·tet
oc·to·ge·nar·i·an
oc·to·pus (–pus·es or –pi)
odd·i·ty (–ties)

odd·ly
odi·ous
odom·e·ter
odor·ant
odor·ous
od·ys·sey
of·fend·er
of·fense, of·fence
of·ferred
off·hand
of·fi·cer
of·fi·cial
of·fi·ci·ate
of·fi·cious
off·set
off·spring (off·spring or off·springs)
ohm
oil·er
oily
oint·ment
okra
old-fash·ioned
old·ster
ole·ag·i·nous
ol·fac·to·ry
ol·i·gar·chy (–chies)
ol·ive
olym·pi·ad
Olym·pic
om·e·let, om·e·lette
om·i·nous
omis·sion
omit
om·ni·bus
om·nip·o·tence
om·ni·science
om·niv·o·rous
on·col·o·gy
on·com·ing
oner·ous
on·ion
on·line
on·o·mato·poe·ia
on·set
on·shore
on·side
on·slaught
on·tol·o·gy
onus
on·ward, on·wards
on·yx
oo·long
opal·es·cent
opaque
open
op·er·a·ble
op·er·ate
op·er·at·ic
op·er·a·tion
op·er·et·ta

oph·thal·mol·o·gist
opi·ate
opin·ion
opin·ion·at·ed
opi·um
opos·sum
op·po·nent
op·por·tune
op·por·tu·nis·tic
op·por·tu·ni·ty (–ties)
op·po·site
op·pres·sion
op·ti·cal
op·ti·cian
op·ti·mism
op·ti·mum (–ma or –mums)
op·tion
op·tom·e·trist
op·tom·e·try
op·u·lent
opus (opera or opus·es)
or·a·cle
oral (relating to the mouth; see aural)
or·ange
orate
or·a·to·ry (–ries)
or·bit·al
or·chard
or·ches·tra
or·chid
or·dain
or·deal
or·der
or·di·nance
or·di·nary (–nar·ies)
or·di·nar·i·ly
or·di·na·tion
ord·nance
ore
oreg·a·no
or·gan
or·gan·ic
or·gan·ism
or·ga·ni·za·tion
or·ga·niz·er
or·gasm
or·gi·as·tic
or·gy (or·gies)
ori·en·tal
ori·en·ta·tion
or·i·fice
orig·i·nal·i·ty
orig·i·na·tor
ori·ole
or·na·men·tal
or·na·men·ta·tion
or·nate
or·nery
or·ni·thol·o·gy (–gies)
or·phan·age

or·tho·don·tist
or·tho·dox
or·tho·pe·dic, or·tho·pae·dic
os·cil·late
os·mo·sis
os·prey
os·si·fi·ca·tion
os·si·fy
os·ten·si·ble
os·ten·ta·tious
os·te·o·path
os·tra·cize
os·trich
ot·to·man
ought
ounce
our (relating to us; see *hour*)
oust
out·age
out·break
out·dis·tance
out·fit·ter
out·land·ish
out·pour·ing
out·put
out·ra·geous
out·ward
out·weigh
out·wit
oval
ova·ry (–ries)
ova·tion
over·alls
over·bear·ing
over·board
over·cast
o·ver·con·fi·dent
over·dose
over·draft
over·ex·pose
over·haul
over·joyed
over·lap
over·rate
over·seas
over·seer
over·sight
overt
over·ture
over·whelm
over·wrought
ow·ing
own·er
ox·i·da·tion
ox·ide
ox·i·dize
ox·tail
ox·y·gen
ox·y·gen·ate

oys·ter
ozone

P

pace·mak·er
pac·er
pa·cif·ic
pac·i·fi·er
pack·age
pack·et
pact
pad·ding
pad·dle
pad·dock
pad·lock
pa·gan
page
pag·eant·ry
pag·i·nate
pa·go·da
paid
pail (container; see *pale*)
pain (suffering; see *pane*)
pains·tak·ing
paint
pair (two; see *pare, pear*)
pa·ja·mas
pal·ace
pal·at·able
pal·ate (roof of mouth; see *palette*)
pa·la·tial
pale (deficient in color; see *pail*)
Pa·leo·lith·ic
pal·ette (painter's board; see *palate*)
pal·in·drome
pal·i·sade
pal·la·di·um (–la·dia)
pall·bear·er
pal·met·to
palm·ist
pal·o·mi·no
pal·pa·ble
pal·pi·tate
pal·sy (palsies)
pal·try
pam·per
pam·phlet
pan·a·cea
pan·cre·as
pan·da
pan·de·mo·ni·um
pan·der
pane (sheet of glass; see *pain*)
pan·el
pan·han·dle
pan·ic
pan·icked
pan·o·ply (–plies)

pan·o·rama
pan·sy (pansies)
pan·the·ism
pan·ther
pant·ing
pan·to·mime
pan·try (pantries)
pa·pa·cy (–cies)
pa·pal
pa·pa·ya
pa·pier-mâ·ché
pa·pri·ka
pa·py·rus (pa·py·ri *or* pa·py·rus·es)
par·a·ble
pa·rab·o·la
para·chute
pa·rade
par·a·digm
par·a·dise
par·a·dox
par·af·fin
par·a·gon
par·a·graph
par·a·keet
par·al·lel
par·al·lel·o·gram
pa·ral·y·sis (–y·ses)
par·a·lyt·ic
par·a·lyze
pa·ram·e·ter
par·a·mount
par·amour
para·noia
para·noid
par·a·pet
par·a·pher·na·lia
para·phrase
para·ple·gic
par·a·site
par·a·sol
para·troop·er
par·boil
par·cel
parch
parch·ment
par·don·able
pare (shave off; see *pear, pair*)
pa·ren·tal
pa·ren·the·sis (–ses)
par·en·thet·i·cal·ly
pa·ri·e·tal
pa·rish·ion·er
par·i·ty (–ties)
par·ka
park·way
par·lay (two or more bets in advance; see *parley*)
par·ley (conference; see *parlay*)
par·lia·ment

par·lia·men·ta·ry
par·lor
par·mi·gia·na, par·mi·gia·no
pa·ro·chi·al
par·o·dy (–dies)
pa·role
par·quet (French: type of flooring)
par·rot
par·ry
parse
par·si·mo·ni·ous
pars·ley
pars·nip
par·son·age
par·terre
par·tial
par·tic·i·pate
par·ti·cip·i·al
par·ti·ci·ple
par·ti·cle
par·tic·u·lar·ly
par·ti·san, par·ti·zan
par·ti·tion
par·ti·tive
part·ner
par·tridge
par·ve·nu (French: one with new
     wealth, lacking social standing)
pas·chal
pass·able
pas·sage
pas·sé (French: behind the times)
pas·sen·ger
pass·er·by (pass·ers·by)
pas·sion·ate
pas·sive
pass·port
past
paste
pas·tel
pas·teur·ize
pas·tille, pas·til
pas·time
pas·to·ral
past·ry (pastries)
pas·ty (pasties)
patch·work
patchy
pat·ent
pa·ter·nal·ism
pa·ter·ni·ty
pa·thet·ic
pa·thol·o·gy (–gies)
pa·thos
path·way
pa·tience
pa·tient
pa·ti·na (–nas or –nae)
pa·tio
pa·tois (plural also pa·tois)

pa·tri·arch
pa·tri·cian
pat·ri·cide
pat·ri·mo·ny
pa·tri·ot·ic
pa·trol
pa·tron
pa·tron·age
pat·ter
pat·tern
paunch
pau·per
pause
pave·ment
pa·vil·ion
pawn
pay·able
peace (state of tranquility; see *piece*)
peace·ful
peachy
pea·cock
peak (sharp *or* pointed end; see
     peek, pique)
peal (loud ringing of bells; see *peel*)
pea·nut
pear (fruit; see *pair, pare*)
pearl
peas·ant·ry
peb·ble
pe·can
pec·ca·dil·lo (–loes *or* –los)
pec·to·ral
pe·cu·liar·i·ty (–ties)
pe·cu·ni·ary
ped·a·gogue, ped·a·gog
ped·a·go·gy
ped·al (foot lever; see *peddle*)
pe·dan·tic
ped·dle (travel with wares to sell;
     see *pedal*)
ped·es·tal
pe·des·tri·an
pe·di·a·tri·cian
pe·di·at·rics
ped·i·cure
ped·i·gree
ped·i·ment
pe·dom·e·ter
peek (look furtively; see *peak, pique*)
peel (strip off; see *peal*)
peer (equal; see *pier*)
peer·age
pee·vish
pei·gnoir
pe·jo·ra·tive
pe·koe
pe·lag·ic
pel·i·can
pel·let
pel·vic

pel·vis (pel·vis·es *or* pel·ves)
pe·nal·ize
pen·al·ty (–ties)
pen·ance
pen·chant
pen·ciled
pen·dant, pen·dent
pen·du·lum
pen·e·trate
pen·guin
pen·i·cil·lin
pen·in·su·la
pen·i·tence
pen·i·ten·tia·ry (–ries)
pen·man·ship
pen·nant
pen·ni·less
pen·sion
pen·ta·gon
pent·house
pe·o·ny (–nies)
peo·ple
pep·per
per·cale
per cap·i·ta
per·ceive
per·cent
per·cent·age
per·cen·tile
per·cept
per·cep·ti·ble
per·cep·tive
per·cep·tu·al
perch
per·chance
per·cip·i·ent
per·co·late
per·co·la·tor
per·cus·sion
per di·em
per·di·tion
pe·remp·to·ry
pe·ren·ni·al
per·fect
per·fec·ta
per·fo·rate
per·force
per·for·mance
per·fume
per·func·to·ry
per·haps
per·il·ous
pe·rim·e·ter
pe·ri·od·ic
pe·riph·er·al
pe·riph·ery (–er·ies)
peri·scope
per·ish·able
peri·to·ni·tis
per·i·win·kle

per·jure
per·ju·ry
per·ma·frost
per·ma·nent
per·me·able
per·me·ate
per·mis·si·ble
per·mis·sion
per·mit·ted
per·mu·ta·tion
per·ni·cious
per·o·ra·tion
per·ox·ide
per·pen·dic·u·lar
per·pe·tra·tor
per·pet·u·al
per·pe·tu·i·ty (–ities)
per·plex
per·se·cu·tion
per·se·ver·ance
per·sis·tence
per·snick·e·ty
per·son·able
per·son·age
per·son·al (private, relating to a person;
    see *personnel*)
per·son·al·i·ty (–ties)
per·so·na non gra·ta (Latin: being
    unwelcome)
per·son·i·fi·ca·tion
per·son·nel (body of employees;
    see *personal*)
per·spec·tive
per·spi·ca·cious
per·spi·ra·tion
per·sua·sion
per·tain
per·ti·nent
pe·ruse
per·vade
per·verse
per·vert
pes·si·mism
pes·ter
pes·ti·lence
pes·tle
pet·al
pe·tit (French: small)
pe·ti·tion
pe·trel (sea bird; see *petrol*)
pet·ri·fy
pet·rol (gasoline; see *petrel*)
pe·tro·leum
pet·ti·coat
pet·ti·ness
pet·ty
pet·u·lant
pe·tu·nia
pew·ter

pha·lanx (pha·lanx·es *or* pha·lan·ges)
phan·tasm, fan·tasm
phan·tas·ma·go·ria
phan·tom
phar·ma·ceu·ti·cal
phar·ma·cist
phar·ma·cy (–cies)
phar·ynx (pha·ryn·ges *or* pha·rynx·es)
phase
pheas·ant
phe·nom·e·nal
phe·nom·e·non
phi·lan·der·er
phi·lan·thro·py (–pies)
phil·o·den·dron (–drons *or* –dra)
phi·lol·o·gy
phi·los·o·pher
phil·o·soph·i·cal
phlegm
phleg·mat·ic
pho·bia
phoe·nix
pho·nate
pho·net·ics
pho·nics
pho·no·graph
pho·ny, pho·ney (pho·nies)
phos·phate
phos·pho·res·cent
pho·to·copy (–cop·ies)
pho·to·elec·tric
pho·to·graph·ic
pho·to·stat
phot·to·syn·the·sis
phrase
phra·se·ol·o·gy (–gies)
phre·net·ic, fre·net·ic
phre·nol·o·gy
phys·i·cal
phy·si·cian
phys·i·cist
phys·ics
phys·i·ol·o·gy
phys·io·ther·a·py
phy·sique
pi·a·nist
pi·az·za (pi·az·zas *or* pi·az·ze)
pi·ca
pic·ca·lil·li
pic·co·lo
pick·et
pick·le
pic·nic
pic·nicked
pic·to·graph
pic·to·ri·al
pic·ture (painting, drawing *or*
    photograph; see *pitcher*)
pic·tur·esque

piece (part of a whole; see *peace*)
pièce de ré·sis·tance (pièces de
    ré·sis·tance) (French: outstanding
    item)
pier (dock; see *peer*)
pierce
pi·e·ty (pi·e·ties)
pi·geon
pig·ment
Pi·la·tes
pil·fer
pil·grim·age
piling
pil·lage
pil·lar
pil·low
pi·lot
pi·men·to
pim·ple
pin·a·fore
pin·cer
pin·cush·ion
pine·ap·ple
pin·na·cle
pi·noch·le
pi·o·neer
pi·ous
pipe
pip·ing
pique (to wound vanity; see *peak, peek*)
pi·ra·cy
pir·ou·ette (French: ballet turn)
pis·ta·chio
pis·til (plant organ; see *pistol*)
pis·tol (gun; see *pistil*)
pitch·er (container for liquids;
    see *picture*)
pitch·fork
pit·e·ous
pit·fall
pithy
piti·able
piti·ful
piti·less
pit·tance
piv·ot·al
pix·el
pix·ie, pixy (pix·ies)
pix·i·lat·ed
piz·ze·ria
plac·ard
pla·cate
pla·ce·bo
place·ment
plac·id
plack·et
pla·gia·rize
plague
plaid

plain (level country; lacking ornament;
    see *plane*)
plain·tiff
plane (tool; geometric surface;
    see *plain*)
plan·et
plan·e·tar·i·um
plan·tain
plan·ta·tion
plaque
plas·ma
plas·ter
plas·tic
plas·ti·cize
pla·teau (pla·teaus *or* pla·teaux)
plat·form
plat·i·num
plat·i·tude
pla·ton·ic
pla·toon
plat·ter
plau·si·ble
play·mate
play·wright
pla·za
plead
pleas·ant·ry (–ries)
plea·sure
pleat
plebe
ple·be·ian
pledge
ple·na·ry
pleni·po·ten·tia·ry (–ries)
plen·te·ous
plen·ti·ful
pli·able
pli·ers
plight
plough, plow
plow·share
plum·age
plumb·er
plume
plum·met
plump
plun·der
plunge
plu·ral
plu·ral·i·ty (–ties)
plu·toc·ra·cy (–cies)
plu·to·ni·um
ply·wood
pneu·mat·ic
pneu·mo·nia
poach·er
pock·et·book
po·di·a·trist
po·di·um (podia)
po·em

po·et·ic
poi·gnan·cy (–cies)
poi·gnant
poin·set·tia
point
poi·son·ous
po·lar·i·ty (–ties)
po·lar·i·za·tion
po·lar·ize
pole (long slender object; see *poll*)
po·lem·ic
po·lice (plural also po·lice)
pol·i·cy (–cies)
po·lio
pol·ish
po·lit·bu·ro
po·lit·i·cal
pol·i·ti·cian
pol·i·tics
pol·ka
poll (receive and record votes;
    see *pole*)
pol·len
pol·li·nate
pol·lu·tion
poly·es·ter
po·lyg·a·my
poly·gon
pol·yp
poly·tech·nic
poly·ure·thane
pome·gran·ate
pom·pos·i·ty (–ties)
pomp·ous
pon·cho
pon·der
pon·tiff
pon·tif·i·cal
pon·toon
po·ny·tail
poo·dle
pop·corn
pop·lar (tree; see *popular*)
pop·py (poppies)
pop·u·lace
pop·u·lar (commonly liked; see *poplar*)
pop·u·la·tion
pop·u·list
por·ce·lain
por·cu·pine
por·nog·ra·phy
po·rous
por·poise
por·ridge
por·ta·ble
por·tend
por·tent
por·ten·tous
por·ter·house
port·fo·lio

por·ti·co (–coes *or* –cos)
por·tion
por·trait
por·tray
pos·it
po·si·tion
pos·i·tive·ly
pos·se
pos·ses·sor
pos·ses·sion
pos·si·bil·i·ty (–ties)
post·age
pos·te·ri·or
pos·ter·i·ty
post·hu·mous
post·mor·tem
post·pone
post·script
pos·tu·late
pos·tur·ing
po·ta·ble
po·ta·to (–toes)
po·ten·cy (–cies)
po·tent
po·ten·tial
po·tion
pot·pour·ri
pot·shot
pot·tery (ter·ies)
poul·tice
poul·try
pounce
pound
pov·er·ty
pow·der
pow·er·ful
prac·ti·cal
prac·tice, prac·tise
prac·ti·tion·er
prag·mat·ic
prai·rie
prat·tle
prayer·ful
preach
preachy
pre·am·ble
pre·ar·range
pre·car·i·ous
pre·cau·tion
pre·cede
pre·ce·dence
pre·ce·dent
pre·cept
pre·cinct
pre·cious
prec·i·pice
pre·cip·i·tate
pre·cise
pre·ci·sion
pre·clude

pre·co·cious
pre·con·ceive
pre·con·cep·tion
pre·con·di·tion
pre·cur·sor
pred·a·tor
pre·de·cease
pre·des·ti·na·tion
pre·de·ter·mine
pre·dic·a·ment
pred·i·cate
pre·dict
pre·di·lec·tion
pre·dis·pose
pre·doc·tor·al
pre·dom·i·nant
pre·em·i·nence
pre·empt
preen
pre·fab·ri·cate
pref·ace
pref·a·to·ry
pre·fect
pre·fer
pref·er·a·ble
pref·er·ence
pre·fig·ure
preg·na·ble
preg·nan·cy (–cies)
preg·nant
pre·heat
pre·his·tor·ic
pre·in·duc·tion
prej·u·dice
pre·lim·i·nary (–nar·ies)
pre·lude
pre·mar·i·tal
pre·ma·ture
pre·mier (prime minister; see *premiere*)
pre·miere (first public performance;
    see *premier*)
pre·mise
pre·mi·um
pre·mo·ni·tion
pre·oc·cu·pa·tion
prep·a·ra·tion
pre·pa·ra·to·ry
pre·pared·ness
pre·pon·der·ance
prep·o·si·tion
pre·pos·sess
pre·pos·ter·ous
pre·req·ui·site
pre·scribe
pre·scrip·tion
pre·sent·able
pre·sen·ta·tion
pre·sent·ly
pres·er·va·tion·ist
pre·ser·va·tive

pre·shrunk
pres·i·den·cy (–cies)
pres·sure
pres·sur·ize
pres·tige
pres·ti·gious
pre·sume
pre·sump·tion
pre·sump·tu·ous
pre·tend·er
pre·ten·sion
pre·ten·tious
pre·ter·nat·u·ral
pre·test
pre·text
pret·ti·ness
pret·ty
pret·zel
pre·vail
prev·a·lent
pre·var·i·cate
pre·vent·able, pre·vent·ible
pre·ven·tive, pre·ven·ta·tive
pre·view
pre·vi·ous
prey
prick·ly
pri·ma·cy
pri·ma don·na
pri·ma fa·cie
pri·mar·i·ly
pri·mate
prime
prim·er
pri·me·val
priming
prim·i·tive
pri·mor·di·al
prim·rose
prince·ly
prin·ci·pal (head of school; see
    principle)
prin·ci·ple (fundamental law;
    see *principal*)
print·able
pri·or
prism
pris·mat·ic
pris·on·er
pris·tine
pri·va·cy (–cies)
pri·vate
pri·va·tion
priv·et
priv·i·lege
prize
prob·a·bil·i·ty (–ties)
prob·a·ble
pro·bate
pro·ba·tion·er

prob·lem·at·ic
pro·ce·dur·al
pro·ce·dure
pro·ceed
pro·cess (pro·cess·es)
pro·ces·sion
pro·ces·sor
pro·claim
proc·la·ma·tion
pro·cliv·i·ty (–ties)
pro·cras·ti·nate
pro·cre·ate
pro·crus·te·an
proc·tor
proc·u·ra·tor
pro·cure·ment
prod·i·gal
pro·di·gious
prod·i·gy (–gies)
pro·duce (noun), pro·duce (verb)
pro·duc·tion
pro·fan·i·ty (–ties)
pro·fes·sion
pro·fes·sor
pro·fi·cien·cy (–cies)
pro·file
prof·it (gain; see *prophet*)
prof·li·ga·cy
pro·found
pro·fun·di·ty (–ties)
pro·fuse·ly
prog·e·ny (–nies)
prog·no·sis (–no·ses)
prog·nos·tic
prog·nos·ti·cate
pro·gram
pro·gram·mer, pro·gram·er
pro·gres·sion
pro·gres·sive
pro·hib·it
pro·hi·bi·tion
proj·ect
pro·jec·tile
pro·jec·tion
pro·lif·er·ate
pro·lif·ic
pro·logue, pro·log
pro·long
prom·e·nade
prom·i·nence
pro·mis·cu·i·ty (–ties)
prom·is·ing
prom·is·so·ry (–ries)
prom·on·to·ry (–ries)
pro·mot·er
pro·mo·tion
prompt·ness
pro·mul·gate
pro·nate
pro·noun

pro·nounce·ment
pro·nun·ci·a·tion
pro·pa·gan·da
prop·a·gate
pro·pane
pro·pel
pro·pen·si·ty (–ties)
prop·er·ly
prop·er·ty (–ties)
proph·e·cy (–cies) (inspired
    declaration; see *prophesy*)
proph·e·sy (–sies) (to predict;
    see *prophecy*)
proph·et (one who foretells the future;
    see *profit*)
pro·phet·ic
pro·phy·lac·tic
pro·pi·tious
pro·por·tion
pro·pose
prop·o·si·tion
pro·pri·e·tary (–tar·ies)
pro·pri·e·tor
pro·pul·sion
pro·rate
pro·sa·ic
pro·scribe
pro·scrip·tion
pros·e·cute
pros·e·cu·tor
pros·e·ly·tize
pro·spect
pro·spec·tive
pro·spec·tus (–tus·es)
pros·tate (gland; see *prostrate*)
pros·trate (prone; see *prostate*)
pro·tag·o·nist
pro·tec·tive·ly
pro·tec·tion
pro·té·gé
pro·tein
pro·test·er, pro·test·or
pro·tes·ta·tion
pro·to·col
pro·ton
pro·to·type
pro·to·zo·an
pro·trac·tor
pro·trude
pro·tru·sion
pro·tu·ber·ant
prove
prov·en·der
pro·ver·bi·al
prov·i·dence
prov·i·den·tial
pro·vin·cial
pro·vi·sion·al
pro·vi·so (–sos *or* –soes)

prov·o·ca·tion
pro·voc·a·tive
pro·vo·lo·ne (Italian: a kind of cheese)
pro·vost
prow·ess
prowl
prox·i·mate
prox·im·i·ty
proxy (prox·ies)
pru·dence
pru·ri·ence
pry·ing
psalm·ist
psal·tery, psal·try (–ter·ies *or* –tries)
pseu·do·nym
psy·che·del·ic
psy·chi·a·trist
psy·chi·a·try
psy·chic
psy·cho·anal·y·sis
psy·cho·log·i·cal
psy·chol·o·gist
psy·cho·path
psy·cho·so·mat·ics
psy·cho·ther·a·py
pto·maine
pu·ber·ty
pu·bes·cent
pu·bic
pub·lic
pub·li·can
pub·lic·i·ty
pub·lic·ly, pub·li·cal·ly
pub·lish·er
puck·er
pud·ding
pud·dle
pug·na·cious
pul·ley
pul·mo·nary
pulp
pul·pit
pul·sar
pul·sate
pulse
pul·ver·ize
pu·ma
pum·ice
pum·mel
pump·er
pum·per·nick·el
pump·kin
punch
punc·tu·al
punc·tu·ate
punc·tu·a·tion
punc·ture
pun·dit
pun·gen·cy

pun·gent
pun·ish·able
pu·ni·tive
pun·ster
punt·er
pup·pet
pup·pe·teer
pur·chase
pu·ree, pu·rée (French: to strain cooked
    food)
purge
pu·ri·fi·ca·tion
pu·ri·fy
pur·ist
pu·ri·tan·i·cal
pur·loin
pur·ple
pur·port
pur·pose
pur·pose·ly
pur·su·ance
pur·sue
pur·suit
pur·vey·or
pur·view
pushy
pus·tu·lar
pus·tule
pu·tre·fy
pu·trid
put·ter
put·ty (putties)
puz·zling
pyg·my, pig·my (pygmies, pigmies)
py·or·rhea
pyr·a·mid
pyre
py·ro·tech·nics
py·thon
pyx·ie

Q

quack·ery
quad·rant
qua·dren·ni·al
quad·ri·lat·er·al
qua·dru·ple
quaff
quag·mire
quail
quaint·ly
quake
qual·i·fi·ca·tion
qual·i·fied
qual·i·fy
qual·i·ta·tive
qual·i·ty (–ties)
qualm

quan·da·ry (–ries)
quan·ti·fy
quan·ti·ta·tive
quan·ti·ty (–ties)
quan·tum (–ta)
quar·an·tine
quar·rel
quar·rel·some
quar·ry (quarries)
quar·ter
quar·ter·back
quar·tet, quar·tette
quar·to
quartz
qua·sar
quash
qua·train
quay
quea·sy, quea·zy
queen
queen-size
queer
quell
quench
quer·u·lous
que·ry (queries)
quest
ques·tion
ques·tion·able
ques·tion·naire
queue (ordered list, see *cue*)
quib·ble
quick·en
qui·et (free from noise; see *quite*)
qui·etus
quilt
quince
qui·nine
quin·tes·sence
quin·tet
quin·tile
quin·tu·plet
quip
quirk
quirky
quit
quite (completely; see *quiet*)
quit·ter
quiv·er
quix·ot·ic
quiz (quiz·zes)
quiz·zi·cal
quo·rum
quo·ta
quot·able
quo·ta·tion
quote
quo·tient

R

rab·bit (rabbit *or* rabbits)
rab·ble
ra·bid
ra·bies (plural also ra·bies)
rac·coon, ra·coon
race·way
ra·cial
rac·ism
rack·et, rac·quet
racy
ra·dar
ra·di·al
ra·di·ance
ra·di·ate
ra·di·a·tor
rad·i·cal
rad·i·cal·ly
ra·dio·ac·tive
rad·ish
ra·di·um
ra·di·us (ra·dii *or* ra·di·us·es)
raff·ish
raf·fle
raf·ter
rag·ged
rag·gle-tag·gle
raging
ra·gout
raid·er
rail·road
rain (water falling in drops from the atmosphere; see *reign, rein*)
rain·bow
rainy
raise (to lift; see *raze*)
rai·sin
ral·ly (rallies)
ram·ble
ram·bunc·tious
ram·i·fi·ca·tion
ram·i·fy
ram·page
ram·pant
ram·part
ram·rod
ram·shack·le
ran·cor·ous
ran·dom
rang·er
ran·sack
ran·som
rap·id
ra·pi·er
rap·ine
rap·port
rar·e·fy, rar·i·fy
rar·i·ty (–ties)

ras·cal·i·ty (–ties)
rasp·ber·ry
raspy
ratch·et, rach·et
rate
rat·i·fy
ra·tio
ra·tion
ra·tio·nal (relating to reason; see *rationale*)
ra·tio·nale (underlying reason; see *rational*)
ra·tio·nal·ize
rat·tan
rat·tle
rau·cous
raun·chy
rav·age
rav·en·ous
ra·vine
rav·i·o·li
ray·on
raze (destroy to the ground; see *raise*)
raz·zle-daz·zle
reach·able
re·ac·tion
re·ac·tion·ary
re·ac·ti·vate
re·ac·tor
read·able
read·i·ly
re·align
re·al·is·tic
re·al·i·ty (–ties)
re·al·i·za·tion
re·al·ly
realm
re·al·ty
ream
re·ap·por·tion
re·arm
rea·son·able
re·as·sur·ance
re·bate
re·bel·lious
re·bound
re·buff
re·buke
re·but·tal
re·cal·ci·trance
re·ca·pit·u·late
re·cede
re·ceipt
re·ceiv·able
re·ceiv·er
re·cent·ly
re·cep·ta·cle
re·cep·tion·ist
re·cep·tive

re·cess
re·ces·sion
re·cid·i·vist
re·cip·ro·cate
rec·i·proc·i·ty (–ties)
re·cit·al
rec·i·ta·tive
reck·oned
rec·la·ma·tion
re·cluse
rec·og·ni·tion
re·cog·ni·zance
re·col·lect
rec·om·mend
rec·om·men·da·tion
rec·om·pense
rec·on·cil·able
re·con·nais·sance
re·con·sti·tute
re·con·struc·tion
re·con·vert
re·cord·er
re·coup
re·course
re·cov·er·able
rec·re·ant
rec·re·a·tion
re·crim·i·nate
re·cru·des·cence
re·cruit
rect·an·gu·lar
rec·ti·fy
rec·ti·tude
rec·tor
re·cum·bent
re·cu·per·ate
re·cur·rent
re·cy·cla·ble
re·cy·cle
red·den
re·deem·er
re·demp·tive
re·de·sign
re·dis·trict
red·o·lent
re·dou·ble
re·dound
re·duc·ible
re·duc·tion
re·dun·dan·cy (–cies)
re·elec·tion
re·en·act
re·en·try
re·fec·to·ry (–ries)
re·fer·able
ref·er·ee
ref·er·ence
ref·er·en·dum (–da *or* –dums)
re·fer·ral
re·fi·nance

re·fine·ment
re·flec·tion
re·flec·tor
re·flex
ref·or·ma·tion
re·for·ma·to·ry (–ries)
re·frac·to·ry (–ries)
re·frain
re·fresh·ment
re·frig·er·a·tor
ref·u·gee
re·fund
re·fur·bish
re·fus·al
ref·u·ta·tion
re·gal (royal; see *regale*)
re·gale (to give pleasure; see *regal*)
re·ga·lia
re·gard·less
re·gat·ta
re·gen·cy (–cies)
re·gen·er·ate
re·gent
re·gime, ré·gime
reg·i·men (systematic plan; see
     regiment)
reg·i·ment (military unit; see *regimen*)
re·gion·al
reg·is·ter (to enroll formally; see
     registrar)
reg·is·trar (keeper of records; see
     register)
reg·is·try (–tries)
re·gres·sion
re·gres·sive
re·gret·ta·bly
reg·u·lar·i·ty (–ties)
reg·u·la·to·ry
re·gur·gi·tate
re·ha·bil·i·tate
re·hears·al
reign (sovereignty; see *rain, rein*)
re·im·burse
rein (part of a bridle; stop *or* check;
     see *rain, reign*)
rein·deer
re·in·force, re·en·force
re·in·vest·ment
re·is·sue
re·it·er·ate
re·jec·tion
re·join·der
re·ju·ve·nate
re·lapse
re·la·tion
rel·a·tive
rel·a·tiv·i·ty (–ties)
re·lax·a·tion
re·lay
re·lease

rel·e·gate
re·lent·less
rel·e·van·cy (–cies)
rel·e·vant
re·li·abil·i·ty
re·li·ance
rel·ic
re·lied
re·lief
re·lieve
re·li·gious
re·lo·cate
re·luc·tant
re·main
re·main·der
re·mark·able
re·me·di·a·ble
re·me·di·al
rem·e·dy (–dies)
re·mem·brance
rem·i·nis·cence
re·mis·sion
re·mit·tance
rem·nant
re·mon·strate
re·morse·ful
re·mote
re·mov·able
re·mu·ner·ate
re·nais·sance, re·na·scence
ren·der
ren·dez·vous (plural also ren·dez·vous)
ren·di·tion
ren·e·gade
re·nege
re·ne·go·ti·ate
re·new·al
re·nounce
ren·o·vate
rent·al
re·nun·ci·a·tion
re·open
re·or·ga·ni·za·tion
re·pair·able
rep·a·ra·tion
rep·ar·tee
re·pa·tri·ate
re·peal
re·peat·ed·ly
re·pel·lent, re·pel·lant
re·pen·tance
re·per·cus·sion
rep·er·toire
rep·er·to·ry (–ries)
rep·e·ti·tious
re·place·able
re·plen·ish
re·plete
rep·li·ca
rep·li·cate

re·port·able
re·pose
re·pos·i·to·ry (–ries)
re·pos·sess
rep·re·hend
rep·re·hen·si·ble
rep·re·sen·ta·tive
re·pres·sion
re·prieve
re·pri·sal
re·prise
re·proach
rep·ro·bate
re·pro·duc·tion
rep·tile
re·pub·lic
re·pu·di·ate
re·pug·nance
re·pul·sive
rep·u·ta·ble
re·pute
re·quest
re·qui·em
re·quire·ment
req·ui·site
req·ui·si·tion
re·scind
res·cue
re·search
re·sem·blance
re·sent·ful
res·er·va·tion
res·er·voir
re·shuf·fle
res·i·dence
res·i·den·tial
re·sid·u·al
res·i·due
res·ig·na·tion
re·sis·tance
re·sist·er (one who opposes; see *resistor*)
re·sis·tor (electrical device; see *resister*)
res·o·lute
re·solve
res·o·nance
res·o·nate
res·o·na·tor
re·sound
re·source·ful
re·spect·abil·i·ty
re·spec·tive·ly
res·pi·ra·tion
res·pi·ra·tor
re·splen·dent
re·spon·dent
re·spon·si·bil·i·ty (–ties)
re·spon·sive
re·spon·so·ry (–ries)
re·state·ment
res·tau·rant

res·ti·tu·tion
res·to·ra·tion
re·strain
re·stric·tion
re·struc·ture
re·sult
re·sume (to begin again; see *resumé*)
re·su·mé, re·su·me (short account of career; see *resume*)
re·sump·tion
re·sur·gence
res·ur·rec·tion
re·sus·ci·tate
re·tail·ing
re·tain·er
re·tal·i·ate
re·tar·da·tion
re·ten·tive
ret·i·cence
ret·i·nue
re·tire·ment
re·tract
re·trench
ret·ri·bu·tion
re·triev·al
ret·ro·ac·tive
ret·ro·grade
ret·ro·spect
re·turn·able
re·unite
re·us·able
re·veal
rev·e·la·tion
rev·el·er, rev·el·ler
rev·el·ry
re·venge·ful
rev·e·nue
re·ver·ber·ate
rev·er·ence
rev·er·ie, rev·ery (rev·er·ies)
re·ver·sal
re·vers·ible
re·vert·ible
re·view (to see again; see *revue*)
re·vile
re·vi·sion
re·vi·tal·ize
re·viv·al
re·vive
rev·o·ca·ble, re·vok·able
re·voke
re·volt
rev·o·lu·tion
rev·o·lu·tion·ize
re·volv·er
re·vue (theatrical production; see *review*)
re·vul·sion
re·ward
re·write

rhap·so·dy (–dies)
rheo·stat
rhet·o·ric
rheu·mat·ic
rhi·noc·er·os (–noc·er·os·es *or* –noc·eros *or* –noc·eri)
rhu·barb
rhyme, rime
rhythm
rhyth·mic
rib·ald
rib·bon
rick·ety
rid·dance
rid·dle
ridge
ri·dic·u·lous
ri·fle
rift
rig·ging
right (correct; see *rite*)
righ·teous
ri·gid·i·ty (–ties)
rig·ma·role, rig·a·ma·role
rig·or·ous
ring·er
rinsing
ri·ot·ous
ri·par·i·an
rip·ple
risky
ris·qué (French: off·color)
rite (a ceremonial act; see *right*)
rit·u·al
ri·val·ry (–ries)
riv·er·side
riv·et
roach
roam
roast
rob·bery (–ber·ies)
ro·bot
ro·bust
rock·et
ro·co·co
ro·dent
ro·deo (ro·de·os)
rogue
rogu·ish
rol·lick·ing
ro·man·ti·cize
roomy
roost·er
ro·sette
ros·ter
ros·trum (ros·tra *or* rostrums)
ro·ta·ry (–ries)
ro·ta·tion
rote
ro·tund

ro·tun·da
rouge
rough
rou·lette
rouse
route
rou·tine
roving
row·dy
roy·al·ist
roy·al·ty (–ties)
rub·bery
rub·bish
rub·ble
ru·bric
rud·der
ru·di·men·ta·ry
ruf·fi·an
ruf·fle
rug·by
rug·ged
ru·in·ous
ruling
rum·ba, rhum·ba
rum·ble
ru·mi·nate
rum·mage
ru·mor
run·ner
rup·ture
ru·ral
ruse
rus·set
rus·tic
rus·ti·cate
rust·i·ness
rus·tle
ru·ta·ba·ga
ruth·less
rye

S

sab·bat·i·cal
sa·ber, sa·bre
sa·ble
sab·o·tage
sab·o·teur
sac·cha·rine
sa·chet
sac·ra·ment
sa·cred
sac·ri·fice
sac·ri·fi·cial
sac·ro·sanct
sad·den
sad·dle
sa·fa·ri
safe·ty (safeties)
saf·flow·er

sa·ga
sa·ga·cious
sage
sail (canvas used to propel ship;
    see *sale*)
sail·or
sal·able, sale·able
sal·ad
sal·a·ry (–ries)
sale (act of selling; see *sail*)
sales check
sales·clerk
sales tax
sa·lient
sa·line
sa·li·va
sal·i·vate
sal·low
salm·on (salmon *or* salmons)
sa·lon (elegant living room; see *saloon*)
sa·loon (place selling alcoholic drinks;
    see *salon*)
sal·u·tary
sa·lu·ta·to·ri·an
sa·lute
sal·vage
sal·va·tion
salve
sam·ple
san·a·to·ri·um (–riums *or* –ria)
sanc·ti·mo·nious
sanc·tion
sanc·tu·ary (–ar·ies)
san·dal
sand·wich
san·i·tary
san·i·ta·tion
sap·ling
sap·phire
sar·casm
sar·cas·ti·cal·ly
sar·dine (sardines *or* sardine)
sar·don·ic
sa·ri, sa·ree (Sanskrit: woman's
    Hindu garment)
sar·sa·pa·ril·la
sar·to·ri·al
sas·sa·fras
satch·el
sa·teen
sat·el·lite
sa·ti·ate
sa·ti·ety
sat·in
sat·ire
sat·is·fac·tion
sat·u·rate
sat·u·ra·tion
sat·ur·nine
sa·tyr

saucy
sau·er·kraut
sau·na
saun·ter
sau·sage
sau·té, sau·te
sav·age·ly
sa·van·na, sa·van·nah
sa·vant
sav·ior, sav·iour
sa·voir faire (French: sureness in
    social behavior)
sa·vory, sa·voury
sax·o·phone
scab·bard
sca·brous
scaf·fold
scald·ing
scal·lion
scal·lop, scol·lop
scalp·er
scan·dal
scan·dal·ous
scan·ner
scanty
scape·goat
scap·u·lar
scar·ci·ty (–ties)
scarf (scarves)
scary
scath·ing
scat·o·log·i·cal
scat·ter
scav·enge
sce·nar·io (–i·os)
sce·nar·ist
scen·ery (–er·ies)
sce·nic
scent·ed
scep·ter, scep·tre
sched·ule
sche·mat·ic
scheme
schism
schizo·phre·nia
schnau·zer
schol·ar·ly
scho·las·tic
school
schoo·ner
schwa
sci·at·ic
sci·ence
sci·en·tif·ic
scin·til·late
scis·sors
scle·ro·sis
scoff·law
scone
scope

scorch

scor·ing

scorn·ful

scor·pi·on

scoun·drel

scour

scourge

scram·ble

scrap·ing (grate harshly; see *scrapping*)

scrap·ping (quarreling, converting to scrap; see *scraping*)

scratch

scraw·ny

scream

screech

screen

screen·play

screw

scrib·ble

scrim·mage

scrim·shaw

script

scrip·ture

scrounge

scruff

scru·ple

scru·pu·lous

scru·ti·nize

scru·ti·ny

scu·ba

scuff

scuf·fle

sculp·tor

sculp·ture

scur·ri·lous

scut·tle

scythe

sea (body of water; see *see*)

seamy

sé·ance (French: a session to receive spirit communications)

search

sea·shore

sea·son·al

seat

se·cede

se·ces·sion

se·clu·sion

sec·ond·ary

se·cre·cy (–cies)

se·cret

sec·re·tar·i·at

sec·re·tary (–tar·ies)

se·crete

se·cre·tive

sect

sec·tar·i·an

sec·tion·al

sec·tor

sec·u·lar

se·cu·ri·ty (–ties)

se·dan

se·date

sed·a·tive

sed·en·tary

se·der (seders *or* se·da·rim)

sedge

sed·i·ment

se·di·tion

se·duce

se·duc·tive

sed·u·lous

see (perceive by eye; see *sea*)

seed·ling

seem·ing·ly

seep·age

seer·suck·er

see·saw

seethe

seg·ment

seg·re·gate

seg·re·ga·tion

se·gue

seine

seis·mic

seis·mo·graph

seize

sei·zure

sel·dom

se·lec·tion

se·lec·tive

self-con·scious

self-de·fense

self-por·trait

sell (to exact a price for; see *cell*)

sell·er (one who offers for sale; see *cellar*)

se·man·tics

sem·a·phore

sem·blance

se·mes·ter

semi·an·nu·al

sem·i·nal

sem·i·nar

sem·i·nary (–nar·ies)

semi·pro·fes·sion·al

sem·pi·ter·nal

sen·a·to·ri·al

se·nes·cence

se·nile

se·nil·i·ty

se·nior·i·ty

sen·sa·tion

sense

sense·less

sen·si·bil·i·ty (–ties)

sen·si·tive

sen·si·tiv·i·ty (–ties)

sen·so·ry

sen·su·al

sen·su·ous

sent (past of send; see *cent*)

sen·tence

sen·ten·tious

sen·tient

sen·ti·men·tal

sen·ti·nel

sen·try (sentries)

sep·a·ra·ble

sep·a·rate

sep·a·ra·tion

sep·ul·cher, sep·ul·chre

se·quel

se·quence

se·quen·tial

se·ques·ter

se·quoia

ser·e·nade

se·ren·i·ty

serge

ser·geant

se·ri·al (arranged in series; see *cereal*)

se·ries (plural also series)

se·ri·ous

ser·mon

ser·pent

ser·rat·ed

se·rum (serums *or* se·ra)

ser·vant

serv·er

ser·vice

ser·vice·able

ser·vi·tude

ses·a·me

ses·sion

ses·tet

set·tle

set·tle·ment

sev·enth

sev·er·al

sev·er·ance

se·ver·i·ty

sew·age

sew·ing

sex·ism

sex·tant

sex·ton

sex·u·al

sexy

shab·by

shack·le

shad·ing

shad·owy

shaft

shag·gy

shaky

shale

shal·low

sham·ble

shame·ful

sham·poo
sham·rock
shank
shan·ty (shanties)
shape
shard
share·crop·per
shark
sharp·en
shat·ter
shav·ing
sheaf (sheaves)
shear (cut off; see *sheer*)
sheath (case for a blade; see *sheathe*)
sheathe (to put into a sheath; see *sheath*)
sheer (transparent; see *shear*)
sheet
sheikh, sheik
shelf (shelves)
shel·lac
shel·ter
she·nan·i·gan
shep·herd
sher·bet, sher·bert
sher·iff
sher·ry (sherries)
shib·bo·leth
shield
shifty
shin·gle
shining
shiny
ship·ment
shirk·er
shirt·sleeve
shish ke·bab
shiv·er
shoal
shock
shoe
shop
shoring
short·age
short·en·ing
short·hand
short-term
should
shoul·der
shout
shove
shov·el
show·case
show·er
showy
shrap·nel
shrewd
shriek
shrine
shrink

shriv·el
shroud
shrub·bery
shrug
shud·der
shuf·fle
shut·ter
shut·tle
shy
sib·i·lant
sick·le
sick·ly
sick·ness
side·line
si·de·re·al
siege
sieve
sigh
sight·ly
sign
sig·nal
sig·na·to·ry (–ries)
sig·na·ture
sig·nif·i·cant
si·lent
sil·hou·ette
sil·i·con
silky
sil·ver·ware
sil·very
sim·i·an
sim·i·lar
sim·i·lar·i·ty (–ties)
sim·i·le
si·mil·i·tude
sim·per
sim·ple
sim·pli·fy
sim·u·la·tion
si·mul·ta·neous
sin·cere·ly
si·ne·cure
sin·ew
singe
singe·ing
sin·gle
sin·gly
sin·gu·lar·i·ty (–ties)
sin·is·ter
sin·u·ous
si·nus
si·phon, sy·phon
si·ren
sis·ter·ly
site (place; see *cite*)
situated
sit·u·a·tion
six·ty (sixties)
size
siz·zle

skean, skeane, skein
skel·e·ton
skep·ti·cal
sketchy
skied
skiing
skil·let
skill·ful
skimming
skimpy
skip·per
skirl
skir·mish
skit·tish
skul·dug·gery, skull·dug·gery (–ger·ies)
skulk
sky
slack·en
slack·er
sla·lom
slan·der·ous
slaugh·ter
slav·ery
slea·zy
sledge
sledge·ham·mer
sleek
sleeve
sleigh
slen·der·ize
sleuth
slic·ing
slick·er
slide
slight·ing·ly
slime
slip·pery
slip·shod
slith·er
sliv·er
slob·ber
sloe (fruit; see *slow*)
slo·gan
sloop
slope
slop·ing
slop·py
sloth·ful
slouch
slough
slov·en·ly
slow (not hasty; see *sloe*)
sludge
slug·gish
sluice
slum·ber
slushy
sly
small
smart

smat·ter·ing

smear

smelly

smid·gen, smid·geon, smid·gin, smidge

smile

smirk

smith·er·eens

smoke

smol·der, smoul·der

smooth

smor·gas·bord

smudge

snail

snake

sneak·er

sneer

sneeze

snif·ter

snip·er

snob·bery (–ber·ies)

snor·kel

snow·flake

snow·mo·bile

snug·gle

soap opera

soapy

soar·ing

so·ber·ly

so·bri·ety

soc·cer

so·cia·bil·i·ty (–ties)

so·cial·ism

so·cial·ize

so·ci·e·tal

so·ci·e·ty (–ies)

so·cio·eco·nom·ic

so·ci·ol·o·gy

sod·den

soft·ware

sog·gy

soil

soi·rée, soi·ree (French: evening party)

so·journ

so·lace

so·lar

sol·der

sol·dier

sole (fish *or* bottom of foot; see *soul*)

so·le·cism

sol·emn

so·lem·ni·ty (–ties)

so·le·noid

so·lic·it

so·lic·i·tor

so·lic·i·tous

so·lic·i·tude

sol·i·dar·i·ty

so·lid·i·fy

so·lil·o·quize

sol·i·taire

sol·i·tary

sol·i·tude

so·lo·ist

sol·u·ble

so·lu·tion

solv·able

sol·ven·cy

som·ber, som·bre

son (male child; see *sun*)

so·nar

son·ic

son·net

so·no·rous

soothe

sooty

so·phis·ti·cat·ed

soph·ist·ry

soph·o·more

so·po·rif·ic

so·pra·no (–nos)

sor·cer·er

sor·did

so·ror·i·ty (–ties)

sor·row·ful

soul (spiritual essence; see *sole*)

sought

sound

soup du jour (French: soup of the day)

sour

source

south·ern

sou·ve·nir

sov·er·eign, sov·ran

soy·bean, soya bean

space

spacial

spa·cious

spa·ghet·ti

span·gled

span·iel

spar·ing·ly

spar·kle

spar·row

sparse

spasm

spas·mod·ic

spas·tic

spa·tial

spat·u·la

spay

speak·er

spe·cial

spe·cial·ty (–ties)

spe·cies

spe·cif·ic

spec·i·fi·ca·tion

spec·i·fic·i·ty

spec·i·men

spec·ta·cle

spec·tac·u·lar

spec·ta·tor

spec·tral

spec·trum

spec·u·late

spec·u·la·tion

speech·less

spell-check, spell-checker

spend·thrift

sperm

sphere

spher·i·cal

sphinx (sphinx·es *or* sphin·ges)

spice

spic·ing

spig·ot

spill·age

spin·ach

spin·dle

spin·dly

spin·et

spin·ster

spi·ral

spir·i·tu·al

spite·ful

splashy

splen·dor

splice

splin·ter

splut·ter

spoil·age

spokes·man

spo·li·a·tion

spon·dee

sponge

spongy

spon·sor

spon·ta·ne·i·ty

spon·ta·ne·ous

spooky

spoon·ful (spoonfuls *or* spoons·ful)

spo·rad·ic

spore

sport·ive

sporty

spot·light

spot·ty

spouse

spright·ly

spring·time

springy

sprin·kling

sprock·et

sprout

spry

spunky

spu·ri·ous

spurred

spu·tum (spu·ta)

spy (spies)

squab·ble

squad·ron
squal·id
squa·lor
squan·der
square
squash
squat·ted
squat·ter
squawk
squeaky
squeal
squea·mish
squeeze
squelch
squint
squire
squirm
squir·rel (squir·rels or squir·rel)
squirt
sta·bil·i·ty (–ties)
sta·ble
stac·ca·to
stacked
sta·di·um (–dia or –di·ums)
staff
stage
staging
stag·nant
staid
stair·case
stake (pointed post; see steak)
sta·lac·tite
sta·lag·mite
stale·mate
stalk
stal·lion
stal·wart
stam·i·na
stam·mer
stam·pede
stance
stan·dard·ize
stand·by
stan·za
sta·ple
starchy
star·ry
star·tle
star·va·tion
stash
state
state·ment
stat·ic
sta·tion
sta·tion·ary (immobile; see stationery)
sta·tio·nery (materials for writing; see stationary)
stat·is·ti·cian
sta·tis·tics
stat·ue

stat·ure
sta·tus (sta·tus·es)
stat·u·to·ry
staunch
stead·fast
steak (slice of meat; see stake)
steal (to take the property of another; see steel)
stealthy
steel (a metal; see steal)
stee·ple
steer·age
stein
stel·lar
sten·cil
ste·nog·ra·pher
sten·to·ri·an
step (an advance of a foot; see steppe)
steppe (treeless plain; see step)
ste·reo·type
ste·reo·typ·i·cal
ster·ile
ster·ling
ste·ve·dore
stew·ard
stick·ler
sticky
sti·fle
stig·ma·tize
sti·let·to
stim·u·late
stim·u·lus
stin·gy
sti·pend
stip·u·late
stir·rup
stitch
stock·ade
stock·bro·ker
stodgy
stol·id
stom·ach·ache
stop·page
stor·age
sto·ried
stow·age
strad·dle
strag·gle
straight (free from curves; see strait)
straight·en
strait (a narrow passageway between two bodies of water; see straight)
strang·er
stran·gle
stran·gu·late
strat·a·gem
stra·te·gic
strat·e·gy (–gies)
strat·i·fy
strato·sphere

stra·tum (stra·ta)
streaky
stream·line
strength
stren·u·ous
stress·ful
stretch·er
stri·at·ed
strick·en
stric·ture
stri·dent
strike
strin·gent
strobe
stroll
strong
struc·tur·al
struc·ture
strug·gle
strych·nine
stub·ble
stub·by
stuc·co (stuccos or stuccoes)
stu·dent
stu·dio
stu·di·ous
study (stud·ies)
stul·ti·fy
stum·bling
stu·pe·fy
stu·pen·dous
stur·dy
stur·geon
stut·ter
sty, stye (sties or styes)
style
styl·ish
styl·ized
sty·lus (sty·li or sty·lus·es)
suave
sub·com·mit·tee
sub·con·scious
sub·di·vi·sion
sub·due
sub·ject (noun), sub·ject (verb)
sub·ju·gate
sub·lime
sub·lim·i·nal
sub·ma·rine
sub·merge
sub·mis·sion
sub·or·di·nate
sub·orn
sub·poe·na
sub·scribe
sub·scrip·tion
sub·se·quent
sub·ser·vi·ent
sub·side
sub·sid·i·ary

sub·si·dize
sub·si·dy (–dies)
sub·sis·tence
sub·stance
sub·stan·tial
sub·stan·tive
sub·sti·tute
sub·sume
sub·ter·fuge
sub·tle
sub·trac·tion
sub·ur·bia
sub·ver·sion
suc·ceed
suc·cess·ful
suc·ces·sion
suc·ces·sor
suc·cinct
suc·co·tash
suc·cu·lent
suc·cumb
suck·le
suc·tion
sud·den
sudsy
sue
suede, suède
suf·fer·ance
suf·fice
suf·fi·cient
suf·fo·cate
suf·frage
suf·fuse
sug·ar
sug·ges·tion
sui·cid·al
suit·able
suite
suit·or
sulky
sul·fur, sul·phur
sul·try
sum·ma·ry (abridgment of discourse;
    see *summery*)
sum·mer·time
sum·mery (like summer; see *summary*)
sum·mit
sum·mon
sump·tu·ous
sun (celestial body; see *son*)
su·per·an·nu·ate
su·perb
su·per·cil·ious
su·per·fi·cial
su·per·flu·i·ty (–ties)
su·per·flu·ous
su·per·high·way
su·per·in·ten·dent
su·pe·ri·or
su·per·la·tive

su·per·nat·u·ral
su·per·sede
su·per·sti·tious
su·per·vi·sion
su·per·vi·so·ry
su·pine
sup·plant
sup·ple
sup·ple·men·ta·ry
sup·pli·ant
sup·pli·cate
supply (supplies)
sup·port·ive
sup·po·si·tion
sup·pos·i·to·ry (–ries)
sup·pres·sion
sup·pu·rate
su·prem·a·cy (–cies)
sur·cease
sur·charge
sure·ty (–ties)
sur·face
sur·feit
sur·fer
surge
sur·geon
sur·gery (–ger·ies)
sur·gi·cal
sur·mise
sur·name
sur·plus
sur·prise
sur·re·al·ism
sur·ren·der
sur·ro·gate
sur·round·ings
sur·tax
sur·veil·lance
sur·vey (noun), sur·vey (verb)
sur·viv·al
sus·cep·ti·bil·i·ty (–ties)
sus·cep·ti·ble
sus·pect
sus·pense
sus·pi·cious
sus·te·nance
su·ture
svelte
swad·dling
swag·ger
swampy
swank
swar·thy
swash·buck·ler
swath, swathe
swear
sweaty
sweet·ened
swel·ter
swept

swerve
swin·dle
swing
swirl
swish
switch
swiv·el
swollen
sword
syc·a·more
sy·co·phant
syl·lab·ic
syl·lab·i·fy
syl·la·bus (–bi *or* ·bus·es)
syl·lo·gism
sylph
syl·van
sym·bol·ic
sym·met·ri·cal, sym·met·ric
sym·me·try (–tries)
sym·pa·thet·ic
sym·phon·ic
sym·po·sium (–sia *or* –siums)
symp·tom
syn·chro·nize
syn·di·cate
syn·o·nym
syn·op·sis (–op·ses)
syn·op·tic
syn·tax
syn·the·size
syn·thet·ic
syph·i·lis
sy·ringe
syr·upy
sys·tem·at·ic
sys·tem·a·tize
sys·tem·ic

T

Ta·bas·co
tab·by (tabbies)
tab·er·na·cle
tab·la·ture
ta·bling
ta·ble·spoon·ful (tablespoonfuls *or*
    ta·ble·spoons·ful)
tab·let
tab·loid
ta·boo, ta·bu
tab·o·ret, tab·ou·ret (French: type of
    seat *or* stand)
tab·u·lar
tab·u·late
tab·u·la·tor
ta·chom·e·ter
tac·it
tac·i·turn
tack·le

tacky
tact·ful
tac·tic·al
tac·tile
tad·pole
taf·fe·ta
taff·rail
taf·fy (taffies)
tai·chi, t'ai chi
tail (rear end; see *tale*)
tai·lored
taint
tak·ing
talc
tal·cum
tale (story: see *tail*)
tal·ent
tales·man (juror; see *talisman*)
tal·is·man (charm: see *talesman*)
talk·ative
talk·ie (sound motion picture;
    see *talky*)
talky (too much talk; see *talkie*)
tall·ish
tal·low
tal·ly (tal·lies)
tal·on
ta·ma·le
tam·a·rack
tam·bou·rine
tam·ing
tam·per
tan·a·ger
tan·dem
tan·ge·lo
tan·gent
tan·gen·tial
tan·ger·ine
tan·gi·ble
tan·gled
tan·gling
tan·go (tangos)
tangy
tan·kard
tan·nery (−ner·ies)
tanning
tan·ta·lize
tan·ta·mount
tan·trum
tape
ta·per
tap·es·tried
tap·es·try (−tries)
tap·i·o·ca
tar·an·tel·la
ta·ran·tu·la
tar·di·ly
tar·dy
tare (weed; see *tear*)
tar·get

tar·iff
tar·mac
tar·nish
tar·ot
tar·pau·lin
tar·pon (tarpon *or* tarpons)
tar·ra·gon
tar·ry
tar·tan
tar·tar
task
tas·sel
taste·ful
tasty
tat·tered
tat·too
taught
taunt
taupe
taut
tav·ern
taw·dry
taw·ny
tax·a·tion
tax·ex·empt
taxi·der·my
tax·ied
taxi·ing
tax·on·o·my
tax·pay·er
teach·able
tea·ket·tle
teak·wood
team (group; see *teem*)
team·ster
tear (damage from being torn; see *tare*)
teas·ing
teat
tech·ni·cal
tech·ni·cian
tech·nique
tech·no·log·i·cal, tech·no·log·ic
tech·nol·o·gy (−gies)
tech·no·phile
te·dious
te·di·um
teem (filled to overflowing; see *team*)
teen·age
tee·ter
teethe
tee·to·tal·er, tee·to·tal·ler
tele·cast
tele·com·mu·ni·ca·tion
tele·con·fer·ence
tele·gram
tele·graph
tele·mar·ket·er
te·lep·a·thy
tele·pho·to
tele·scope

tele·vise
te·mer·i·ty (−ties)
tem·per·a·ment
tem·per·ate
tem·per·a·ture
tem·pered
tem·pes·tu·ous
tem·plate
tem·ple
tem·po (tem·pi *or* tempos)
tem·po·ral
tem·po·rar·i·ly
tem·po·rize
tempt
temp·ta·tion
tem·pu·ra
ten·a·ble
te·na·cious
te·nac·i·ty
ten·ant
ten·den·cy (−cies)
ten·den·tious, ten·den·cious
ten·der·ize
ten·der·loin
ten·der·ly
ten·don
ten·dril
ten·e·ment
te·net
ten·or
tense
ten·sile
ten·sion
ten·ta·cle
ten·ta·tive
ten·ter·hook
ten·u·ous
ten·ure
te·pee, tee·pee, ti·pi
tep·id
ter·gi·ver·sa·tion
ter·i·ya·ki (Japanese: spicy meat *or*
    shellfish dish)
ter·ma·gant
ter·mi·nal
ter·mi·nate
ter·mi·na·tion
ter·mi·nol·o·gy (−gies)
ter·mi·nus (−ni *or* −nus·es)
ter·mite
ter·race
ter·ra·cot·ta
ter·rain, ter·rane
ter·rar·i·um (−ia *or* −i·ums)
ter·res·tri·al
ter·ri·ble
ter·ri·er
ter·rif·ic
ter·ri·fy
ter·ri·to·ri·al

ter·ri·to·ry (–ries)
ter·ror·ize
ter·ry (terries)
terse
ter·tia·ry (–ries)
tes·sel·tate
tes·ta·ment
tes·ta·tor
test·ed
tes·ti·cle
tes·ti·fy
tes·ti·mo·ni·al
tes·ti·mo·ny (–nies)
tes·ty
tet·a·nus
tête-à-tête (French: private conversation
    between two people)
teth·er
tet·ra·chlo·ride
te·tram·e·ter
text·book
tex·tile
tex·ture
thank·ful
thatch
the·ater, the·atre
the·at·ri·cal
theft
their (relating to them; see *there*)
the·ism
the·mat·ic
theme
thence
the·oc·ra·cy (–cies)
theo·lo·gian
the·ol·o·gy (–gies)
the·o·rem
the·o·ret·i·cal
the·o·rist
the·o·ry (–ries)
the·os·o·phy
ther·a·peu·tic
ther·a·pist
ther·a·py (–pies)
there (in that place; see *their*)
ther·mal
ther·mom·e·ter
ther·mo·stat
the·sau·rus (–sau·ri *or* –sau·rus·es)
the·sis (the·ses)
thes·pi·an
thew
they
thick·en·ing
thick·et
thief
thiev·ery (–er·ies)
thigh
thim·ble·ful
think·able

thin·ner
third
thirsty
thir·teenth
this·tle
thith·er
thong
tho·rac·ic
thorny
thor·ough
thor·ough·bred
thor·ough·fare
though
thought
thought·ful
thou·sand
thrash
thread·bare
threat·en
three-di·men·sion·al
thren·o·dy (–dies)
thresh·old
thrift
thrive
throat
throe
throm·bo·sis (–bo·ses)
throne
thronged
throt·tle
through
through·out
thru·way
thug
thumb
thump
thun·der·ous
thwart
thyme
thy·roid, thy·roi·dal
ti·ara
tick·et
tick·ing
tick·le
tid·al
tidings
ti·di·ness
tier
tight·rope
tile
till·age
tim·ber (wood; see *timbre*)
tim·bre (quality of sound; see *timber*)
time·ly
time·ta·ble
tim·id
timing
tim·o·rous
tim·pa·nist, tym·pa·nist
tinc·ture

tin·der
tinge
tin·gle
tin·kle
tin·ny
tin·sel
tint·ing
tip·sy
ti·rade
tire
tis·sue
tithe
tit·il·late
tit·i·vate, tit·ti·vate
titled
tit·tle
toasty
to·bac·co (–cos)
to·bog·gan
toc·sin
tod·dle
to·ga
to·geth·er·ness
tog·gle
toil
toile (French: type of fabric)
toil·worn
to·ken·ism
tole
tol·er·a·ble
tol·er·ance
toll
tom·a·hawk
to·ma·to (–toes)
tomb
to·mor·row
to·nal·i·ty (–ties)
tongue
tongu·ing
to·nic·i·ty
to·night
ton·nage
ton·sil·lec·to·my (–mies)
ton·sil·li·tis
ton·so·ri·al
ton·sure
tool·box
tooth·some
to·paz
top·i·cal
to·pog·ra·phy
to·pol·o·gy (–gies)
top·ple
top·sy-tur·vy
toque
to·re·a·dor (Spanish: bullfighter)
tor·men·tor, tor·ment·er
tor·na·do (– does *or* –dos)
tor·pe·do (–does)
tor·pid

tor·por
torque
tor·ren·tial
tor·rid·ly
tor·sion
tor·so (tor·sos *or* tor·si)
tor·ti·lla
tor·toise
tor·tu·ous
tor·ture
to·tal·ing
to·tal·i·tar·i·an
to·tal·i·ty (–ties)
to·tal·ly
to·tem
touch
touchy
tough·en
tou·pee (French: wig)
tour de force (French: a feat of
    strength, skill, or ingenuity)
tour·ism
tour·na·ment
tour·ney
tour·ni·quet
tou·sle
to·ward
tow·el·ing, tow·el·ling
tow·er·ing
tow·head
town house
tox·ic
tox·ic·i·ty
tox·in
tra·chea (–che·ae, –che·as, *or* –chea)
tracing
trac·ta·ble
trac·tion
trac·tor
trade·mark
trad·er
tra·di·tion
traf·fic
trag·e·dy (–dies)
trail
train·ing
trai·tor
trai·tor·ous
tra·jec·to·ry (–ries)
tram·mel
tram·ple
tram·po·line
trance
tran·quil
tran·quil·ize, tran·quil·lize
tran·quil·li·ty, tran·quil·i·ty
trans·ac·tion
trans·at·lan·tic
tran·scen·dence
trans·scen·den·tal

tran·con·ti·nen·tal
tran·scribe
trans·script
tran·sect
tran·sept
trans·fer·al
trans·fer·ence
trans·for·ma·tion
trans·fu·sion
trans·gres·sion
tran·sience
tran·sient
tran·sis·tor
tran·sit
tran·si·tion
tran·si·to·ry
trans·la·tion
trans·lu·cent
trans·mis·si·ble
trans·mit·tance
trans·mute
tran·som
trans·par·en·cy (–cies)
tran·spire
trans·port·able
trans·pose
trans·verse
tra·peze
trashy
trau·ma (traumas *or* trau·ma·ta)
tra·vail
trav·eled, trav·elled
trav·el·er, trav·el·ler
traveling, travelling
trav·el·ogue, trav·el·og
tra·verse
trav·es·ty (–ties)
trawl·er
treach·er·ous
trea·cle
trea·dle
trea·son·able
trea·sur·er
trea·tise
trea·ty (treaties)
tre·ble
trek·king
trel·lis
trem·ble
tre·men·dous
trem·or
trem·u·lous
tren·chant
trep·i·da·tion
tres·pass
tres·tle, tres·sel
tri·an·gle
tri·bal
trib·u·la·tion
tri·bu·nal

trib·u·tary
trick·ery
tri·col·or
tri·cy·cle
tri·dent
tri·fling
trig·ger
tril·o·gy (–gies)
tri·mes·ter
trin·ket
trio
tri·ple
trip·let
trip·li·cate
trip·tych
trite
tri·umph
tri·um·vi·rate
triv·et
triv·i·al
trol·ley, trol·ly (trolleys *or* trollies)
trom·bone
tro·phy (trophies)
trop·i·cal
trou·ba·dour
trou·bling
trough
troupe
trou·sers
trow·el
tru·an·cy (–cies)
tru·cu·lence
true
tru·ism
tru·ly
trum·pet·er
trun·cat·ed
trun·cheon
trun·dle
truss
trust·ee
truth·ful
try
tryst
tsu·na·mi (tsunamis *or* tsunami)
tu·ba
tu·ber·cu·lar
tu·ber·cu·lo·sis
tu·ber·ous
tu·bu·lar
tu·ition
tum·brel, tum·bril
tu·mes·cent
tu·mor
tu·mul·tu·ous
tun·dra
tung·sten
tu·nic
tun·nel·ing, tun·nel·ling
tur·ban

tur·bine
tur·bo·jet
tur·bu·lence
tu·reen
tur·moil
tur·pen·tine
tur·quoise, tur·quois
tur·tle
tus·sle
tus·sock
tu·te·lage
tu·te·lary
tu·to·ri·al
tut·ti-frut·ti
tux·e·do (–dos *or* –does)
twain
tweak
tweed
twee·zers
twelfth
twen·ti·eth
twi·light
twill
twine
twinge
twin·kling
twirl
twist
twitch
twit·ter
two·fer
ty·coon
ty·ing, tie·ing
type·script
type·writ·er
ty·phoid
ty·phoon
ty·phus
typ·i·cal
typ·i·fy
ty·pog·ra·phy
ty·ran·ni·cal, ty·ran·nic
tyr·an·nize
tyr·an·nous
tyr·an·ny (–nies)

U

ubiq·ui·tous
ubiq·ui·ty
ud·der (contains a cow's mammary
    glands; see *utter*)
ug·li·ness
uku·le·le, uke·le·le
ul·cer
ul·cer·ous
ul·te·ri·or
ul·ti·mate
ul·ti·ma·tum (–tums *or* –ta)
ul·tra

ul·tra·vi·o·let
um·ber
um·bil·i·cal
um·brage
um·brel·la
um·laut
um·pire
un·abat·ed
un·able
un·abridged
un·ac·cept·able
un·ac·com·pa·nied
un·ac·count·able
un·ac·cus·tomed
un·adorned
un·adul·ter·at·ed
un·af·fect·ed
un·aid·ed
un·alien·able
un·aligned
un·al·ter·able
un·am·big·u·ous
una·nim·i·ty
unan·i·mous
un·an·tic·i·pat·ed
un·ap·peal·ing
un·ap·pe·tiz·ing
un·ap·proach·able
un·armed
un·ashamed
un·asked
un·as·sail·able
un·as·sist·ed
un·at·trac·tive
un·avail·able
un·avoid·able
un·awares
un·bal·anced
un·be·com·ing
un·be·known
un·be·liev·able
un·bi·ased
un·bri·dled
un·budg·ing
un·can·ny
un·cer·tain·ty
un·change·able
un·char·i·ta·ble
un·cle
un·com·fort·able
un·com·mu·ni·ca·tive
un·com·pli·men·ta·ry
un·con·di·tion·al
un·con·scio·na·ble
un·con·scious
un·con·trol·la·ble
un·couth
un·de·bat·able
un·dem·o·crat·ic
un·de·ni·able

un·der·achiev·er
un·der·gird
un·der·grad·u·ate
un·der·priv·i·leged
un·der·signed
un·der·stand
un·der·state·ment
un·der·tak·er
un·de·sir·able
un·de·vi·at·ing
un·due
un·du·lant
un·dy·ing
un·easy
un·em·ployed
un·en·dur·able
un·equiv·o·cal
un·err·ing
un·fa·mil·iar
un·fash·ion·able
un·fa·vor·able
un·flag·ging
un·flat·ter·ing
un·flinch·ing
un·for·get·ta·ble
un·for·tu·nate·ly
un·fre·quent·ed
un·gain·ly
un·glued
un·gov·ern·able
un·gra·cious
un·gram·mat·i·cal
un·guard·ed
un·hes·i·tat·ing
un·hinged
uni·corn
uni·di·rec·tion·al
uni·fi·ca·tion
uni·for·mi·ty (–ties)
uni·fy
uni·lat·er·al
un·imag·in·able
un·im·pas·sioned
un·im·peach·able
un·in·hib·it·ed
un·in·tel·li·gi·ble
un·in·ten·tion·al
un·in·ter·rupt·ed
union
unique
uni·sex
uni·son
unit
uni·tary
unite
uni·ver·sal
uni·ver·si·ty (–ties)
un·kempt
un·know·able
un·known

un·law·ful
un·less
un·lim·it·ed
un·man·ner·ly
un·men·tion·able
un·mis·tak·able
un·mit·i·gat·ed
un·nec·es·sary
un·oc·cu·pied
un·of·fi·cial
un·or·tho·dox
un·pal·at·able
un·par·al·leled
un·par·lia·men·ta·ry
un·pleas·ant
un·plumbed
un·prec·e·dent·ed
un·pre·dict·able
un·prej·u·diced
un·pre·ten·tious
un·prof·it·able
un·qual·i·fied
un·ques·tion·ing
un·rav·el
un·re·al·is·tic
un·rea·son·able
un·re·lent·ing
un·re·spon·sive
un·re·strained
un·ri·valed, un·ri·valled
un·ruly
un·sad·dle
un·safe
un·sat·u·rat·ed
un·saved
un·sa·vory
un·scathed
un·sci·en·tif·ic
un·scram·ble
un·scru·pu·lous
un·sea·son·able
un·seat
un·seem·ly
un·seg·re·gat·ed
un·se·lect·ed
un·self·ish
un·set·tle
un·shack·le
un·sheathe
un·shod
un·sight·ly
un·skill·ful
un·snap
un·snarl
un·so·cia·ble
un·so·phis·ti·cat·ed
un·sought
un·sound
un·spar·ing
un·speak·able

un·sports·man·like
un·spot·ted
un·sta·ble
un·steady
un·stop·pa·ble
un·stressed
un·struc·tured
un·stud·ied
un·sub·stan·tial
un·suc·cess·ful
un·suit·able
un·swerv·ing
un·tan·gle
un·tapped
un·taught
un·ten·a·ble
un·think·able
un·ti·dy
un·tie
un·til
un·time·ly
un·ti·tled
un·touch·abil·i·ty
un·touch·able
un·trod·den, un·trod
un·truth·ful
un·tu·tored
un·twine
un·used
un·usu·al
un·ut·ter·able
un·var·nished
un·veil
un·ver·bal·ized
un·voiced
un·war·rant·able
un·wary
un·whole·some
un·wieldy
un·wise
un·wit·ting
un·wor·thi·ness
un·wound
un·writ·ten
un·yield·ing
un·yoke
un·zip
up·beat
up·braid
up·bring·ing
up·com·ing
up·date
up·grade
up·heav·al
up·hol·ster
up·lift
up·load
up·on
up·right·ness
up·ris·ing

up·roar·i·ous
up·set
up·side down
up·stage
up·stand·ing
up·surge
up·swept
up·tight
up·turn
up·ward, up·wards
up·wind
ura·ni·um
ur·ban (relating to a city; see *urbane*)
ur·bane (suave; see *urban*)
ur·ban·ite
ur·chin
ure·mia
ure·ter
ure·thra (–thras *or* –thrae)
urg·ing
ur·gen·cy (–cies)
uric
uri·nal
uri·nary
urine
urn
us·able, use·able
us·age
use·ful
use·ful·ness
ush·er
usu·al
usu·al·ly
usu·rer
usu·ri·ous
usurp
usu·ry
uten·sil
uter·ine
uter·us (uteri *or* –us·es)
util·i·tar·i·an
util·i·ty (–ties)
ut·most
uto·pi·an
ut·ter (to speak or pronounce; see *udder*)
ut·ter·ance
ut·ter·most
uvu·la (–las *or* –lae)

V

va·can·cy (–cies)
va·cant
va·cate
va·ca·tion·ing
vac·ci·nate
vac·cine
vac·il·late
vac·il·la·tion

va·cu·i·ty (–ties)
vac·u·ole
vac·u·ous
vac·u·um
vag·a·bond
va·ga·ry (–ries)
va·gran·cy (–cies)
va·grant
vague
vain (worthless; see *vane*)
va·lance (drapery: see *valence*)
val·e·dic·tion
val·e·dic·to·ri·an
val·e·dic·to·ry (–ries)
va·lence (combining power or
    chemical element; see *valance*)
val·en·tine
va·le·ri·an
va·let
val·iant
val·id
val·i·date
va·lid·i·ty
val·late
val·ley (valleys)
val·or
valu·able
val·u·ate
val·u·a·tor
val·ue
val·ued
val·ue·less
valve
val·vu·lar
va·moose
vam·pire
va·na·di·um
van·dal·ism
van·dal·ize
vane (weathercock; see *vain*)
van·guard
va·nil·la
van·ish
van·i·ty (–ties)
van·quish
van·tage
va·pid·i·ty (–ties)
va·por
va·por·i·za·tion
va·por·iz·er
va·por·ous
var·i·abil·i·ty
var·i·able
var·i·ance
var·i·ant
var·i·a·tion
var·i·cose
var·i·cos·i·ty (–ties)
varied
va·ri·e·ty (–ties)

var·i·ous
var·mint
var·nish
var·si·ty (–ties)
vary
vas·cu·lar
vase
va·sec·to·my (–mies)
Vas·e·line
vast·ly
vaude·ville
vaude·vil·lian
vault
vaunt
veal
vec·tor
veer
ve·gan
veg·e·ta·ble
veg·e·tar·i·an
veg·e·tar·i·an·ism
veg·e·tate
veg·e·ta·tive
ve·he·mence
ve·hi·cle
ve·hic·u·lar
veiled
veined
vel·lum (leather binding; see *velum*)
ve·loc·i·ty (–ties)
ve·lour, ve·lours (plural also ve·lours)
ve·lum (ve·la) (part of soft palate;
    see *vellum*)
vel·vet
vel·vety
ve·nal
vend
ven·der, ven·dor
ven·det·ta
ve·neer
ven·er·a·ble
ven·er·ate
ven·er·a·tor
ve·ne·re·al
ven·ery
ve·ne·tian blind
ven·geance
venge·ful
ven·i·son
ven·om
ven·om·ous
vent
ven·ti·late
ven·ti·la·tor
ven·tral
ven·tri·cle
ven·tril·o·quist
ven·ture
ven·ture·some
ven·tur·ous

ven·ue
ve·ra·cious
ve·rac·i·ty (–ties)
ve·ran·da, ve·ran·dah
ver·bal·ly
ver·ba·tim
ver·be·na
ver·biage
ver·bose
ver·dict
verge
verg·ing
ve·rid·i·cal
ver·i·fi·able
ver·i·fi·ca·tion
ver·i·fy
ver·i·ly
veri·si·mil·i·tude
ver·i·ta·ble
ver·i·ty (–ties)
ver·mi·cel·li
ver·mil·ion, ver·mil·lion
ver·min (plural also ver·min)
ver·min·ous
ver·mouth
ver·nac·u·lar
ver·nal
ver·ni·er
ver·sa·til·i·ty
verse
ver·si·cle
ver·si·fi·ca·tion
ver·si·fi·er
ver·sion
ver·sus
ver·te·bra (–brae *or* –bras)
ver·te·brate
ver·tex (ver·ti·ces *or* ver·tex·es)
ver·ti·cal
ver·tig·i·nous
ver·ti·go (–goes *or* –gos)
verve
very
ves·sel
ves·ti·bule
ves·tige
vest·ment
ves·try (–tries)
ves·ture
vetch
vet·er·an
vet·er·i·nar·i·an
vet·er·i·nary
ve·to (–toes)
vex·a·tion
vex·a·tious
vi·a·ble
via·duct
vi·al (small container; see *vile*)
vi·and

vi·at·i·cum (–cums or –ca)
vibes
vi·brant
vi·brate
vi·bra·tor
vi·bur·num
vi·car·i·ous
vi·chys·soise
vic·i·nage
vi·cin·i·ty (–ties)
vi·cious
vi·cis·si·tude
vic·tim·ize
vic·to·ri·ous
vic·to·ry (–ries)
vict·ual
vid·eo·tape
view·ing
vig·i·lance
vig·i·lan·te
vi·gnette
vig·or·ous
vile (wretchedly bad; see vial)
vil·i·fi·ca·tion
vil·i·fy
vil·lag·er
vil·lain
vil·lainy (–lain·ies)
vin·ci·ble
vin·cu·lum (–lums or –la)
vin·di·cate
vin·dic·tive
vin·e·gar
vin·ery (–er·ies)
vin·tage
vi·nyl
vi·o·la
vi·o·la·ble
vi·o·late
vi·o·lence
vi·o·let
vi·o·lin
vi·per
vir·gin·al
vir·gin·i·ty (–ties)
vir·i·des·cent
vi·rid·i·ty
vir·tu·al
vir·tu·al·ly
vir·tue
vir·tu·os·i·ty (–ties)
vir·tu·o·so (–sos or –si)
vir·tu·ous
vir·u·lence
vi·rus (vi·rus·es)
vis·age
vis-à-vis (French: face to face with)
vis·cer·al
vis·cos·i·ty (–ties)

vis·count
vis·cous
vis·i·bil·i·ty (–ties)
vis·i·ble
vi·sion·ary
vis·i·ta·tion
vis·i·tor
vi·sor, vizor
vis·ta
vi·su·al
vi·su·al·ize
vi·su·al·i·za·tion
vi·tal
vi·tal·i·ty (–ties)
vi·ta·min
vi·ti·ate
vit·re·ous
vi·va·cious
viv·id
viv·i·fy
vi·vip·a·rous
viv·i·sec·tion
vix·en
vo·cab·u·lary (–lar·ies)
vo·cal·ist
vo·ca·tion
voc·a·tive
vo·cif·er·ate
vo·cif·er·ous
vod·ka
vogue
voice
void
vol·a·tile
vol·ca·nic
vol·ca·no (–noes or –nos)
vo·li·tion
vol·ley (volleys)
volt·age
vol·ta·ic
vol·u·ble
vol·ume
vo·lu·mi·nous
vol·un·tary
vol·un·ta·rism
vol·un·teer
vo·lup·tu·ous
voo·doo (voodoos)
vo·ra·cious
vo·rac·i·ty
vor·tex (vor·ti·ces or vor·tex·es)
vo·ta·ry (–ries)
vo·tive
vouch
vouch·safe
vow·el
voy·age
voy·eur
vul·gar

vul·gar·ism
vul·ner·a·ble
vul·ture
vying

W

wacky, whacky
wad·ding (soft mass; see wading)
wad·dle
wad·ing (step through water; see
    wadding)
wa·fer
waf·fle
waft
wage
wag·ging (to be in motion; see waging)
wag·gle
wag·ing (to engage in; see wagging)
wag·on
waif
wail
waist (narrowed part of body above
    hips; see waste)
wait·er
wait·ress
waive (relinquish voluntarily; see wave)
wak·ened
walk·ie-talk·ie
wal·let
wal·lop
wal·low
wall·pa·per
wal·nut
wal·rus (walrus or wal·rus·es)
waltz
wan·dered
wan·der·lust
wan·ing
wan·ton
war·bled
war·den
ward·robe
ware·house
war·fare
war·i·ly
war·mon·ger
warmth
warn
warp
war·rant
war·ran·tee (person to whom warranty
    is made; see warranty)
war·ran·tor
war·ran·ty (–ties) (written guarantee;
    see warrantee)
war·ren
war·ring
war·rior

wash·able
wast·age
waste (refuse from human habitations;
    see *waist*)
waste·land
watch·dog
watch·ful
wa·ter·proof
wa·tery
watt·age
wat·tle
wave (moving swell on sea surface;
    see *waive*)
wave·length
wavy
wax·en
waxy
way·far·er
way·lay
way·side
way·ward
weak·ened
wealthy
wean
weap·on
wear·able
wea·ried
wea·sel (–sels)
weath·er (state of atmosphere;
    see *whether*)
weave
web·bing
Web site
web·cam
web·cast
web·mas·ter
wed·ding
wedg·ing
wed·lock
weedy
weep·ing
wee·vil
weigh
weighty
weir
weird
weird·ly
wel·com·ing
weld·er
wel·fare
well·ness
welsh
welt
wel·ter
were·wolf (were·wolves)
west·ern
west·ward
whack
whale

wham·my (–mies)
wharf (wharves *or* wharfs)
what·so·ev·er
wheel·ing
wheeze
whelp
whence
when·ev·er
where·abouts
where·as
where·fore
where·so·ev·er
wher·ev·er
wheth·er (alternative condition;
    see *weather*)
whey
which·ev·er
whiff
while
whim·per
whim·si·cal
whim·sy, whim·sey (whim·sies *or*
    whim·seys)
whine
whin·ny
whip·pet
whirl·ing
whirl·wind
whis·ker
whis·key, whis·ky (whiskeys *or*
    whiskies)
whis·pered
whis·tle
whis·tling
whit·en·er
whith·er
whit·tle
whoa
whole·sal·er
whole·some
whol·ly
whoop
whose
why
wick·er
wide·awake
wid·ow·er
width
wield
wie·ner, wei·ner
wife (wives)
wig·gle
wig·wam
wil·der·ness
wile
will·ful, wil·ful
wil·lies
wil·lowy
wim·ple

wince
winch
wind·ing
wind·lass
win·dow
wind·swept
windy
wine
wined
wing·span
win·ner
win·now
win·some
win·ter·ize
win·ter·time
win·try, win·tery
winy
wip·ing
wire·less
wiring
wiry
wis·dom
wise
wish·ful
wishy-washy
wispy
wist·ful
witch·ery (–er·ies)
with·al
with·drawn
with·er
with·hold
with·out
wit
wit·less
wit·ness
wit·ti·cism
wit·ty
wiz·ard
wiz·ened
wob·ble, wab·ble
woe·be·gone
woe·ful, wo·ful
wolf (wolves)
wolf·ish
wom·an·ish
womb
won·der·ful
won·drous
wont (habit; see *won't*)
won't (will not; see *wont*)
wood·en
woody
woof·er
wool·en, wool·len
woo·zy
wordy
work·able
work·a·day

work·man·ship
world·ly
world·wide
wormy
wor·ri·some
wor·ry (worries)
wors·en
wor·ship
worst
wor·thy
would
wound·ed
wrack
wran·gle
wrap·per
wrath·ful
wreak
wreath (wreaths)
wreathe
wreck·age
wrench
wres·tle
wretch·ed
wrig·gle
wrist·watch
wring
wrin·kle
writ
writhe
writ·ing
wronged
wrought
wry

X

xe·non
xe·no·phile
xe·no·pho·bia
xe·rox

X-ray
xy·lo·phone

Y

yacht
ya·hoo
yak
yak·king
yam
Yan·kee
yap·ping
yard·age
yar·mul·ke
yar·row
yawn·ing
yawp, yaup
year·ling
year·ly
yearn
yeasty
yel·low·ish
yelp·er
yes·ter·day
yield
yip·pee
yo·del
yo·ga
yo·gurt, yo·ghurt
yoke (wooden bar; see *yolk*)
yo·kel
yolk (yellow portion of egg;
    see *yoke*)
yon·der
yoo·hoo
yore
you
young
young·ster
your (relating to you; see *you're*)
you're (you are; see *your*)

5/27/11

your·self (your·selves)
youth·ful
youth·ful·ness
you've
yowl
yo-yo
yuc·ca
yum·my

Z

zag·ging
za·ny (–nies)
zapped
zeal·ot
zeal·ous
ze·bra
ze·nith
zeph·yr
zep·pe·lin
ze·ro (zeros *or* zeroes)
zesty
zig·zag
zilch
zil·lion
zinc
zin·nia
Zi·on·ism
zip code
zip·per
zir·con
zith·er
zo·di·ac
zom·bie, zom·bi
zone
zonked
zoo (zoos)
zoo·log·i·cal, zoo·log·ic
zo·ol·o·gy
zoom